Spiritual Dimensions of Pastoral Care

of related interest

Spirituality in Mental Health Care

John Swinton
ISBN 1 85302 804 5

Spiritual Caregiving as Secular Sacrament
A Practical Theology for Professional Caregivers

Ray S. Anderson
ISBN 1 84310 746 5

In Living Color
An Intercultural Approach to Pastoral Care and Counseling, Second Edition

Emmanuel Y. Lartey
ISBN 1 84310 750 3

The Spiritual Dimension of Ageing

Elizabeth MacKinlay
ISBN 1 84310 008 8

Spirituality, Healing and Medicine
Return to the Silence

David Aldridge
ISBN 1 85302 554 2

Spirituality in Health Care Contexts

Edited by Helen Orchard
ISBN 1 85302 969 6

Working Relationships
Spirituality in Human Service and Organisational Life

Neil Pembroke
ISBN 1 84310 252 8

Spiritual Dimentions of Pastoral Care

Practical Theology in a Multidisciplinary Context

Edited by

David Willows and John Swinton

Jessica Kingsley Publishers
London and New York

First published in the United Kingdom in 2000 by
Jessica Kingsley Publishers Ltd
116 Pentonville Road
London N1 9JB, England
and
29 West 35th Street, 10th fl.
New York, NY 10001-2299, USA

www.jkp.com

Copyright © 2000 *Contact: The Interdisciplinary Journal of Pastoral Studies* and the contributors

Second impression 2004

Library of Congress Cataloging in Publication Data
A CIP catalog record for this book is available from the Library of Congress

British Library Cataloguing in Publication Data
A CIP catalogue record for this book is available from the British Library

ISBN 1 85302 892 4

Printed and Bound in Great Britain by
Athenaeum Press, Gateshead, Tyne and Wear

Contents

Acknowledgements

The authors and publisher are grateful to Contact Pastoral Trust (registered office: New College, Mound Place, Edinburgh EH1 2LX) for permission to reprint these articles that were originally published in *Contact: The Interdisciplinary Journal of Pastoral Studies*.

The publishers also acknowledge permission to quote from the following copyright sources:

Excerpt from *Siddhartha* by Herman Hesse, 1978. Reproduced by kind permission of Peter Owen Publishers Ltd, London, and copyright © 1951 by New Directions Publishing Corp. Reprinted by permission of New Directions Publishing Corp., New York in the US. Excerpt of about 25 words from *The Brothers Karamazov* by Fyodor Dostoyevsky, translated by David Magarshack, (Penguin Classics, 1958 p. 376). Copyright © David Magarshack, 1958. Reproduced by kind permission of Penguin Books Ltd, London. Two lines from The *Earliest English Poems* translated by Michael Alexander, (Penguin Classics 1966 p.123, Third revised edition 1991) Copyright © Michael Alexander, 1966, 1977, 1991. Reproduced by kind permission of Penguin Books Ltd, London. Excerpt from *Gitanjali* by Rabindranath Tagore, 1974. Reproduced by kind permission of Visva-Bharati Publishers, Calcutta, India. Excerpt from *Poetry and Prose of William Blake* edited by G. Keynes, 1961. Reproduced by kind permission of Nonesuch Press, London. Excerpt from *The Complete Talking Heads* by Alan Bennett, reprinted on p. 95 is reproduced with the permission of BBC Worldwide Ltd. Copyright © Alan Bennett 1998, and from PFD on behalf of Alan Bennett. Excerpt from *The Peacock and the Phoenix* by Richard Shannon, 1975. Reproduced by kind permission of David Higham Associates, London. Excerpt from *Visitors Laugh At Locksmiths / Hospital Doors Haven't Got Locks Anyhow* by Ogden Nash cited in Sergeant and Sergeant (eds) 1968, originally published in 1942. Copyright © Ogden Nash 1942, renewed. Reprinted by kind permission of Curtis Brown Ltd, New York. Excerpt from Selected Poems by Stevie Smith, 1962. Reproduced by kind permission from the Estate of James MacGibbon. The extract from *The Prophet* by Khalil Gibran, 1976, is used by kind permission of the National Committee of Gibran, all rights reserved.

Foreword

Every so often within the life of a discipline, it is necessary to stop and reflect upon where it has been, and where it wants to go. The past forty years or so have witnessed the emergence of a fresh vision of practical theology as an exciting, vibrant, multidisciplinary way of doing theology that incorporates and challenges both accepted theory and forms of practice. However, significant as many of the contemporary developments have been, if any discipline is to grow healthily, it must learn the art of critical reflection. Critical reflection on praxis lies at the heart of the practical theological task. Critical reflection on the discipline itself will encourage growth and positive new directions. This book provides an opportunity for the discipline to stop and reflect on what it has been, what it is and what it desires to be in the future.

Contact: The Interdisciplinary Journal of Pastoral Studies has had a significant role to play in the development of practical theology within the United Kingdom and beyond. During the forty years of its existence, *Contact* has documented many of the most significant changes and developments within the field. As such it constitutes an invaluable historical and contemporary record of what practical theology is and how it is done within a British context. I am delighted that this collection of some of the best essays published in *Contact* has been put together. The breadth of scholarship along with the wide variety of disciplines represented makes this text an invaluable resource for teachers, students, religious professionals, pastoral workers, and those with research interests in this area. It is my pleasure to commend this text and to recommend that it be taken seriously as a significant contribution to the field.

Don Browning
Alexander Campbell Professor of Religious Ethics and Social Sciences
University of Chicago

Introduction

The spiritual dimension of pastoral care is something that most of us would acknowledge during the course of our professional practice, even if 'spiritual' refers only to that part of the caring relationship that lies beyond rational explanation and scientific method. Within all caring encounters there is a transcendent dynamic that encompasses, yet lifts us beyond, our professional skills and competencies into the realms of mystery. To speak of the spiritual dimensions of pastoral care is thus, at very least, to admit that the caring relationship is always more than the sum of its parts (Willows 1999, p.65). Beyond this, however, there are many who would argue that this 'something other' has to do with the introduction of 'God' into our understanding of ourselves and the world in which we live.

One of the central aims of this book is to show how 'practical theologians' have recognized, and sought to articulate, these spiritual dimensions by exploring the relationship between our language of God (theology) and contemporary forms of pastoral practice. In order to set this in some kind of context, however, it is necessary to give some brief consideration to the practical theological task.

The practical theological task

Practical theology is arguably one of the most fascinating aspects of contemporary theology and is currently one of the fastest growing areas of theological study within the UK, with increasing numbers of courses and modules being offered at universities and seminaries throughout the country, each giving students the opportunity to explore the interface between theology and practical living. More precisely what practical theology entails, however, remains the subject of a good deal of debate and controversy. Indeed, as one surveys the wide range of methods and approaches used by practical theologians, one would perhaps be forgiven for assuming that practical theology is whatever any particular practical theologian says it is! For ministers it is a way of applying theology to their daily encounters; for academics, a way of looking at theology that acknowledges the significance of practice in the process of theological reflection; for the counsellor, practical theology works itself out as a critical dialogue partner within the ongoing conversation with contemporary psychological theories; for the politically aware, practical theology provides a method and a perspective within which the need for social change can be highlighted and initiated; whilst for others, practical theology has to do with telling stories that create meaningful human existence.

All of the perspectives noted above are represented within this book, and weave themselves together to provide a richly textured picture of what practical theology is and how it has been understood over the past forty years. Of course, such diversity might lead one to conclude that practical theology is nothing more than a baffling patchwork of disparate ideas and approaches that are difficult to tie down and make sense of. It is our conviction, however, that such diversity is the strength and the beauty of a discipline that, in various ways, is committed to the possibility of encountering God within the diversity of human experience.

In so far as practical theology takes seriously and incorporates fully the diversity of human experiences (regarding them, not simply as illustrative material, but as unique 'moments' in the drama of divine revelation), the practical theological task therefore appears to be necessarily diverse. After all, rooted as they are in the complexities of human lives, cultures and ever-changing contexts, the 'texts' that practical theologians work with are 'living' (Gerkin 1984) and will always demand a spectrum of different approaches and methodologies, if only to mirror the contrasting experiences of human beings as they live out their lives amidst the complexities and uncertainties of an unpredictable world.

The breadth and diversity that marks out this collection of articles is thus, in the end, symptomatic of the way in which practical theology has grown out of various methodological positions and adopted the guise of a conversation. Far from detracting from the practical theological task, however, this admixture of different voices and contrasting perspectives has enriched a discipline that has continually managed to extend itself beyond the relative safety of its own linguistic and conceptual framework and invited others to become working partners in the practical theological task. Of course, as with any conversation, an inevitable feature of this approach is a tendency for some differences to remain unresolved and for the conversation to drift along unexpected paths. Similarly, there are times when some voices appear to dominate to a disturbing degree. Yet despite these signs of human fallibility, one can nevertheless clearly discern within this 'conversation' (particularly with the advantage of hindsight) several strong tides of opinion and insight that have come to be determinative for the discipline as a whole.

The papers in this book have been arranged around six discernible 'tides of opinion' that, we believe, best illustrate the movement and process of British practical theology both historically and contemporarily; a process that has become integrally bound up with *Contact: The Interdisciplinary Journal of Pastoral Studies*. Indeed, since its inception in 1960, *Contact* has been and remains the major journal of practical theology within the UK and has undoubtedly played a major part in tracing, recording and actively participating in the formation and shaping of practical theology within the UK.

Drawing upon the rich resource that *Contact* has come to represent, the papers that can be found within this book illustrate the significance of practical theology as it has presented itself within a British context. Individually, they represent key moments of change and reconstruction in the history of the discipline. Taken together, they provide a unique insight into British practical theology as it has worked itself out in the past and as it is continuing to develop in the present.

In reading these various contributions, the reader should note that there has been no attempt made to update (e.g., through inclusive language) or alter what was originally written (the only exception being a conscious decision by the editors to reference bibliographic sources as far as possible). Essentially, therefore, they remain unedited in order accurately to represent a distinct contribution to the discipline at a specific moment in time. Each of these papers in their own way has affected the course of practical theology in Britain. Reading them again with fresh eyes and within a new context, it is very possible that they will affect its course again.

Before moving directly to the papers themselves, however, let us make some brief comments and observations that may help the reader to discern the rationale that underpins the way in which we have structured what is to follow.

The emergence of practical theology

From its roots in applying theology primarily to the training needs of the clergy, practical theology has emerged as a vibrant and challenging mode of theology that not only applies, but also constructs and clarifies theological understandings, including our understanding of the spiritual dimensions of pastoral care. The journey from 'Cinderella' to 'princess' (Wesson 1986), however, has been long, complicated and at times, quite controversial. We therefore begin our exploration in this book by looking at some of the historical and contemporary attempts that have been made to understand and develop practical theology, both as an intellectual discipline and as a way of being in the world. None of the authors in part one attempt to present a definitive understanding of practical theology. Yet for the discerning reader they clearly provide a rich intellectual and artistic interpretation of the practical theological task that captures something of the emergent and dialectical nature of the discipline.

Practical theology and the art of theological reflection

Alongside this quest to articulate the determinate features of practical theology, various questions arise as to the nature of the knowledge that it purports to reveal and the manner in which it is acquired. For many contemporary practical theologians, theological truth is not viewed as a set of propositions that simply need to be applied to certain situations, quite apart from their unique contexts. Rather, it is assumed to arise out of the continuing dialogue between context, the social sciences, the Christian tradition and the continuing praxis of the church in the world. This understanding of theological truth and its acquisition has led to new developments in the ways in which practical theology is done. The art of theological reflection – the critical conversation between context and tradition, leading to revised theological understandings and ways of being in the world – has thus established itself as a particular method that forms the heart of the practical theological task. Part two explores some of the ways in which this method has been developed to enable academics and practitioners working in a variety of contexts, to reflect theologically on the nature of their tasks.

Practical theology in search of practical wisdom

Implicit in this emphasis upon the art of theological reflection is the conviction that practical theology is a praxis-based discipline. The word *praxis* essentially means 'action'. However, properly understood, practical theology refers to a particular form of action that should not be directly equated with the word 'practice'; for whereas practice implies the simple non-reflective performance of a task in a dispassionate, value-free manner, praxis denotes a form of action which is value-directed, value-laden and profoundly saturated with meaning. In short, praxis thus refers to a practical form of knowledge that generates actions through which the church community lives out its beliefs.

> Praxis is reflective, because it is action that not only seeks to achieve particular ends, but also reflects upon the means and the ends of such action in order to assess the validity of both in the light of its guiding vision. Praxis is theory-laden because it includes theory as a vital constituent. It is not just reflective action, but reflective action that is laden with belief. (Swinton 2000, p.11)

Engagement in such praxis results in the development of *phronesis*, or practical wisdom: a form of knowledge that informs practice, rather than knowledge which is sought for its own sake.

> [A] knowing in which skill and understanding cooperate; a knowing in which experience and critical reflection work in concert; a knowing in which the disciplined improvisation, against a backdrop of reflective wisdom, marks the virtuosity of the competent practitioner. (Fowler cited in Wesson 1986, p.60)

Part three focuses on this practical theological search for practical wisdom by exploring various expressions of being and active practice that capture something of the mystery of the divine human encounter as it works itself out in the lives of both the church and the world.

Practical theology in critical dialogue

Practical theology has a history of critical engagement with other disciplines. Over the past few years the most popular dialogue partner has been psychology, particularly as it has worked itself out in the area of counselling and psychotherapy. The dialogue has not always been friendly. In fact, at times it has been more than a little acrimonious, leading to significant rifts over what the heart of spiritual care should be and the appropriate tools to fulfil it faithfully.

Given such critical dialogue, questions have been plentiful: Is the church called to a ministry of counselling, or a ministry of pastoral care? Is counselling simply another symptom of Western individualism with a spiritual gloss? Are religion and psychotherapy compatible, or are they so much at odds as to be wholly incompatible? The papers in part four highlight some of these fundamental controversies and debates. Each of the contributions takes us on a fascinating and challenging journey through the complexities of interdisciplinary care and raise challenging questions as how best to maintain a constructive, critical tension between the various and at times apparently disparate disciplines without one side collapsing into the other.

Practical theology and social action

In recent years there has been a general recognition, across a variety of disciplines, that the legacy of modernism has given too much emphasis to the notion of the individual. Pastoral care is certainly no exception. On the contrary, its continuing conversation with psychology has led to an emphasis (some would argue a dependency) on the ministry of counselling, often to the exclusion of wider social and political aspects that are of great significance to the caring process.

Critical prophetic voices from within practical theology have, for many years, consistently sought to challenge such individualistic tendencies and remind us of the need for greater involvement in, and reflection on, the wider social and political aspects of the pastoral task. The three papers in part five are representative of early attempts to challenge the individualism of pastoral care and to move it in a more political and socially oriented direction.

Practical theology as story

Practical theology has consistently given voice to the fact that listening to and telling stories lies at the heart of all human experiencing and forms part of the fabric of the practical theological task. We locate ourselves in the world, know who we are, where we have been, and where we are going in and through the stories that we tell about ourselves and through the 'metanarratives' by which we chose to live. Formative experiences, for example, such as suffering, alienation, chaos and confusions, are invariably communicated and interpreted through the stories that people tell about themselves and their experiences. Moreover, it could be argued that the essence of faith itself has to do with the possibility of encountering stories that transform who we are and the way in which we see the world.

A highly significant development within recent years has been the reclamation of the significance of creativity, story-telling and other narrative themes as key components of practical theological reflection. The final essays in this book, in quite contrasting ways, explore this medium of story, and illustrate possible ways in which listening to and telling stories can provide opportunities for both revelation and healing.

It is our conviction that these six themes offer the reader a framework within which they can begin to develop a rounded picture of the discipline of practical insight into the spiritual dimensions of pastoral care. Of course, in pointing to this rich tradition that has grown up through a generation of thinkers and practitioners, there is much that has not been said and many voices that regretfully have not been included. Notwithstanding such limitations, however, it is the hope and the prayer of the editors that this text will contribute to the development of the discipline of practical theology, and that those who reflect on the insights presented within these pages will emerge stimulated, refreshed and challenged to move the discipline on towards new horizons.

David Willows and John Swinton

PART ONE

The Emergence of
Practical Theology

1

Pastoral Theology

Towards a New Discipline (1983)

Anthony Dyson

In this essay I shall argue that, for both religious and secular reasons, it is desirable for greater recognition and institutional support to be given to that enterprise sometimes known as *pastoral theology*; that a precondition of such recognition and support is a greater and more precise awareness by pastoral theology of itself as an intellectual and academic discipline; and that such self-awareness will only come about through a wider theological commitment to a discipline of thought about the task, content and limitations of this discipline. Thus the title of my essay deliberately plays on the word 'discipline' both as a certain quality of intellectual activity and as the visible and usable product of that activity. My considerations are undertaken in the conviction, which I shall later spell out in more detail, that a satisfactory pastoral theology is an *applied* discipline with important contributions to make as much to the human sciences and social policy in general as to theology in particular.

I begin with some brief observations about the origins and early development of pastoral theology. I shall then indicate some of the factors which crucially call that inherited pastoral theology into question and which also begin to indicate the possible shape of things to come. This will lead to a consideration of three reasons why a development of pastoral theology will helpfully respond to needs both in society at large and in the churches. I argue in some detail that this kind of development leads to a critical stance towards many values and practices both in society and in the Christian tradition. I end the essay with some modest suggestions for practical change.

Perhaps different stories must be told to account for the beginnings of pastoral theology in the different Christian traditions. Certainly today there are notable differences between denominations and national cultures in this respect. But what is found in the Church of England appears to represent, at least in part, a not uncommon history. Namely, the matter of pastoral theology is bound up with the practical tasks of the ordained minister, whether in more outward activities such as visiting or baptizing or in more inward activities such as spiritual direction. This severely practical and clerical approach to pastoral theology is found in countless handbooks for the clergy in the last part of the 19th and the first part of the 20th century. This practical and clerical understanding of pastoral theology still lingers in the definition found in the *Dictionary of Christian Theology* of 1969: 'pastoral theology, or pastoralia, is that branch of theological education which concerns the theoretical and practical training of clergy and ministers for their proper work' (Richardson 1969, p.253). A similar emphasis on the side of spiritual direction is found in a revealing quotation from the 1939 volume *The Study of Theology* prepared by Kenneth Kirk. Here pastoral theology is the '*ars artium* of guiding and influencing souls', which is one of a number of theological disciplines which, 'fascinating though they are to those who have time for pursuing them, are predominantly the affair of the professional ecclesiastic, pastor, confessor, or guide of souls' (Kirk 1939, p.13). In general, the origins of this clerical pastoral theology lie with a practice-based discipline with limited theoretical content. The body and tradition of practice was only loosely tied to theological or scientific principles, though there was often general and pious reference to the ministry of Jesus as the norm of pastoral activity. When writers on pastoral theology became aware of the wider social context – and that, in a rapidly urbanizing Britain, a dispiriting one – in which pastoral activity was being undertaken, there are signs of modest dealings with theory in the forms of educational method and psychology. In fact, however, it is only since World War Two that the major impact of psychotherapy on British pastoral theology has occurred. The influence of that development is limited, and still breeds suspicion among those who think in terms of a practice-based discipline. Nonetheless it deserves attention in view of its effect upon ministerial training since about 1960. I should be inclined to treat this appeal to psychotherapy as symptomatic of the search for a trouble-free zone of inwardness in which Christian theology and practice could maintain integrity at a time when, externally, the threats of biblical criticism, secular functionalism and the natural sciences were keenly felt.

The origins and modern development of pastoral theology must now seriously be called into question for a number of reasons. Some of these also relate to theology in general and I mention these first before noting others that have a special reference to pastoral theology.

First, pastoral theology has to involve itself in the wider debate about the authority of the bible and tradition, and of the meaning and content which may be given to the notion of revelation in relation to other sources of knowledge to which pastoral theology refers.

Second, pastoral theology is involved with the question of the historical Jesus and of the extent to which he may be regarded as the historical and/or theological norm for pastoral theology and practice.

Third, pastoral theology has to take note of the related issues concerning the time-bound character of theological statements. How far are the various traditional themes and outlooks of pastoral theology determined by prevailing cultures and what interpretative procedures are available to work with these questions?

I now turn to a series of challenges, which bear upon pastoral theology more particularly.

First, pastoral theology will be required to register, as theological ethics has to some extent already done, a greater interest in the debates in the sciences about the nature and determinants of the self. The warm personalism of much pastoral theology, still thinking of an independent self-directing consciousness largely unaffected by physical and social processes, must give way to more complex and more severe accounts of the self.

Second, the challenge to individualism, which in political economy has come from various forms of socialism, and which in social work has come from community work, must now make itself felt against individualistic pastoral theology, perhaps from the direction of political and liberation theology. What is at stake are not only questions of the correct human locus for pastoral theology, but also the further challenge as to whether pastoral theology's traditional concern with the individual does not fall prey to the charge of manipulation, of a social control which actually *inhibits* social change and individual development.

Third, the practice-based origins of pastoral theology have already been in part challenged by the increasing professionalization of the clergy (parallel with professionalization in other spheres too), where a body of theory and practice is evolved which is more sophisticated in content but which serves to keep a closed profession closed. Also, paradoxically, this very process of professionalization has become confused because the nature and function of the clergy is no longer clear to clergy or to their clients. Connected with that lack of clarity is a rising *lay* self-consciousness, which blurs the image of the clergy and fundamentally questions the notion that pastoral theology is the preserve of clergy.

Fourth, it is a commonplace, though an important one, that the rapid extension of pastoral-social work by statutory and voluntary agencies since the 19th century raises searching questions about *whose* practice pastoral theology refers to, and *to whom* that practice is directed.

Fifth, practice-based pastoral theology is seen by some as theologically imbued with a 'Pelagian' optimism about humankind. So in one form or another (e.g. Barthianism) a plea arises for the restoration of a more transcendental, super-naturalist, judgemental quality to this discipline. This and other similar pleas clearly pose searching questions to pastoral theology about its necessary connections with a particular announcement of good news (gospel) in all its radical challenge.

Sixth, feminist theology has, in my opinion, succeeded in demonstrating beyond reasonable doubt the largely androcentric character of Christian tradition in theology and church practice. The resultant attempts to reconstruct the doctrine of the human person in the light of that criticism have direct consequences for pastoral theology. For example, the possibility that the character of the religious quest may be quite different in men and women must put a question-mark upon a range of pastoral beliefs, assumptions, practices and rituals shaped by the androcentric tradition. Again, if it is correct that notions of hierarchy, of distancing the 'other', are products of the androcentric tradition, pastoral theology may have to revise some of its most basic assumptions about the nature and purpose of interventions into people's lives.

Seventh, and last, I want to draw especial attention to a challenge, which seems in some respects recent and relatively unexamined. The inherited practice-based theology used, consciously or unconsciously, the concept of *apprenticeship*. For the most part, ministers would work out their pastoral theology in the early years of their ministry largely through imitation of older and allegedly wiser ministers. Thus the *theoretical* basis of pastoral practice was not seriously addressed. Doubts and difficulties would be resolved within the terms of the apprentice-relationship. The study, on any serious scale, of theoretical subjects in the pastoral sphere as a precondition of ordination was certainly not required in the Church of England. This state of affairs has changed only recently with the result that *pastoral studies* has rapidly grown in importance and curricular visibility in many theological colleges and seminaries. In this rise to prominence of pastoral studies, confusion and conflict understandably reign in many quarters. An analogy may be drawn with recent developments in social work teaching, and with the emergence of diplomas of education in an earlier generation. Originally social work consisted in a number of practice-based professions with a limited amount of theoretical material attached loosely to each. In more recent times, and most especially after Seebohm, the necessity has arisen of teaching a generic course to a wide variety of candidates who will engage in a wide range of activities. It is hardly surprising if the picture has seemed to be one of fragmentary, disparate, and even incompatible subjects in search of a coherent structure, in search of some theory, which might hold together elements of widely different subjects and disciplines. H. Richard Niebuhr found a very similar state of affairs when he surveyed theological education in the United States in the mid-1950s – a situation that has reproduced itself in Britain some decades later. The problems, which arise today in pastoral studies, reflect similar problems in education and social work: the question of theory; supervised practice; the pattern of interdisciplinarity. But these problems are compounded by the deep emotions variously felt as people bemoan or rejoice at the loss of simplicity, at the tendencies to politicization, all overlaid by the obsessive anachronisms of British divisions of churchmanship (Dyson 1982).

Such, in outline, are some of the principal challenges which today bear upon the discipline of pastoral theology, challenges which cannot adequately be faced without the introduction of greater intellectual and institutional ordering in respect of the challenges and of the search for responses.

I turn now to consider briefly why a disciplined response to these challenges is more than a domestic churchly matter.

(1) It seems clear that Christian (systematic) theology will not long sustain itself as a credible discipline with bearing upon social realities as long as it retains the generalized and abstract character it has traditionally possessed. This is not to deny that there is a continuing place for systematic, philosophical and doctrinal theology. But the complexity, fluctuation and multi-sided change of societies in late, middle or early stages of

modernization point to the need for *mediating, flexible, applied disciplines*, which can relate adequately to the modern conditions without being engulfed by them. Pastoral theology appears to be the theological discipline potentially most easily developable in these terms.

(2) After decades of relative buoyancy and self-confidence, perhaps deriving from the traditions of Victorian middle-class philanthropy, many of the caring professions, and the bodies of theory attached to them, are in disarray. On a widespread scale, rational enquiry about ends and means is being replaced by strident appeals to ideology, by a new conservatism, which simply reintroduces all the unresolved problems of practice-based work, or by a pragmatism in which moral ideals and values disappear from the vocabulary, and where preoccupation with theory is regarded as pretentious and irrelevant. If, as for example in penal theory and practice, the most fundamental purposes are now in question, is it possible to envisage pastoral theology finding a secular voice and discovering a public vocation?

(3) In the Christian sphere there is a good deal of evidence today of sinister gaps between believing and praying, and between praying and exercising worldly responsibility. For complex historical reasons theology, ethics and spirituality have lost their connections with each other, and each with a secularizing society. Again the only discipline potentially in contact simultaneously with all three areas might appear to be pastoral theology, which, in this case, would increasingly have to be accorded a greater primacy among the theological disciplines, indeed as a discipline to which the others significantly contribute.

I have deliberately cast these three remarks about the potential wider utility of pastoral theology in broad terms. I accept that this kind of reasoning would have to be expounded in much greater detail. But the limited remarks made are intended to serve at least as an indication that in my view the question of pastoral theology is both more important and more comprehensive than is often allowed.

I want now to examine two major issues which arise for pastoral theology from the position, which I have developed so far. One of these issues concerns the teaching of pastoral theology; the other concerns the public vocation of Christian pastoral theology.

Teaching

A 1974 Higher Education Policy Group, *Some Policy Issues in Higher Education*, identified three distinctive objectives for higher education: competence; enjoyment; critical awareness and commitment. There is much evidence to suggest that in higher education the *de facto* emphasis is upon 'competence', and that this is no less so in pastoral studies, being the primary explicit or implicit criterion in curriculum design.

'Enjoyment', which the Report defines as 'exploration of a field of knowledge for its own sake', and 'critical awareness and commitment', which include the examination of values, an ensuing concern with the nature of human life, the meaning of imagination and intuition in life, and the meaning of compassion and of aspiration, are much less readily and quantifiably realizable objectives of education than 'competence'. But there appears to be a considerable optimism in some parts of higher education, and in the sphere of pastoral studies, that such further objectives beyond 'competence', and the resources for their attainment, are realizable out of the interplay of carefully chosen elements on a curriculum, or in terms of the mutual friction of theory and practice, or through the self-questioning and questioning of the environment which skilled supervision will provoke. Others admit that these further objectives are hardly achieved by educational engineering, but instead go on to talk very loosely about 'the doing of theology', and 'community life' as the elements which engender intuition and imagination out of the raw material of competence. This second kind of optimism seems no more convincing than the first, making far too great claims for fashionable forms of contextual theology and for the none too healthy common life generally prevalent in seminaries and other religious institutions. The problem is a far deeper one. It is the problem which can be described in terms of the contrast between the analytical and fiduciary views of language, and where the cultivation of imagination and intuition presupposes Coleridge's understanding of the primary response to language being in terms of a complex act of inference and of assent, the very opposite of the method of doubt commanded by Descartes and his followers to this day (Coulson 1970, chapter 1). Coleridge's approach is especially apt for pastoral theology where words and things and experiences and relationships cannot be simply equivalated, where aspects of experience cannot be committed to single precise images, and where contradictions cannot be removed. It seems to me that the apparent bustle of much contemporary pastoral studies, with the demand to master and co-ordinate several different intellectual elements, the pressures of often inadequately mounted and supervised fieldwork, together with parallel and extraneous demands upon the individual from other sources, are hardly calculated to serve the causes of imagination and intuition, compassion and aspiration. But nor will these causes by served by adding yet further things in a desperate search for the pearl of great price. If pastoral theology depends upon a syllabus integrating several different elements of theory and practice (and we are not yet in a position to say that it does not), then is it not a primary desideratum to control that syllabus, to create time and space for silence and reflection, for absorption and digestion, for responding to the richness and diversity of language around us? The Report quoted earlier observed: 'the main objective in higher education ... should be to provide the soil, rather than choosing all the plants.'

Public vocation

It is surely justified, as some writers have done, to raise questions about expressions of pastoral theology which simply take over the norms of other disciplines with the addition of a thin theological veneer. For pastoral theology is part of theology, a discipline which makes a series of striking claims about the world – claims which are not easily accommodated without loss to the positions of other sciences. This is an important question, not only at the intellectual level, but at the level of pastoral practice too. Is pastoral theology obliged to fit in with the assumptions and conventions of the wider intellectual firmament? Is pastoral practice in a Christian context part of a roughly homogeneous group of helping-caring activities in society? Has pastoral theology a distinctive Christian axis?

Some of these questions are helpfully, if indirectly, explored in a recent essay by Donald Houston on 'Affirmation and sacrifice in everyday life and in social work' (Houston 1978). Houston distinguishes between *unilateral* affirmation where each person is who he or she is without much regard to the experience and enactment of the being of others. *Reciprocal* affirmation is where each person experiences himself or herself in the light of an awareness of how other persons are experiencing themselves. Houston argues that most relationships in contemporary British society are of the unilateral type where we always define ourselves as winners in relation to others as losers. We can make unilateral affirmation more palatable as we can make boring work superficially more acceptable by so-called job-enrichment. But whatever the appearances, in unilateral affirmation we always win, are always in a position of strength. The only way of breaking free of this pattern is to move into the realm of reciprocal affirmation where we are 'essentially living in the light of change.' But to proceed thus is to go against the grain of society, in which we must expect much risk and the payment of many costs.

Houston's is an important argument which can be developed from another direction in terms of feminist theology's treatment of the theme of *hierarchy*. Houston's account must by implication be very critical of various kinds of one-way pastoral relationships in which the identity and position of the carer is not called into question. Such an indictment would, for example, probably be true of almost all of the churches' pastoral responses to the 'working classes' since the beginning of the industrial revolution. It would also be true of many types of formal counselling in which clergy are engaged. But these unilateral assumptions flourishing in Christian context, are incompatible with basic Christian assertions about the mutual self-giving of God and human persons, in a reciprocity of grace and freedom, and about the self-giving to others of the Incarnation. It would seem to me that pastoral theology should expect to explore the reciprocal mode in all its aspects as nothing less than an exposition of the Gospel. But this would certainly challenge the way in which Christian pastoral conscience and practice have adapted themselves to expressions of unilateral affirmations, as these occur in state provision of the social services, of law, of the penal system, of education, and so on.

I have tried here to show how it is possible to begin critically relating pastoral theology on the one hand to fundamental theology, and on the other hand, to social and political arrangements about us. It is possible to see how, without ceasing to learn from other disciplines, without retiring from the fray, it is quite possible, on a Christian argumentation, to come up with a direction of social policy which is radically untypical of current practice, but which cannot be ignored simply because it differs from the prevailing wisdom. This can, however, only be done if we are also prepared to probe critically a Christian tradition redolent of androcentrism, hierarchy and the unilateral mode.

In conclusion I offer three observations about ways in which some of the concerns expressed in this essay may be further explored at the institutional level.

(1) Disregarding cries of 'irrelevance' which might ensue, there is an urgent need to concentrate theological energies upon basic questions of the task, epistemology, sources and hermeneutical procedures of pastoral theology, if the discipline is not to go on lurching drunkenly from one practical fashion to another. This means research, writing, colloquy on a far broader basis than at present occurs.

(2) A good deal of research is happening in pastoral theology – more than outsiders will suppose. But there is a need to find ways and means of coordinating it, listing it, describing it, and commenting upon it. An information body on the model of a *research council* might be a helpful device.

(3) Pastoral theology urgently needs to find modes of entry, on a reciprocal basis, into other cognate disciplines. The present moment of retraction and reorganization in higher education might serve as an important opportunity.

2

Can Theology be Practical?

(1992)

Paul Ballard

Recently, in a seminar for post-graduate students there was a discussion on the nature of Practical Theology, a topic that is currently widely debated. In the course of the conversation one of the participants asked why the academics were so anxious to analyze the nature of theological activity. After all, he said, as a working minister, he had to get on with the job on the basis of a convenient and appropriate working theological model. It was not necessary continuously to be peering under the bonnet when the car had to be out on the road.

This intervention highlights the issue that is before us. There are, of course, those who would dismiss theology out of hand, either out of obscurantism or from an impatience with anything that may detract from doing. But this was not the implication here, coming from a group that was precisely anxious to develop theological insights and skills. Yet it pointed to something real: the sense of alienation between much academic theology and the needs of the practical situation. Ironically, however, this tension is precisely what the theologians in their way are trying to come to grips with. Concern for the essential task of theology is the attempt to respond to this sense of frustration. It is a very practical issue to know if and how theology functions in the concrete reality of daily action.

Theology as a practical activity

The first thing is to affirm that theology is in fact an essentially practical activity. Its task is to provide a resource for a working Christian understanding that can inform practice. There is a proper reflective theological stance, which holds back from the cutting edge of practice. Theology is, indeed, a critical, evaluative activity that tests, refines and explores the possibility and nature of belief. But this is done in the service of and as part of the community of faith and must be related creatively and positively to the task of living and working Christianity in the present with all its ambiguities and demands. The questioner was surely right to voice concern that the pleasures of analytical niceties and esoteric interest (however intrinsically right) seem too often to turn attention away from the creation of a working theology.

This is sometimes exhibited in the tension found between the expectations and demands of the academic context and the expectations and demands of the community of faith. Properly there are specialist fields of study, examining, for example, historical issues in relation to scripture and tradition or engaged in philosophical discussions concerning belief. It is essential for theology to be part of academic enquiry. At the same time, however, the place of theology is at the heart of the Church's life, giving reason for the hope that is within us (1 Peter 3:15), making the treasures of scripture and tradition accessible to the People of God. Too often these drift apart, setting one over against the other. In truth, however, they belong together. Theology is the intellectual awareness of faith and must stand at the bar of reason and truth as well as the service of the Gospel.

This is the reasoning behind theology normally being the core of training for ordination or other forms of ministry. In our own day, however, this has been augmented by an increasing number of students with no necessary professional interest, who see it not only as an academic subject but as a way of having a better understanding of the Christian faith and its implications or at least asking those questions of meaning and purpose that are fundamental to life. Outside the universities and colleges there has also been a proliferation of other agencies, in the churches and elsewhere, engaged in making theological education accessible both as a means of training within the Church and as a way of becoming better informed about their Christian commitment. It would seem, therefore, that theology retains and ever increases its interest and that for practical reasons. Thomas Ogletree usefully sums this up:

> Theology is practical in the sense that it concerns, in all of its expressions, the most basic issues of human existence. (Ogletree in Browning 1983a, p.85)

Is practical theology Practical Theology?

There is a parallel issue that needs to be addressed at this point. It is an understandable inference to suppose that Practical Theology mediates between critical or theoretical theology and practice. This is, indeed, the inherited Protestant tradition (with its Catholic parallels), classically set out by Friedrich Schleiermacher. Theology, he argued, is essentially geared to practice, by which was meant the Church's ministry in its widest sense. Practice, however, was the application of principles uncovered by fundamental, historical and systematic theology. Unfortunately, such a model helped to open up the way for the split between theory and practice that bedevils so much contemporary theology, which has been compounded by the assimilation, on one hand, of theoretical theology into philosophy and history and, on the other hand, of practical theology into skills based on the human sciences.

Yet it is clear that no such hiatus can be sustained without undermining the foundation of theology. Each field of theology is part of the practical demands for Christian understanding in contemporary society. There is no purely theoretical or critical enquiry that remains detached from involvement with action, however indirectly or remotely. So, for example, Biblical studies is not merely archaeology, history or textual criticism but informs doctrine, prayer, preaching and ethics. There may be tensions, even conflict, between different interests, but they have to be held together. Moreover, Biblical studies itself is part of the theological response in and to the modern world, working at the frontiers of scholarship in the marketplace of ideas, trying to make sense of the material in the light of questions asked of it. Further, as James Barr (1973) has pointed out, the majority of biblical (and other) scholars have always understood their task precisely as part of their ministry in the Church. Far from setting out to secularize the Bible, whatever the actual result, the intention was to bring the tools of critical scholarship into the service of biblical exegesis in the support of faith.

Practical Theology, therefore, is not simply the bridge between theory and practice. Practical Theology is but one of a number of fields in theology, each of which draws on the concerns and resources of the others, but each of which has its own focal concern, and each of which is part of that total theological activity which is there to equip the People of God in the service of the world. The special task of Practical Theology is to start with the concrete, historical, immediate reality critically evaluating and enabling the practical life of the Church in all its many forms, drawing on the findings of fundamental, historical and systematic theology. At the same time, however, Practical Theology will be needed by these others as they too wrestle with the task of enabling the Church to stand faithfully in today's world.

If, therefore, it is right to assert, in the first instance, that all theology is essentially practical, it is necessary, in the second instance, to affirm that all theologians are practical theologians. The Practical Theologian, whether as academic, minister, or believer, does not stand in a different place from other theologians. All are wrestling with the pressures, challenges and opportunities they find in relation to their concern. It is a shared task, a common calling to articulate in word and deed the Christian reality.

Theoria and praxis

All this has led us into one of the current major debates in theology: the relation between theory and practice. If theology is essentially practical, at the service of the community of faith, then the question cannot but be pivotal. As Matthew Lamb (1976), in an important survey article, claims:

> The relationship of theory and praxis goes right to the core of the entire philosophical enterprise; it involves the relationship of consciousness to being, of subject to object, of idea to reality, of word to deed, of meaning to history. Similarly in theology, this relationship goes beyond a discussion of contemplative or active ways of life to raise such fundamental issues as the relations of faith to love, of Church to world, of orthodoxy to orthopraxis, of salvation to liberation, of religion to political concerns, of historical and systematic to moral and pastoral theology. (p.149)

Lamb goes on to set out a useful 'framework of models or types' by which to categorize the way the theory–praxis relationship is used in modern theology. Despite the threat of over-simplification, this can provide a convenient starting point from which to develop our own model further.

The first type Lamb presents is 'the primacy of theory', in which praxis is understood as being the application of theory which is 'the knowledge of necessary and eternal truths or first principles' (p.155). This has been the classical model in Western Christianity in which traditionally both doctrine and practice have been deduced from either dogmatic presuppositions or from some form of natural theology that establishes primary axioms.

The second type Lamb presents is 'the primacy of praxis', in which theory is deduced from experience or built up from empirical evidence. This alternative has emerged with the Enlightenment and may take several forms, including Liberal Protestantism and Marxism.

Our interest, however, is on the next three types which are variations and refinements of the first two.

The third group Lamb calls 'the primacy of faith-love', where 'the self-referent of the theologians is a dialectical appropriation of the basic attitudes of the Christian faith, trust and agapic love, while the object-referent is the 'wholly other God of Jesus Christ' (p.162). Here are found Karl Barth and Hans Urs von Balthasar. Practice and theory, it is claimed, are taken up into an absolute obedience to the norms of revelation which has its own dynamic. It tends to absolutize Christian faith, detaching it from any historical reality.

However, it may be possible to begin to modify Lamb's typology by suggesting that the fundamental affirmation that is contained in this type can be retained without some of its limitations. What is being asserted is that there is a giveness at the heart of Christianity, a concept of revelation. But this does not have to be lost when we also recognize that this is mediated in and through the relativities of history.

One of the important sources of some contemporary theology has been Michael Polanyi's (1958) analysis of the structure of human thought. He points out that there is always a fundamental *a priori* that is the basis of any kind of meaning. Without such an assumption it is impossible to observe the world rationally at all. *Credo ut intellegam.* It is not unreasonable to suggest that such an *a priori* is a form of revelation that both makes reason possible and is confirmed by reason. Revelation, therefore, is not alien from reason. Revelation is a primary axiom which is the basis of reason that tests, evaluates, enlarges and completes revelation. And reason is the mediating vehicle of that revelation which provides a constant critical reference point for reason. The point of this distinction comes out when we turn to the last two types in Lamb's typology, for they too presuppose a sense of giveness which is characterized as 'the tradition'.

The fourth group Lamb gives us is the 'critical theoretic correlations' model in which tradition and contemporary theory are brought together attempting to do justice to 'both the socio-historical and existential demand of Christian faith and practice' (Lamb 1976, p.166). This is the model that has shaped much recent Practical Theology following the correlation approach developed from Tillich or the hermeneutic theories of Gadamer and Ricoeur. At the heart of this model is a dialogue between the tradition and (usually) the findings and theories of contemporary social sciences with a view to providing a theoretical basis for practice. Its strength lies precisely in the recognition of the need for theoretical dialogue. In a differentiated and pluralistic world, where sciences and professions claim autonomy, there is a need to have a critical appraisal of underlying assumptions that inform action. It is too easy to assume a facile compatibility between different fields of theory and practice. Within pastoral care, for example, there has been considerable concern that the understanding of human nature has frequently been taken from humanistic psychologies rather than theological principles. Such an exchange will lead towards a more effective and soundly based theory by which to undergird practice.

The fifth and last group that Lamb provides is the 'critical praxis correlation' model in which the emphasis is placed on praxis as the determining partner in the dialogue. Here we find recent political theologies, including liberation theology, and those forms of Practical Theology that practice an 'action-reflection' methodology. The strength of this model lies in the insistence on the concrete reality of the present. It is impossible to escape from the arena of experience and responsibility. Here is the crucible in which theology is done.

However, it is necessary to ask whether these last two models are so distinct as to be seen as polarized opposites. Turning again to Polanyi, he argues that human knowing does not start with either theory or practice but is a constant dialogue between conceptual frameworks that interpret experience and the evidence that has to be accounted for. Understanding is having a credible, coherent, but never final, picture that allows us to cope with experience. There is, therefore, another dialogue – between theory and practice which constantly inform one another.

Moreover, if we return to the nature of tradition, that itself is not a simple reality but is the varied, and often distorted, expression of faith through history. How do we identify the tradition, except in some fairly loose sense? Also, the Christian story does not happen in a vacuum but is interwound with the whole history of our culture. Tradition is a living stream that bears us all along even though we need to find means of taking bearings and mapping the shoals and currents so that in some way we can navigate our passage. Yet, at the same time, there is the sense of giveness, the reality that is manifesting itself through the flux and uncertainties of history. One would appear to be driven to acknowledging that the locus of truth, and thus the theological task, is to be found in the midst of living where theory, practice and chance meet. It is there that we have to discern the face of God.

At this point, to Lamb's fivefold typology I want to add a sixth model. Edward Farley (1983) has pointed out that the earliest understanding of the theological task was spiritual illumination.

> From its beginnings, the Christian Community has laid claim to a knowledge of God, to a divine illumination of the human intellect operative in the salvation of the human being. Pseudo-Dionysius called this knowledge the mystical theology. (p.35)

And this tradition has persisted. Today, for example, Catholicism is concerned with 'formation' and conservative evangelicals continue the pietistic tradition of theology as 'saving knowledge'. So, in this sense, Farley concludes: 'theology is *a practical,* not theoretical, habit, having the primary character of wisdom' (p.35).

So he argues that what is needed is a recovery of *theologia*: that is a reflective discipline that combines the necessary demands of intellectual rigour and quest for truth that is harnessed to a vision of God and a personal commitment.

> *Theologia* is a sapiential (existential) personal and praxis-orientated understanding and as such is the way faith rises to self-conscious dealing with the world. *Theologia* is salvation viewed as a self-conscious interpretive activity. (p.170)

Out of doing theology comes not primarily information or skills or theory, but the informed heart and mind that has learnt the art of discernment and is oriented towards the truth as found in Jesus, which is able, in all the demands and pressures of the coming and going of life, to recognize intuitively, out of *habitus,* what is true, honourable, just pure and lovely (Philippians 4:8).

What then emerges for our interlocutors from this somewhat condensed and difficult section on theory and practice? I would suggest two further points.

First, those gathered round the table in that seminar room, each engaged in some kind of specialized ministry, knew that they were indeed at the heart of the theological process. They may have come together to reflect and learn but they had not come away to the source of a golden thread that would lead them through their labyrinth to a solution. They had come together with their tutors, to share in the essential theological enterprise which takes place in the concrete reality of history. Their fundamental instincts were just right. Theology is done at the point where one is set and with the tools that are to hand. This is the form of the life of faith.

Second, it has also helped us confirm that theology is not foremost a discipline or a body of knowledge but a process of discovery, the pursuit of wisdom and the discovery of salvation. The root of practicality is the informed disposition, the engaged personality.

Contemporary pressures

There was, however, another undertone in the discussion in the seminar; a sense of confusion in the face of disarray in the theological world. The pastoral context is complex and pressured enough, how is it also possible to cope with theological diversity well?

There are some who can remember when it did not always feel like this. It was assumed that it is possible to read off from the Bible and tradition, using accepted scholarly methods and findings, a distinctive Christian perspective that could enable the renewal of discipleship in technological industrial society. Perhaps there was a fey naivety about Biblical theology, though its achievements are not inconsiderable or irrelevant. However, history does not stand still. Today, increasing secularism and pluralism have shifted familiar landmarks and opened up fissures in society, not to mention the impact of the advances of science and technology. This has been reflected in a theological pluralism and insecurity, together with a neo-confessionalist backlash. All this may be exciting, even worthwhile, but it does make for uncertainty in an already uncertain world. What, however, can be said from the Christian perspective that can provide both acceptance and support in the struggle to discern the Gospel in today's rapid social change? What is the pastoral word for both the pastor and the people in these circumstances? Can we discern basic themes that suggest that theology is properly done from within the tension of our human ambiguity?

First, there is the notion of eschatology. Christianity looks to a fulfilment which grows out of history and yet is beyond history. But meanwhile all is provisionality, a building up and casting down. At the heart of the tradition stands Jesus as the pledge of all that is valued and hoped for; but we also await the Kingdom. We are on a journey that has yet to be completed. This is not to play down the present but is an affirmation of the provisional as the place where Christ can be found, where something of the future may be experienced. Only from the perspective of the end may all be understood, but that which is to be revealed will take up into itself what we have made of today.

Second, part of the Christian virtue of faith is patience, the willingness to bear the dark and not give up under adversity. If we have to be patient with God, trusting where we cannot see, so too God is patient with us, giving us time and opportunity to grow towards him. Theology may be fragmented, marginalized, hesitant; but to do theology at all is itself an act of faith and an affirmation of the worthwhileness of the search for wisdom and truth.

Third, the journey is not undertaken alone. We belong to the community of faith and share together in the common struggle. So it does not all depend on me. Faith is embraced and expressed in and through the communion of saints. Theology is a function of the whole People of God. It is possible to trust others in our weakness and to share together in comfort and wisdom, being formed together in the common life. The Christian does not have to live in isolation but with friends and allies which help to guide our choices and shape our perspectives.

Fourth, Christian theology is essentially incarnational. Truth is discovered in the swirl and buffeting of our existence. Here we are plunged right back to the fundamental perspective that has informed these remarks. In the end there is no escape from the ambiguities of history because that is how we human beings are, that is where we find joy and hope, anxiety and pain, truth and falsehood; and above all, that is where, in Christian terms, God is found, revealed and yet hidden, the beyond in the midst.

The theologian as artist

Finally, who is this theologian who stands in the midst of the Church and in the midst of the world seeking to articulate and inform faith? Perhaps the image that best gathers up all that has been suggested is the theologian as artist.

The artist brings to the creative act, first of all, skills and experience, which are constantly trained and nurtured, often with long practice and patient repetitive copying. Yet techniques are there to become servants, giving freedom to employ them at will and to be dispensed with at need.

The artist brings to the creative act, second, a sense of discipline, the knowledge of how to work with material that has its own properties, strengths and beauty. The task is to draw out the best and to facilitate the creative potential of what lies to hand.

The artist brings to the creative act, third, imagination and attention, the ability to see in the ordinariness the tender realities of the joy or pain, fear and wonder; and so to bring them out that others are enabled to see with new eyes that which is now true yet has, in a real sense, always been true.

The artists brings to the creative act, fourth, a vision of the world, a glimpse of the ultimate that is both beyond reach and yet infinitely near. In our fragment of existence we can recognize the web of transcendence. Henri Nouwen (1986) refers, in one of his diaries, to Rilke's comments on Cézanne:

> Not since Moses has anyone seen a mountain so greatly ... only a saint could be so united with his God as Cézanne, in Rilke's view, was able to be fully present to the present and could therefore see reality as it is. (p.96)

The artist brings to the creative act, fifth, the ability to pour out one's being into the beloved object, to know that what is made is greater than the maker. In religious language this would be spoken of in terms of sacrifice and redemption.

The artist is the most individual of all people yet never alone. The artist has a compulsion, an energy that cannot but express itself. Charles Morgan, in his play, *The River Line*, has a fugitive RAF pilot in occupied France burn, under orders, a poem he had just written, though no one else had read it. No matter, for he had himself been engaged in the act of creation. That which demanded to come into existence had taken form. Nor was it wasted for its existence had been affirmed, even if only by the writer. Yet art essentially communicates. Its aim is to enable others to catch a vision, discover a truth, experience renewal. Art is a public activity, growing out of and speaking to communal experience. It can focus celebration and shared events; or speak in prophetic judgement. Art can be housed in galleries and mansions or be part of the life of the street or marketplace.

The artist participates in and is created by the artistic process. Through the act of creation the artist both bares the inner spirit and exposes it to being transformed into a new image, re-created through the struggle. Yet there is also a sense of presence, of serving that which commands through gentle persuasion, of being caught up in that which is greater and nobler. Even failure or exhaustion is not shame because there is further opportunity, a true vocation: being called out to fresh ventures.

So the artist embodies what Pascal called the greatness and misery of humanity, for in the one person is found both the broken contingency of being human and the glory that is only found in the earthen vessel. John De Gruchy (1986) describes the theologian as being there to enable the community of faith critically to understand its faith and express answers to the questions: Who is God? Where is God to be found today and what does this God require of us here and now? (p.55).

But Dorothy Sayers, in *The Mind of the Maker* (1941), reverses the process; for if we are made in the image of God, then our creative activity mirrors forth that image of God himself.

> If you ask me, What is this pattern which I recognize as the true law of my nature, I can only suggest it is the pattern of the creative mind – an eternal Idea, manifested in material form by an unresting Energy, with an outpouring of Power that at once inspires, judges and communicates the work. And this I observe, is the pattern laid down by the theologians as the pattern and being of God. (pp.172–173)

3

A Vision of Pastoral Theology

In Search of Words that Resurrect the Dead (1994)[1]

Stephen Pattison with James Woodward

Pastoral theology is like a lake where experiences and theories mingle and are creatively transformed – they suffer a 'sea change', to mix images slightly. The lake image is, I hope, both picturesque and useful in grasping some of the broad features of pastoral theological activity, that is, the process whereby experiences and events are held and mixed together. It gives an overall sense of the size, scope and nature of pastoral theology. (Actually, it is more accurate to talk of pastoral theologies in the plural, all of which have some concern with the understanding and transformation of theory and practice, but which have very different concerns, focuses, methods and outcomes.) However, it does not do much to answer the question: How is pastoral theology done? There are a number of ways and methods for undertaking pastoral theological activity. My own preferred image or model for this is that of critical, creative conversation between (a) my own ideas, beliefs, feelings, perceptions and assumptions; (b) the beliefs, perceptions and assumptions arising from the Christian community and tradition; and (c) the contemporary situation, practice or event which is under consideration. The model of conversation has several positive features to it. Conversation often lies at the centre of human and pastoral encounters so it seems natural to extend its usage analogously into the formulation of pastoral theologies. Conversations can be short or long, deep or superficial, involve two or more parties or factors, and they do not necessarily proceed in a straightforward direction or at the same level. Used in pastoral theology, a conversational model does not necessarily require a lot of previous knowledge (e.g. about theology or a particular event or situational, but it does presuppose a willingness to attend, to listen and to learn. The skills and conventions of conversation can be learned and benefit from practice with other people. In the end, good, creative conversations change people and their view of the world, perhaps not profoundly and immediately, but definitely and gradually. (It is helpful here to remember that, as in the Bible, words are in some sense deeds and they shape events and actions.) Conversation and talk is the stuff of individual and social life. There are advantages in seeing pastoral theological process as an enjoyable, illuminating and often demanding conversation which draws participants onwards and outwards without prescribing exactly where they should end up or what they should do.

I want now to look at some of the main actual or possible features which characterize contemporary pastoral theological conversations in all their diversity. What follows is partly prescription (what I hope pastoral theologies will be and take into account), partly description (observation of what is already going on). The list of features presented here may be characteristic of what some pastoral theologies might be in practice. They are in no particular order of importance or significance.

Transformational

Aristotle distinguished between practical reasoning, which helps to distinguish the proper course of action or conduct, and theoretical reasoning, which helps one to arrive at true statements and beliefs (Hampshire 1978, pp.23ff). Pastoral theologies arise in the sphere of practical reasoning and that they need to engage more of the person than the faculty of reason. They help people to distinguish how they should act and be. More than this, the kind of knowledge which is contained and expressed in pastoral theologies, even in their written form, is transformational knowledge.

Transformational knowledge is *soft* knowledge.

> [It] involves intuition, wisdom, and mystery in contrast to technical control ... Transformational knowledge is a 'peculiar' amalgam, different from the methodological knowledge sought by the humanities in their academic and scholarly pursuits. Members of the transformational disciplines are always faced with the 'messy' aspects of human life. (Patton 1990, p.70)

Transformational knowledge emanates in large part from the transitional realm of the symbol. Here reason and emotion, conscious and unconscious, intersect and interconnect to generate fundamental, if not necessarily verbally expressible, understandings, hopes, fears and world views. It is in this dimension that religion operates and from which it gains its importance and significance. Transformational, knowledge is messy. It amounts to informal knowledge, personal knowledge and that elusive thing *wisdom*: the kind of knowledge which is very difficult to evaluate and assess by any kind of examination process. It arises from people's experience of living and their dialogue (at all sorts of different levels) with experience. Arising from 'talking back' to experience and activity, it is both knowledge in action and knowledge as action (Schön 1991). It cannot be produced apart from action. Because of this, it is partial knowledge. While it has objective and communicable aspects, it cannot be exhausted in words and it is difficult to describe. It is knowledge that makes a difference, changing and transforming people and situations even as it is itself transformed and changing (Pruyser 1987, p.5).

Increasingly we are living in an environment where all activity must be measured and clearly described in terms of actual behaviour. Vague concepts of 'education' are giving way to more limited, concrete ideas of vocational training through the National Vocational Qualification scheme, designed to produce particular skills and competencies for specific defined roles. However, at the very moment when a narrow, ratio-technocratic, instrumental view of life seems about to triumph, the realization that not everything can be reduced to these terms is beginning to emerge. Senior managers in the public sector, for example, are starting to show an interest in nebulous topics such as ethics; they want to develop skills of judgement and discernment which are not easily categorizable. Some nurses are revolting against the idea that all their activity can be reduced to itemizable and separable acts – the actual task of nursing, they say, is more than the sum of its separate parts. The time has come for practical wisdom or transformational knowledge to re-emerge as a major resource for practice.

Browning, who works with a strongly cognitive, rational view of practical theology, suggests that it should be action guiding (Browning 1983b). If the process of pastoral theological activity and reflection makes no difference to what people do or how they see the world it becomes a limited, abstract and disconnected intellectual quest. However, I think it is better to describe pastoral theologies as transformational rather than action guiding. Action guiding implies a process of straight translation of theory into practice – you set your theoretical objective, identify your goals and make your plans for proceeding from here to there in as straight a line as possible. Things are never as simple as this; people are not wholly rational, and reality is complicated.

Theological aims and principles, worked out in theory, are not implemented in action in a straightforward way. That is why the Kingdom of God has still not come on earth, despite centuries of religious education and training. The process of undertaking pastoral theology transforms people, their views of the world and their actions, producing new ways of seeing and possibilities for acting. It does not necessarily produce clear actions and easily measurable outcomes. What can be measured is not necessarily what is most wanted or most valued anyway; what price wisdom, care, or love? Pastoral theology stands for a complex view of reality which incorporates meanings, images, metaphors, stories and feelings as well as thoughts and actions. This is a kind of practical wisdom which is more valuable and more elusive than action guiding plans; it is part of what a religious world view distinctively has to offer.

Not just propositional, rational and logical

Christian theological activity has been dominated by dogmas, propositions and arguments to which 'believers' have been invited to give basically cognitive assent. Theologians since the Enlightenment have devoted much time and effort to showing how rational Christianity is. A good performance in such theology is one that is reasonable, well-argued, logical, linear, abstract, analytic and orderly, one which appeals to that which is rational in all people. This is consonant with the idea of God as a principle of rationality whose main gift to humankind is that of reason which is regarded as the chief feature of the God's image in us.

While this approach has many strengths, e.g., liberating Christianity from superstition, it is deficient. People are more than their minds. They have emotions and non-logical parts; these are as important as reason in determining how they react and behave (Kitwood 1990). A feminist perspective suggests that cognitive rationality, far from being the highest and most important part of all human beings, is just the self-conscious state of men: 'Objectivity is a word men use to talk about their own subjectivity' (Rich, cited in Morris 1992, p.159). Faith itself can be seen as an act of trust in the being of God rather than cognitive assent to proposals about the deity. Religion derives much of its real significance precisely from the fact that it speaks to the preconscious and unconscious part of the person and the community, the transitional part where symbol and pre-linguistic perception holds sway. This aspect of existence is not primarily addressed or expressed by linear logic and clear proposition, but more by myth, metaphor, image, symbol and story that nuance and colour perceptions of self and world.

Awareness of the hiddenness of much of the personality leads me to argue for the need to express theology in terms of rich story, symbol, image, metaphor and myth. All discourse is filled with these elements anyway, but they are often not easy to spot, particularly if they closely reflect what we take to be common-sense or scientific reality (Midgley 1992; Rorty 1989). The power of these elements cannot be underestimated. The metaphor of the marketplace which has been made a reality in the NHS, for example, has rendered some features of reality very visible (competition, 'customers', suspicion) while hiding features which were visible under the old mythology of the state-provided welfare system (co-operation, patients, trust). Indeed, the whole of British public service has been transformed by a language full of vivid images, many ironically drawn from apocalyptic Christianity, such as 'mission', 'vision' and 'doom scenario'. Rationality does not need to be excluded from pastoral theological process, but its dominance needs to be relativized (Oakley 1992).

Paradoxically, at a time when people outside religion are drawn to exploring the potential of images, metaphors and myths to motivate and change, theologians can feel embarrassed and de-skilled in their use (Soskice 1985). Words, images and myths by which people can understand and lead their lives are vital in an age of mass communication (Campbell 1976; May 1991). It is important that pastoral theologies should rediscover a ministry of the word which transforms and brings to life, cracking open new possibilities. If, as R.S. Thomas (1992) has suggested, God is a great metaphor, then this metaphor has been enormously generative and creative over the centuries, creating new possibilities from people's reflections upon and refractions of metaphorical truth. A truthful fiction may be worth any amount of argument and pseudo-rationality in transforming the world – hence the enduring power of fairy-tales and stories from the Bible. The words used in pastoral theology, like the word spoken in and through Jesus, should be fruitful, full of surplus meaning. They point beyond themselves to something more, and express the eschatological tension between what is and what might be.

I have already alluded to the work of Alves (1984), Cupitt (1991), Sölle (1981; 1993), McFague (1987; 1993) and R.S. Thomas, suggesting that their skilled use of metaphors and words is a way of breathing new life into situations and experiences as well as into theology. The same could be said of approaches to pastoral theology which take narratives and stories seriously. Cupitt (1991) points out that we all live our lives as linear narratives, not as expressions of abstract theoretical or theological ideas. Christianity is full of powerful stories but has not valued the temporal narrative, preferring the eternal abstraction. Pastoral care has, however, always had to pay attention to the stories of individuals, mingling these with aspects of the traditional Christian narrative. It is good to see some pastoral theologians paying more attention to the mingling and clash of narratives, individual and corporate, contemporary and historical, which could be so fruitful for a pastoral theology that remains close to the actual texture of the lived reality of communities and individuals (Jacobs 1988; Woodward 1990).

Pastoral theologies which spring from people's own words and stories must learn to be creative with them. They have to discover how to dance and move, to speak not only to people's minds but to their whole being. Christianity is familiar with the creative use of word, symbol, ritual and image. It is pastoral theologies that will elicit new ways of working with these life-giving traditional elements. In doing this, they will render a considerable service both to the church and to the world where false and destructive myths may otherwise have free reign.

Confessional and unsystematic

By describing pastoral theological activity as confessional I want to suggest that it is prepared to find its own expression of faith and personal and group experience and to speak directly about this, as did the early Christian apostles. It is confessional, too, in that it helps people to bear witness to the truths and questions of religion in a particular context.

It is partly because it is the product of direct reflection of particular and immediate situations and events that pastoral theology finds it hard to be systematic. Traditionally, the aspiration of theology has been to provide reasoned and ordered utterance at a high level of abstraction which has consistency and coherence, covering many eventualities, themes and areas in an even and illuminating way. Pastoral theologies cannot (and perhaps should not wish to) aspire to this level of second- or third-order theology (Fierro 1977, p.317). It takes time and effort to develop complex systematic theologies and they may be of limited practical use once they have been manufactured. Pastoral theologies will need to content themselves with being, for the most part, fragmentary, partial and unsystematic. In the modern world this should perhaps be recognized as grounds for pride rather than an inferiority complex! It is not only well-ordered theoretical systematic theology (second- or third-order theological activity) which covers all the bases in the game which is real theology and worth doing.

Truthful about reality

The great monotheistic religions have been unswerving in their stand against idolatry. That which is less than God should be named as such and should not be worshipped or obeyed. This tradition, exemplified by prophets and other 'paradigmatic performers' of the lived language of faith, can be married up of finding God in present reality exemplified by mystics such as Caussade and Meister Eckhart; there is nowhere that we can find God except in the realities of the present time and God is not absent from that reality (Caussade 1959; Eckhart 1980). One of the most important functions of pastoral theologies formulated within the Christian tradition is to be faithful to, and truthful about, reality, however difficult that may be.

Of course, it can be argued that there are many realities, and there are many different interpretations of reality even amongst contemporaries ostensibly observing the same circumstances. In complex situations and institutions truth is contested and not immediately apparent. It is not that different interpretations should be crushed in favour of one unitary idea or explanation but that part of any worthwhile pastoral theology is likely to be bearing truthful witness to reality as it is perceived. This may include a refusal to be simplistic about the complexities of a situation, however hard they may be to live with.

Witness, which may be costly, is part of the vocation of pastoral theology. It is fundamental if this activity is to be seen as relevant and authentic. In the modern world, in public service organizations for example, there seems to be a willingness for deception of self and others to creep in. All is for the best in the best of all possible worlds, we are told. What makes pastoral theology an important activity is its consonance with a spiritual tradition that requires truth and the facing of reality not the attempt to wishfully pretend that things are actually different. This kind of witness is essential to the integrity of pastoral theologians. It is also part of the genuinely practical service that they can offer to others, both inside and outside the church (Church of England 1985; Pattison 1994, pp.261ff).

Apophatic

In a sceptical age much pastoral experience has to do with exploring gaps, holes, shadows and uncertainties. There are huge chasms between confident theological assertions about the unfailing love of God and, say, the death of five million Jews in Nazi Germany or the death of a child at the hands of other children. Because of its central concern with the realities of experience which contains much to perplex and upset it is part of the task of pastoral theology to be apophatic, i.e. to follow the tradition of asserting the difference and strangeness of God as well as asserting the deity's similarity and closeness to human beings (Bondi 1983). Pastoral theology lives close to the dark, unexplained and unacceptable parts of life and treats of a God whose face is hidden in reality, whose presence is known more by its perceived absence and revealed in the longing desire which is part mourning over loss, part hopeful expectation (Alves 1984, chapter 2). In pastoral theologies much can be learned from the gaps and silences exposed in existence by paying close attention to the real experience of human beings. This kind of *via negativa* cannot be spurned or neglected if pastoral theologies are to have credibility and relevance. Darkness can bear within it a kind of transfiguration, but only if it is acknowledged as darkness in the first place.

Contextual and situationally related

Pastoral theologies need to be contextual and situationally related; they must forgo the desire to address all people in every place. If they are to be useful and authentic, pastoral theologies will emerge out of particular experiences and situations and they may have little significance beyond these situations. Attempts to generalize and universalize often render theologies suspect (consider the churches' teaching on matters sexual which often pays little or no attention to the actual sexual experience of real people).

Pastoral theology at its best, like cultural anthropology, is probably a small-scale enterprise which pays minute attention to particular situations and is more remarkable 'for the delicacy of its distinctions not the sweep of its abstractions' (Geertz 1991, p.25). It needs to pay minute attention to seeing and understanding a particular phenomenon and to listen before moving into carefully chosen words. Contextually and situationally sensitive pastoral theologies will be modest in their claims and assertions. This is a welcome feature amidst the past grandiosity of many theological enterprises which have sought to control and order the world rather than to understand it and to set particular individuals and communities free.

According to context and situation, pastoral theologies will vary greatly in terms of content, method and practical implications. A pastoral theology relating to care of cancer patients in the NHS will probably look very different from one that tries to reflect upon care in prisons. This raises the problem of orthodoxy and conformity to central aspects and norms and methods of the religious tradition. While there may be a danger of destructive heterodoxy here, for pastoral theology to be a creative, related activity there must be the possibility of developing new insights and directions. The alternative is death and irrelevance; conformity and orthodoxy can be over-rated virtues.

Flexible and provisional

Orthodox Christianity has prized the permanent, the unitary, the eternally true and valid. One of the most valued features of the deity has been unchangingness and constancy. A definite aspiration has been to rise above the changes and chances of this life to attain that which is solid, lasting and lies 'above'. One way in which permanence and certainty has been sought has been to privilege the beliefs, documents and values produced and espoused by the Christian community in the past whence the highest and most reliable truth is felt to come. This bias is reproduced in theological courses and training for ministry where a lot of time is spent reflecting on tradition and the past.

The desire for conformity with the past (actually a selective modern view of what the past was like which excludes as much as it includes) is challenged by pastoral theologies. These tend to focus on the present, the 'living human document' rather than the dead written one. There is a theological rationale for this. The Christian God is god of the living and of the present and so it is important to discern how this being is involved in contemporary reality.

In an age of rapid change more significance must be given to the transitory. To respond adequately to the present, the work of pastoral theologians must have a considerable degree of provisionality. To feel that one can only engage in activity or thought if it is going to have universal significance for centuries is to opt out of meaningful pastoral theological activity altogether. Pastoral theologies must be flexible and provisional phenomena which change over time and, indeed, seek positively to value the change which is a real sign of life in the world. Flowers are transitory, but this contributes to their value rather than negating it!

Practically, pastoral theorists and practitioners should expect to change their working theories and theologies fundamentally several times in a lifetime. It cannot be a question of acquiring one set of beliefs and methods at an early point in life and continuing to operate with these unchanged until death. While Dean Inge's adage that 'he who would marry the spirit of the age must needs soon find himself a widower' is worth remembering here: theology has for too long been biased towards dalliance with the spirit of yesterday.

Pluralism of form and content

We live in a pluralistic world. Due to ease of travel and communication, we are increasingly aware not only of both our unity and commonality with other people but also our mutual strangeness and differences. While the rhetoric of unity and belonging to a common human race or European Community trips off the tongue, closeness to others reveals that we are separated by great gulfs of language, belief, attitude and culture. In a consumer society the choice of individuals is emphasized and there has been a collapse of socially binding institutions and ideologies. This is reflected on the intellectual level by the post-modern world view which maintains that we are in a kind of Tower of Babel. There are no common, over-arching theories, belief systems, symbols or languages which will enable everyone to see the world from the same angle or to boil down differences into some kind of unity based on rationality (Stout 1988).

In the churches there is increasing recognition that people and groups are very different. Sociologist Peter Berger (1980) argues that we are under a 'heretical imperative' whereby each individual has to choose their own faith. This has set people free to discover and affirm their own world-views, perceptions of God and theologies. Experiential and locally-based theologies such as liberation theology in

Latin America and feminist theology in North America affirm the contemporary experience of the poor or of women and then interrogate the theological tradition from this standpoint. What was once taken to be a unitary body of truth encapsulated in tradition and mediated by the teaching authority of the church has come under attack as people have discovered the human (therefore biased and distorted) basis of traditional theologies which often served as ideological justifications for an oppressive social order. The Platonic God who guaranteed a single truth which could be discovered and used by all within a single, holy, catholic and apostolic church has become less credible in a fragmented world. People allow themselves to express uncomfortable questions about the nature of belief rather than subordinating their doubts and experience to obedient compliance with the interpretations offered them by distant theologians living comfortably in foreign lands (Schreiter 1985).

The pluralism of form and content which is implied here does not necessarily imply isolationism or solipsism. People doing different kinds of pastoral theologies can continue to talk to each other and may do so with greater interest. Although there is some danger in the long run that locally based pastoral theologies may draw so far apart from one another that pastoral theology fragments, at the moment it seems appropriate to say, 'Let a thousand flowers blossom'. We have only just begun to explore the possibilities of practice-related theologies; experimentation and plurality of approach are inevitable but also welcome at this point.

Experiential and practical

In Britain we often have contempt for the practical and resort to ideas and concepts as an ideological way of avoiding experience and practice. So, for example, the ancient Universities of Oxford and Cambridge for a long time rejected courses that focused on professional training for jobs, preferring 'pure' theory as a preparation for life. In theological education, practice mostly comes after theory when people have done a good deal of theology which is based on the reading of books and the writing of essays. Practice and experience are thus regarded as an afterthought or an extra in theology. We are only just beginning to take them seriously as primary sources for pastoral theology.

We owe this liberation from text-centred theologies which are only available to the highly educated and literate to the new theologies of practice which have come out of the deeply practical struggles to change the world. Latin American liberation theologians and other theologians of practice have blown the lid off the idea of theoreticians disconnected from reality in some ideal world of intellectual abstraction (Gutierrez 1974). It is now apparent that all theory is practice- and experience-laden to a large extent and that it has practical implications (Browning 1991). So, for example, some theories, theologies and perspectives will uphold social norms (e.g. the idea that the individual soul is the locus of salvation so individuals conversion is the key to desirable social change) while others will challenge those norms (e.g. the idea that the Kingdom of God is a social entity suggests that salvation should be seen in corporate terms).

This brings me to feminist approaches to pastoral theologies which are amongst the most exciting and fruitful. Much feminist activity has been about entering a cloud of unlearning to find ways of knowing about and expressing experience which values the daily reality of women's lives. There is not much room for, or interest in, abstract ideas that do not reflect present realities here. Feminist pastoral theologians are intellectually extremely rigorous but they have chosen to find a large place for important aspects of women's experience that have been subordinated or ignored within patriarchal pastoral theologies. Thus they give a lot of attention to the actual everyday experience and stories that women tell about their own lives (Glaz and Moessner 1991; Graham and Halsey 1993). Feminists have used mythology, symbols and rituals to explore their own spiritual and theological experience using poems and pictures as much as academic articles to explore and creatively subvert personal and political reality (Daly 1979; 1984). Feminist pastoral theology in its protest against dehumanizing forces, its refusal to turn away from reality, however unpleasant, and its engaged playfulness expressed through many means and media presents a kaleidoscopic range of possibilities for pastoral theologies. Feminist pastoral theologies are not only good with words, they are good with symbols, rituals, images and people. They deserve a lot more attention.

We still have a lot of difficulty in valuing and interpreting experience and practice and relating it to the world of theories. Fortunately, however, there is an increasing number of practitioners and theorists outlining methods which may help us to do this. As embodied inhabitants of earth with one life here it behoves us to take our experience and practice more seriously, though we must beware the danger of experiential fundamentalism whereby we think (a) only experience is important; and (b) our own personal experience is the same as everyone else's, so our experience is normative for everyone.

Reflectively based

A central feature of contemporary pastoral theologies is that of reflection on events and experience in the light of theory and faith. There are several writers who have advanced different methods of reflection on practice or what is sometimes called theological reflection and this is one of the best developed features of the critical conversation which constitutes pastoral theologies today (Foskett and Lyall 1988; Patton 1990). It could be argued that all theology since theology began is reflectively based since none of it has been done in a vacuum separated from the world. Thus, writers like St Augustine might be seen as precursors of modern pastoral theologians. I would certainly affirm the practice-laden and -influenced nature of all theologies down the ages. However, modern pastoral theologies differ in important respects from their predecessors. First, they are self-conscious that their situation is one of engaging in human discourse which says more about humans and present reality than it does about God. Second, they positively value the knowledge and insight that is to be gained from reflection on ordinary human experience, i.e. not just that which comes from prayer and participation in spiritual activities. Last, the reflective process is itself ordered, consciously adopted, reflected upon and can be critically revised if thought to be unsatisfactory.

Dialectical and disciplined in method

Many contemporary pastoral theologies are dialectical in method. They proceed by way of critical conversation between two or more different elements. There are a number of elements or polarities which can form the dialectical poles of pastoral theologies. Some of these are as follows:

theory – practice

past religious tradition – present religious experience

situation – theoretical principle

ideal – reality

theology – other disciplines

church community – secular community

These are just some of the corners of conversation which may be included in pastoral theological activity; the list is suggestive rather than exclusive. The more polarities and tensions that are included in the conversation the more complex it can become. Being clear about the nature of the dialectic polarities being included in 'the 'conversation' is helpful in structuring this activity and assessing its significance.

It is also useful to structure and discipline the 'conversation' so that different voices are clearly heard and attended to instead of there being an unstructured cacophony. This is where methods of theological reflection and hermeneutic circles come in. While these methods can be accused of abstraction, oversimplification, idealization, and encouraging a pooling of ignorance, they can be useful structuring devices. A typical example of this is Lartey's (1996) model of theological reflection used with university students. It starts with an experience arising, for example, from a placement. This is subjected to a situational analysis in which perspectives from non-theological disciplines, for example, sociology and psychology, are introduced to help understand the experience. After this, some aspects of the theological, faith tradition are mobilized to illuminate the situation. Next, a situational analysis of the theological tradition is conducted to expose its limitations and presuppositions. Then possible responses to the situation or experience are conceived and discussed. The process ends with some kind of changed action within the situation.

Interrogative, critical, suspicious

In so far as they are intellectual, rational activities which make use of ideas and theories, pastoral theologies are interrogative, critical and suspicious (Lash 1981).

One way of looking at Jesus is to see him as a question mark. Not only did Jesus spend a great deal of time challenging and questioning his contemporaries by his words and his actions, he is also something of an enigma. It is not possible to know with certainty much of who Jesus was and what he was all about (Bowden 1988; Hamilton 1993). This Jesus, incarnated in church and tradition, interrogates and challenges contemporary action and thought, opening up new ways of seeing and different ways of acting. In this spirit, it is possible to rehabilitate the art of asking good questions as a central skill and virtue for theology. Religion has often tried to provide the comforts of certainty, to assert propositions and to claim knowledge. Jesus' example and the *via negativa* tradition in the Christian theology suggests that there is a very important place of asking and living with questions (Tinsley 1983). Having some of the 'right' questions may be more valuable than having all of the wrong answers.

Pastoral theology can help people to develop the art of asking and living with good, if difficult, questions in particular situations. Some of these may come directly from the theological tradition and scripture. These might include:

- what is being worshipped here?
- what sort of god is being served here?
- what sort of a world do we think we are in?
- what are the possibilities for loving human relationships?
- in what should we put our trust and faith?
- are we serving idols instead of a living God?
- how do we categorize and deal with issues of good and evil?

There are other sources of questions than the traditional discipline of theology. The principle of being critical and suspicious owes as much to 'secular' theories as it does to theology which has frequently encouraged unthinking conformity and obedience. It is once again from the praxis-based theologies of feminism and liberation, heavily influenced by the social sciences and the thinking of Freud and Marx, that we need to learn the arts of criticism and suspicion. These prevent pastoral theologies from being unwittingly conformist and passive in relation to personal and social reality.

Interdisciplinary

One effect of the dethroning of theology as 'Queen of the Sciences' and the realization that it is only one, very human way of understanding and analysing reality has been to make it clear that it needs to draw on other academic and applied disciplines to fully comprehend reality. Psychology, sociology and literary theory are but three of the disciplines which may be used by pastoral theologians in different circumstances. There are substantial difficulties here; there are so many disciplines, sub-disciplines, schools, fields and perspectives for pastoral theologians to choose from in trying to analyse particular phenomena or situations. It is not possible to look at a situation from every possible perspective, so pastoral theologians need to think carefully about which disciplines or combinations of disciplines they are going to use, what significance they are going to give them, and how they will use them. This is a stimulating process, giving pastoral theology much of its attraction and vigour, but it is inevitably frustrating and partial too. And it must not be forgotten that different disciplines in, for example, arts and social sciences, have their own implicit values and theologies which may influence the nature and outcomes of the pastoral theological quest (Ballard 1986).

Socio-politically aware and committed

This feature of contemporary pastoral theologies is implied in many of the others mentioned above. From feminism and other practical liberationist movements we have become aware that no human attitude or activity is politically innocent in a world divided between oppressed and oppressors. Issues of race, class and gender impinge on every aspect of life and pastoral theologies do not stand above this. Indeed, it is the realization that pastoral theology is, *inter alia*, a political activity with important political outworkings that is providing much of the impetus of regeneration for this activity (Pattison 1994).

Communal

Pastoral theologies emerge out of human encounters and institutions, i.e. from real conversations with actual human beings. They are best and most usefully constructed within communities, whether ecclesiastical or other, where they are enriched, made relevant and have a positive value in helping people understand and grasp their situations. And it is in communities and between communities that these theologies will best be criticized, modified and expanded. If a theology is seen as a local language, or at least a locally nuanced language, then acquaintance with other linguistic worlds, conventions and denotations can have a positive, expansive effect which prevents a local language from becoming narrow, exclusive and distorted.

Many of the praxis-based theologies which have emerged in recent years emphasise the importance of groups of ordinary Christians (and others) working together to produce new languages, insights and methods so theology is relevant to particular situations and bears the stamp of communal authenticity. Since theologies reflect the needs and interests of particular communities it is important to ensure that the appropriate people are involved in formulating theologies. So, for example, there should be no formulation of pastoral theologies of homosexuality without homosexual people themselves being involved in the conversation. Theologies should also be communally owned, neither the product nor property of an elite minority group. There is beginning to be a good deal of knowledge about how to create and develop theology-producing communities beyond that of traditional scholarly academics. The rediscovery of the central place of the whole community in the production of relevant theologies is one of the great resources for undertaking the pastoral theological process today.

Analytical and constructive

Pastoral theological activity will often have both analytical and constructive aspects. Pastoral theologies can help people to understand the reality of the situation they are in and how to ask relevant, apposite questions. The importance of this kind of critical analysis cannot be overstated. Although it may sound rather dull, or even destructive, it is important to have a clear understanding of where you are if you wish to see the drawbacks and opportunities in a situation and in your role in that situation. Without a good analytic grasp of a situation you have limited options in seeking to affirm or change it. So analysis is an important 'moment' or point in the overall process of pastoral theological activity. This helps to question situations, institutions and our place within them. It will suggest ways in which things could and should be different.

However, analysis is not the last word, nor an end in itself. Becoming aware of the complexities of a situation can lead to an inability to act or discern a direction, producing 'paralysis by analysis'. Although the importance of description and analysis is vital and should not be hurried or skimped, it is essential that pastoral theologies should go on to construct positive directions for proceeding when this is possible. It is not enough to stoically expose the nature of situations only to opt out when it comes to changing them. New visions and directions are required; pastoral theology can do much to indicate what these might be while being mindful of the need not to move from description to prescription in an over-hasty or over-dogmatic way.

Public and clearly expressed

Theologies of all kinds are in danger of being dismissed as irrelevant in a secularized world. Theologians generally have an unfortunate habit of writing and speaking in a kind of private language which is only understood by a very limited number of people. Their books are only read by other theologians. They are published by specialist religious publishers, and they are not taken seriously unless they appear to be challenging the government on some issue. Thus most theological activity has become marginal, private and of little interest to non-specialists. This must be resisted because, as we have seen, a main aim of pastoral theologies is to make a difference in the contemporary world. If pastoral theologies are to be worth engaging in at all they must respond to the real situations of and strive to express themselves in words and concepts that ordinary people will understand so they will be of some use as transformative knowledge. J.L. Austin (Austin in Phillips 1993, p.xi) warns, 'it is not enough to show how clever we are by showing how obscure everything is'. It is here that images and metaphors can economically and interestingly encapsulate much truth – consider the power of David Jenkins image of 'a conjuring trick with bones' to denote some of the issues and problems surrounding the events of Easter.

The challenge to pastoral theologians is to address issues which are of significance to people and to find imaginative ways of discussing these and encapsulating them in language so that a wide variety of people can become involved in transforming pastoral theological activity.

Skilful and demanding

I have portrayed pastoral theological activity as being like a conversation to emphasize the fact that it is comprehensible, normal, ordinary and approachable. Pastoral theologies can only benefit from having width of involvement from a range of people and perspectives and this is desperately needed. However, it would be unfortunate if the impression was given that there is no skill, discipline or learning required for pastoral theology so that it is seen as no more than 'common sense'. Pastoral theology is demanding and requires the acquisition of new knowledge and skills. Every method and model of doing pastoral theology implies a curriculum and a set of skills to be learned. So, for example, people who want to use a liberationist methodological circle for group reflection might potentially need to acquire a knowledge of sociology, of politics and of economics, as well as needing groupwork skills and some knowledge of relevant aspects of the theological tradition! (Green 1987; Pattison 1994).

Those adopting different paradigms might need other skills and knowledge. People wishing to explore the pastoral theological potential of narratives and stories could benefit from acquiring skills of textual interpretation, literary criticism, listening, speaking and story-telling, while those who want to explore the potential of imagistic or preconscious aspects of personality for theological insights may need to grasp skills of verbal free-association from therapists or poets, as well as understanding something of the nature of the mind and personality. The relevant knowledge and skills need not be narrowly academic or cognitive, however. Artistic and emotional training may be essential for some kinds of pastoral theologies; perhaps the most important generic skill of all will be that of being able to exercise sustained attention to people and events (Murdoch 1970).

Editorial Note

1   This chapter has been extracted from a Contact Pastoral Monograph by Pattison and Woodward (1994) under the same title.

PART TWO

Practical Theology and the Art of Theological Reflection

4

Pastoral Action and Theological Reflection (1989)

David Lyall

While the phrase 'theological reflection' is widely used there have been comparatively few attempts to make explicit what this might mean in practice. This paper explores the implications of one model set out by Edward Farley (1987) in a recent important book. The pastoral situation is perhaps described as being 'fictional but informed by the experience of more than one hospital chaplain.'

The situation: The chaplain's story

It had been a good afternoon. I had spent most of it in the Kidney Transplant Unit, all the patients who had had transplants were doing well and it was easy to reflect on how advances in medical science were, quite literally, giving some people a new lease of life. There were problems of course and, as we chatted, the staff made me aware of them.

Then my bleep went. A few minutes later I was in the Neurosurgical Unit. Three days previously a 35-year-old man had been admitted after sustaining a severe head injury at work. His condition had deteriorated and he was now on a life-support system. All the tests had been done and brain-stem death confirmed. The man carried a kidney donor card and his family had agreed that his kidneys could be used. The transplant team had been alerted. The machine was due to be switched off soon. The family had asked if a chaplain could come and say a prayer. (At least that is what I was told – one is never quite sure.)

I entered the room where the patient lay. It was full of relatives, sitting or standing, not knowing where to put themselves; it was hot and smelt of humanity – and the rhythmic sound of the machine filled the unspeakable silence. The words of my prayer I do not remember but I recall the anxiety about what to pray for in that situation – obviously not for physical healing – at least it was obvious to me.

Part of my anxiety related to the fact that I had not previously met the family. His wife was there and his mother – and the rest of the room seemed to contain a football team and their wives. Precipitated into that room, it was difficult to give any structure to pastoral care. If it was a prayer they wanted it was a prayer they would get, and I guess I prayed for peace, for peace for the dying man at the end, for peace for his family in their distress and (silently) a prayer to God to help me cope with the situation.

As I finished the prayer I opened my eyes and saw the wife and mother standing on either side of the patient, each with a hand upon his chest, as it heaved up and down to the rhythm of the machine. I saw their eyes meet. Silently they moved together into the corridor and made a beeline for the sister. I followed them and overheard them say, 'Sister, they won't switch of that machine until he stops breathing will they?' The ward sister was somewhat taken aback. After all, she had been there when the Registrar had explained everything to them. She thought they had understood. The sister sent for the Registrar who came and explained again. But no, the mother and wife were adamant. The machine was not to be switched off until he had stopped breathing. Wife and mother returned to the patient's room to mount guard into the evening and through the night. The rest of the family went home.

Eventually dawn broke and in a state of utter exhaustion, the two women did go home saying that they would return later. At 9 a.m. the Consultant arrived back, having been away for a few days. Once the situation had been described to him he took the only decision which could be taken. The brain death tests had been done twice and there was no doubt at all the criteria had been met. The machine had to be switched off as soon as contact could be renewed with the transplant team. No one disagreed with this decision. The question was – could the situation be handled in a way which was pastorally sensitive and at the same time save the kidneys for two very sick people who had already been alerted to the possibility of a transplant?

The sequence of events was then as follows. Just as the family returned the machine was switched off and the family was told that the man had died. I then took the wife and mother into the room where the dead body lay. We spent a few minutes there after which they were ready to move to another room. I spent a while with them as formalities such as death certificate, etc. were completed, and linked them up with a local minister. Meanwhile, as I spent time with the family, the body was quietly removed to a theatre where the kidneys were removed.

Two days later the story ends where it began, in the Transplant Unit. I met a new patient who had been on dialysis for years. He had been given a new kidney and was doing well. He wondered where it had come from. I did not encourage further exploration.

Theological reflection

The model of reflection used can be described as hermeneutical because it is concerned with the interpretation of situations. This approach is part of a much bigger phenomenon and that is the rediscovery of Practical Theology as a theological discipline. New approaches are moving Practical Theology beyond what

Farley describes as 'the clerical paradigm', beyond a focus upon the training and work of the ordained ministry, to a Practical Theology which is concerned with critical theological reflection upon the life of the whole church and, even more important, with critical theological reflection upon Christian presence and action in the midst of contemporary society. I propose first of all to describe Farley's methodology, then explore it to what extent it helps us to interpret the situation already described.

Interpreting situations

Farley's thesis is that 'the interpretation of situations be self-conscious, self-critical, and disciplined. In other words, similar demands are placed on the believer's interpretation of situations as on the believer's interpretation of ancient texts.'

He begins by defining a situation (which like reality itself is never static) as the way various items, powers and events gather together so as to require responses from the participants, who need not be individuals but may also be groups and communities. He then identifies four tasks.

The first is simply to identify and describe the distinctive and constituent features. This task may sound neutral and relatively simple – but it is not, and for two reasons. The first reason is that we human beings filter all situations not only through our own world views and the taken-for-granted 'knowledge' of our social worlds but through our idolatries. There is therefore much more in a situation than appears on the surface. To discern the components is itself an act of serious and even theological self-criticism. We need to be aware of our own bias, our theological presuppositions, in describing the situation.

The second reason is that the components of situations are always entities of different 'genre': human beings as individuals, world views, groups of various sorts, the pressures of the past, 'futurity', various strata of language and social power. 'Reading the situation' is the task of identifying these genres of things and discerning how they hang together.

The second task has to do with the past. Human historical situations do not present to us the whole past. What does persist into the present is what has not been repressed. While tradition hands on some of the past, that same tradition disguises and even conceals much of the past. The present is comprised of and structured by these disguised repressions of the past.

The third task is to correct the abstraction which has been committed by the focus upon a single situation. Situations occur within systems. We need to identify the place of a situation within a total system. The internal analysis of a single situation is not adequate.

The fourth task may be the most complex of all. While theological perspectives and criticism must be operative in all the tasks of discerning the situation, in this fourth task the theological element becomes central. Why? Because a situation is not neutral. It demands a response. It is a concentration of powers which impinges upon us as individual agents or as communities. Situations may offer promise and possibility or situations may require obligation. But neither the promise nor the obligation are straightforward. As Farley puts it:

> A theological version of this task cannot avoid the insights of its own mythos into the corruption and redemption of human beings. Because of that corruption human beings shape the demand of the situation according to their idolatries, their absolutized self-interests and their participations in the structures of power. Faith then interprets situations and their demands as always containing these elements of corruption and redemption. Situations pose to human beings occasions for idolatry and redemption.

What Farley seems to be saying is that theological reflection consists of something more than making tidy intellectual connections with theological concepts from outside the situation, but rather of examining a situation and identifying the structures of idolatry and redemption which are inherent in the situation. It seems to me that this takes our understanding of theological reflection beyond the application of biblical texts, naively interpreted, to concrete situations especially when, as is so often the case, no hermeneutical principles are applied to the interpretation of the biblical texts themselves.

There are, of course, unspoken assumptions in Farley's hermeneutical method. One is that the central Christian themes of idolatry and redemption can be taken as normative for the interpretation of situations. A second is that we know what is meant by the words 'idolatry' and 'redemption', and this must be filled out by our understanding of the biblical background.

'Applied Farley'

It will be recalled that Farley's first hermeneutical task is the accurate description of the situation. It must be recognized from the outset that the situation has been filtered through the eyes of a hospital chaplain, with his own taken-for-granted knowledge of the hospital, his own prejudices and attempts at self-justification. It would perhaps (indeed almost certainly) have been described differently by the wife and mother of the dying man or by the ward sister. What I have attempted to do is to describe my own attempt to minister to a family in crisis. But I do not wish at this stage to get caught up in the clerical paradigm, but rather to look at the total situation. It is as we try to identify the components of the situation that we will begin to grasp its complexity.

And what are the components of the situation? Obviously there are people – the dying man, his grieving family, an overworked staff who are trying to do their best for everybody, and in the shadowy background, two very sick people who may or may not get new kidneys. And there are other components in the situation of different genre, the hospital's protocols (or lack of them – for these were early days) for coping with a situation like this. And behind the protocols, the ethical issues. If a dying man has signed a Donor Card should that be sufficient authority for the hospital to act? There is also the question of priorities. What is most important – the wishes of the dying man, the needs of the grieving relatives, or the needs of the potential recipients.

Thus simply to describe the situation raises issues of ethical and theological significance. At least one of the theological issues has to do with our understanding of death. Death may be defined (or not defined) biologically, but is there not also a theological contribution to our understanding of when a human life ceases to exist in this world? And when it comes to the issue of competing priorities, whose needs should be considered most important? Does the doctrine of Man not give us some clue about what it means to be human in the eyes of God?

Farley's second task was concerned with identifying the influence of the past. The past impinged upon this situation in several ways. It happened soon after a BBC *Panorama* programme which alleged that in some cases life-support systems had been switched off when the patient might have recovered. And behind the *Panorama* programme there were the cases to which it referred, with all the myths and rumours which come to be associated with these stories.

Our attitudes to death are again brought into question as past understandings make their impact. The traditional attitude has been that where there is breathing there is life. The general public still finds it hard to accept the concept of corpses with beating hearts.

The past also impinges through my own relationship with that unit. It was a unit in which I had always been deeply involved, perhaps more part of the team there than in many other parts of the hospital. Maybe, as chaplain, I had become too much part of that team, taking on board many of their implicit assumptions. The theological issue here is the tension between the pastoral and prophetic. While my own conviction is that one cannot exercise a prophetic role within an institution other than from a pastoral base, this view must be set alongside Old Testament understandings of the relationship between prophecy and priesthood.

And so to Farley's third task, the correction of the abstractions committed by the focus on a single situation in its brevity and specific locality. Obviously the situation on the ward that day occurred within larger situations:

- there are the advances in medical science. The new ethical and pastoral issues are themselves a product of the technology and maybe we need to explore more fully the relationship between technology and ethics (and theology).

- there are political decisions about the allocation of resources. If there is not enough money for dialysis machines, the pressures for transplantation become even stronger. Thus issues of pastoral care cannot be separated from political decisions. And behind the political decisions there are theological issues about the value of human life.

Finally, the fourth task is to identify the structures of idolatry and redemption inherent in the situation:

- the value which society places upon a National Health Service in relation to other (possibly) desirable ends, for example, tax cuts.

- the organization of hospitals in such a way that a constant battle must be waged to prevent the dehumanization of people.

- the God of folk religion, the Lone Ranger who is expected to ride into town just when needed, to clear up the mess and ride off into the sunset making no demands. (This is not meant to be judgemental, simply descriptive.)

And the structures of redemption, the signs of grace? Where was God at work in the midst of that tragic situation? Were there not signs of transcendence in the following?

- in the man who in the first place signed a kidney donor card. Here was a man who believed if he died some good should come of it.

- in the wife and mother who wanted to watch over their man to the very end.

- in the ward sister who held the show together, managing a multi-ringed circus with a deep concern for people amidst the chaos.

- in the good side of the double-edged sword of medical technology, creating possibilities of new life.

- in the wonder and the gratitude of the man who got a new kidney. For some of these folk their experience is akin to resurrection.

- and was there not a word of grace in the weeping thank you of the bereaved wife as she left the hospital, affirming once again the truth that God works in spite of ministry as often as He does through it?

Finally, can this method of interpreting situations help us to think about ministry? Interestingly, having urged us to move beyond the clerical paradigm, Farley reinstates it. But we are not to make it the sole focus of theological reflection. Ministry may simply be part of the situation to be interpreted, nothing more and nothing less. There is a freedom to reflect upon ministry rather than a compulsion to do so. This model is, I believe, characterized not by compulsion but by a freedom to respond to people in a situation out of the riches of the Gospel according to how one interprets the needs of those involved. There is freedom to speak and a freedom to stay silent, a freedom to do and a freedom to do nothing, a freedom to minister through the Word and a ministry of presence, and, as Henri Nouwen (1994) puts it, there is a ministry of presence and a ministry of absence. Interpretation is always prior to acting and speaking.

5

The Case Study Method in Theological Education

(1990)

Michael Northcott

The use of case studies has been a significant feature of vocational training in North American business and law schools, and in medicine, for many years, and they are increasingly used in Britain in the same fields. The case study method in pastoral theology had its origins in the influence of medical and psychotherapeutic practice on the founders of the pastoral theology and counselling movement in the United States, though its first recorded use in pastoral theology was by a nineteenth-century American pastor, Ichabod Spencer, whose pastoral sketches were made better known by Seward Hiltner in his seminal *Preface to Pastoral Theology* (1958). North American pastoral counsellors, most notably Carl Rogers and Russell Dicks, and psycho-therapists such as John Bonnell, used the method of verbatim recording of case interviews extensively, but in pastoral theology it was Seward Hiltner who first showed a theological method by which principles of pastoral theology and practice might be elicited from the study of concrete situations captured in interview and case study material (p.253).

The purpose of recording case material by psychologists and therapists was initially to record details of clients' records and case history (Nouwen 1972). The method then developed into a record of the interaction of therapist and client, and finally into a tool of analysis for the therapeutic relationship. Hiltner adapted the method in a more specifically theological direction, using it to explore how the resources of religion might be brought into therapeutic relationships. Case studies, particularly the verbatim case style, became a standard training procedure in clinical pastoral education in North America in the Fifties and early Sixties, but it is not until the mid-Sixties that we find the method moving beyond the restrictions of the verbatim style and being appropriated for the mainstream of training for pastoral ministry in the parish, most notably by James Glasse (1972, chapters 7 and 8).

The Case Study Method has however not been widely used in Britain in ministerial training and I believe there may be cultural factors at work here in relation to varying educational philosophies in North America and Britain which it is not the primary purpose of this paper to explore. But briefly, Henri Nouwen (1972) rightly points out that the reluctance of pastors to write up case studies of their own interaction with their people is linked to the model of theological education in which they were trained, this being a classroom model where the student is encouraged to write and critically reflect on subjects with a strong theoretical emphasis. Theology represents a package of theoretical disciplines, historical, doctrinal, philosophical, literary. Students are not encouraged to 'do theology' in relation to data from personal or previous professional experience, inter-personal relationships or even societal change. Instead they receive a theological deposit, albeit changing in the light of current scholarly opinion, which in the parish is more often than not deposited quite literally on the shelves of the study, to be consulted for the preparation of sermons. Set in the midst of this theoretical approach, which is still a dominant characteristic of university theology in Britain, the Case Study Method would be a strange, if not alien, style of teaching and theological reflection, but I believe nonetheless a valuable means for bridge-building between theoretical theology and the empirical realities of church and society.

I began using the Case Study Method in 1986, in the Seminar Theology Malaysia, an ecumenical seminary in Kuala Lumpur, Malaysia, both with candidates for the ministry in the weekly field Education Seminar, and with experienced pastors on a pastors' school, and I have now introduced the method into the Diploma/MTh in Ministry in New College, Edinburgh. In this paper I explore the utility of the Case Study Method as a model of theological reflection, and suggest that the method should be more widely adopted in Pastoral Studies, and in in-service clergy training in Britain.

The Case Study Method in practice

James Glasse (1972) describes the Case Study Method as 'a way to present concrete instances of practice to a group of peers for purposes of learning' (p.85). The purpose of the case presentation by each student is not, as in Clinical Pastoral Education (CPE), to record verbatim a conversation with a parishioner, but to describe an 'event' which may be defined as 'an occasion in which the profession (presented) acts as a responsible agent' (p.86). The event is not just a happening which the student observes or a general issue in which the student is interested but something in which the student was genuinely committed and involved and where the effectiveness, competence and consequence of his actions may be observed (p.86). Participants are required to write all the relevant details of the case, confining themselves to one side of a sheet of paper, and to present the case study in four parts. Part of the discipline of case writing is to discover what is relevant to other participants in understanding the event and what is not. Some students typically underestimate the amount of description needed, while others tend to write short stories with numerous biographical details and a series of events over some weeks. The case should be a 'time slice' at a particular stage in an ongoing relationship rather than a total description of a pastoral relationship, and the particular slice of time being described should contain within it an important decision which the presenter had to take within that relationship. Direct quotation from conversations arising during the event may be used sparingly, but the emphasis of the method is on describing the event in narrative form. The four stages in which the Case Study is written up, and which also provide the format of the Seminar procedure are as follows.

1. *Background* The presenter attempts to include as many facts about the actors in the events as are relevant to understanding it, such as personal history, family background, cultural and social information, and Christian formation.

2. *Description* The presenter describes the particular event which is the focus of the case including how the presenter came to be involved, who were the principal actors, what happened, what was said – brief verbatim quotes may add precise colour to the presentation – and what action was taken and with what expectations.

3. *Analysis* The presenter attempts to analyse what was involved in the event: its inner dynamics, the relationships, the tensions and conflicts, the blocks and frustrations, changes and turning-points, the roles being played, and the meanings, understandings and possible motivations which underlay the actions described. The analysis should operate at a number of different levels – inter-personal, psychological, sociological, ethical, cultural, spiritual, theological.

4. *Evaluation* The presenter offers his or her own evaluation of the event and the particular action taken as a piece of professional pastoral practice, whether what was hoped for was achieved, whether it was a good instance of pastoral practice or not and what they might have done differently with the benefit of hindsight (Glasse 1972, p.87).

The case is circulated in advance of the Case Study Seminar to the members of the group. The seminar is chaired by a different student each time, and a scribe records the discussion, preferably on an overhead transparency. The seminar lasts for around one hour and is divided up as follows, again broadly following Glasse's schedule. The first five minutes is for clarification of the information presented in the case, when additional information which may not have been included in the written case may be obtained by questioning from the group. In the two central periods of the seminar the presenter stays silent while her peers explore and reflect on the case. The next twenty-five minutes are for analysis when the group tries to discover what has happened, and the dynamics of the interaction, looking at the event from a variety of perspectives, including insights from the Bible, theology and secular disciplines such as psychology and sociology. The seminar leader has to prevent the group at this stage from evaluating the case before fully analysing it, and her role is also to encourage the participants to engage with the event in full theological seriousness, not simply reacting to it from prejudice or non-reflective presupposition, but drawing on the resources of the Bible, Christian tradition and theology, and secular insight in the discussion. The next fifteen minutes are for evaluation of the professional performance of the presenter and of the theological adequacy of the event. The group asks whether the presenter achieved what was intended and what could have been done better. The group goes on to ask the critical and more theological question as to whether this was worth doing:

[A]t this point theological norms, historical traditions, social needs etc. become critical. What is at stake is the adequacy of the action in relation to the nature of the church, the meaning of ministry, the hierarchy of needs and values of persons and society. (Glasse 1972, p.87)

The final ten minutes of the seminar are for feedback between the presenter and the group where students may say whether the group's discussion was helpful and what additional insights the discussion may have stimulated for the presenter about the event.

Subjects for case studies should and normally do draw on a wide range of ministry experiences. Examples of cases presented in seminars in Malaysia included pastoral encounters involving bereavement, poverty, racial prejudice and family problems, issues over worship such as the type of music or controversy over charismatic styles, people seeking deliverance from perceived oppression by evil spirits, demons or curses, financial corruption in a local church, conflict between a family and a pastor with the student caught in the middle, housing rights on a squatter settlement, and relationship problems between the sexes in youth groups.

The Case Study Method is highly effective as a mechanism of evaluation of student performance on field education placements. The seminar provides an opportunity to students and teachers for regular weekly critical reflection on and assessment of what is taking place on field education placements, both the intensive placements which occur at the end of each academic year and the weekly placements occurring during term. Supervision is a three-cornered relationship between field supervisor, student and the pastoral studies co-ordinator. It is vital that this three-way relationship is recognized in the design of classroom and student review of placement experience. Too often the weak point in vocational training is the link between the placements (including supervision relationship, placement diary and essay, and supervisor's report), and classroom teaching and reflection on pastoral practice and theology.

The Case Study Method is more thoroughly dialectical than courses of theoretical lectures and placement work running side by side which is more typical of pastoral studies training in Britain (Pattison, Bellamy and Easter 1989). The Case Study Method draws on the new experiences and encounters which the student may find the most engaging part of pastoral studies training, and brings them into the centre of classroom-based theological education. My experience of the seminar is that it becomes a popular learning forum which is perceived as student centered, and highly user-friendly. Very occasionally I have been unable to attend the seminar and I find that students are happy to continue the seminar process without a lecturer being present, demonstrating that the method is a genuinely enabling education tool where the focus is on a shared process of peer learning rather than on a bank of learning through which the student is led.

The case study and theological action-reflection

In a recent paper on the subject of theological reflection, Stephen Pattison (1989) proposes a method of critical conversation as a fruitful avenue for constructive theological reflection. His definition of the three corners of a triangular model of theological reflection (the participant's presuppositions, the Christian tradition, and the realities of the empirical situation) is all right as far as it goes, though I wonder if there is not a need for a fourth category of insights from secular disciplines including psychology, sociology and organization theory. However, his idea of a critical conversation lacks the disciplined coherence and simplicity of the Case Study Method. Furthermore without a normal and agreed method by which empirical realities are brought into interaction with presuppositions and the Christian tradition, there is a danger of solipsism in the conversation. The Case Study Seminar is a disciplined and empirically focused model of theological reflection. It is an inter-disciplinary crucible in which the operative theology and vocational motivation of students are manifested and tested, and it functions at a number of different levels.

First, both for the presenter and participating students the method is effective in presenting to them their own presuppositions concerning the pastorate and methods and styles of ministry. The formation of a perception or image of pastoral leadership may arise from a number of places, most typically, the student's own experience of being pastored in her local church, the experience of being fathered or mothered in the family, experiences of leadership, or examples of leadership in educational institutions or national political life. A central aspect of theological formation for ministry is to produce real interaction with these strongly held paradigms of leadership and pastoring which may be deeply embedded in an individual's psyche or personal history, and also closely tied to the sense of call to ministry that the individual perceives. For formation and not just confirmation to occur some development in the individual paradigm of leadership and ministry must take place and the Case Study Method provides an opportunity for this.

In the Case Study Seminar the interaction is primarily between peers. This interaction produces a much greater degree of challenge, even of threat, to the presuppositions about ministry, personality, leadership, counselling and theology which are revealed in, or elicited from, the presenter's case than a series of lectures on ministry. The resultant heightening of consciousness of the implicit or explicit presuppositions in the case being presented produces the opportunity for the individual to begin to adapt her paradigm of pastoring by means of authoritative norms such as biblical models, theological images, ethical ideals or types of professional practice outside of her own paradigm. Robert Towler (Towler and Coxon 1979) has demonstrated that peer group interaction is one of the most powerful forces in the process of personal and professional formation which takes place in theological institutions. The case provides an opportunity to use these forces creatively in a structured and controlled setting.

Second, the method helps the student to begin to learn to juggle with the different disciplines and perspectives of the theological curriculum in analysing and evaluating ministerial practice. Sociological, psychological insight, ethical judgement, exegetical conclusion, and theological proposition may all interact in the group's analysis and evaluation of the dynamics and decisions of a particular case. Students used to being exposed to these disciplines, perspectives in lectures and seminars need to develop skills in building inter-disciplinary bridges with the social and empirical realities of ministry. The Case Study Method provides for this interaction within an action-reflection framework, which enables the student to begin to bridge the gulf between the classroom or library, and pastoral and ministry practice in the church. It is a common assumption of much British professional training, whether for engineering or for Christian ministry, that the bridge between professional theory and professional practice will be created by the student after formal training has ceased. Experience shows that if this bridge is not created within the formal educational process then the new professional will find it difficult within the exigencies and the task orientation of professional practice to establish a bridge for herself. Instead the received habits, norms, practices and perspectives of colleagues or superiors become determinative and normative. If theological formation is to contribute to the renewal and reformation of the ministry and mission of the church in a secular society then theological educators must ensure that the bridging of the gulf between theory and practice commences within the structured educational environment.

Third, the Case Study Method may be effective as a means for the student to identify and develop her own operative theology. The base assumption involved in the contextualization of theology (Asian theology, African theology, Celtic theology) is that theology, talk about God, is essentially related to the language in which we speak about God, the culture in which that language is formed, the experiences of the people who speak that language and their shared assumptions and world view, cultural, spiritual, social, economic and political. A Malaysian student approaching the syncretistic and phenomenological insights of Asian theology needs also to have some idea of her own theology The formation of local theologies at its core involves the relating of individual and group stories and biographies to the paradigmatic biography of Jesus Christ and the corporate biography of God's people in the world and the church. It is in the relating of our individual biographies with the biographies of Christ and his people that contextual theology is created (Hopewell 1989). For students to become active participants in this process, to become doers of theology and not hearers only, a process has to be experienced by which they learn to explore their own theological presuppositions in relationship with their psychosocial and cultural history, their Christian and denominational identity, and their call as theologian and pastor. The Case Study Seminar may represent a significant locus in the exploration and creation of a distinctively Malaysian or Scottish, rural or urban theology.

Fourth, students who have participated in the Case Study Seminar over one or two years of Pastoral Studies training find that, having learnt a disciplined method of reflection on practice, they can apply it to their subsequent ministry experiences without difficulty. The Case Study Method begins to imbue in the participants a capacity for self-review and evaluation as the habit of analysis of particular instances of pastoral practice develops within the group. The variety of perspectives that each participant brings to the seminar, especially when the seminar is ecumenical, extends and sharpens each individual participant's evaluative skills and framework. In future situations of ministry where the student needs to find and establish a method of self-evaluation and self-supervision in ministry s/he can return to the Case Study Method. Ideally it will be a method which can be used with the person who supervises their early parish work, and later it may be a method shared with colleagues in nearby parishes and ministries.

The abstract and non-vocational bias of higher education in Britain is, after the considerable pummelling it has received from the educational 'reforms' of the Eighties, at last beginning to change. As well as the shift to practical pastoral education in theological colleges, university theology must find ways of responding to the needs of the church and community if it is to maintain its place in the widening societal and public focus of higher education in this country. Theological educational methods which relate to the realities of ministry in church and society, and in particular the Case Study Method, should play a significant role in this response, and not only in the field of Pastoral Studies. Case studies may also provide a valuable teaching method in the other disciplines of practical theology including ethics and social theology. Even Systematic Theology could benefit from a judicious use of case material, relating theological construction and reflection to the empirical realities of following Christ in secular society (Evans and Parker 1976).

6

The Personality Profile
of Anglican Clergymen
(1994)

Leslie Francis and Raymond Rodger

Personality theory

The psychological quest to identify the personality characteristics of ministers, clergy and priests has long roots, although as yet few firm conclusions can be drawn (Nauss 1973). The quest is made no easier by the significant disagreements within psychology regarding what are to count as the major dimensions of personality and how such dimensions are to be assessed or measured (Pervin 1990). It is virtually impossible to integrate the findings of those studies which have attempted to research the personality of clergy since many different definitions and models of personality have been employed by them. It is also doubtful whether findings generated in the USA apply equally within the UK, or whether findings based within one denomination apply equally within another denomination.

One promising strand of research into the personality characteristics of male clergy within England has utilized Eysenck's dimensional model of personality (Eysenck and Eysenck 1985; Furnham 1992). Following the successful application of this model among a number of other professional and occupational groups, six studies have set Eysenck's theory to work among male ordinands and clergy in England.

Eysenck's model

Eysenck's dimensional model of personality proposes the three key constructs of neuroticism, extraversion and psychoticism. Eysenck's model also contains a 'lie scale' which may function as a personality dimension in its own right.

Eysenck's neuroticism scales measure emotional liability and over-reactivity. The opposite of neuroticism is emotional stability. The high scorer on the neuroticism scale is characterized by the test manual as an anxious, worrying individual, who is moody and frequently depressed, likely to sleep badly and to suffer from various psychosomatic disorders. Eysenck suggests that if the high scorer on the neuroticism scale 'has to be described in one word, one might say that he was a worrier; his main characteristic is a constant preoccupation with things that might go wrong, and with a strong emotional reaction of anxiety to these thoughts'. Eysenck characterizes the high scorer as anxious, depressed, tense, irrational, shy, moody, emotional, suffering from guilt feelings and low self-esteem. The low scorer on this dimension is characterized by the absence of these traits.

Eysenck's extraversion scales measure sociability and impulsivity. The opposite of extraversion is introversion. The high scorer on the extraversion scale is characterized by the test manual as a sociable individual, who likes parties, has many friends, needs to have people to talk to and prefers meeting people to reading or studying alone. The typical extravert craves excitement, takes chances, acts on the spur of the moment, is carefree, easy-going, optimistic, and likes to 'laugh and be merry'. Eysenck characterizes the high scorer as sociable, lively, active, assertive, sensation-seeking, carefree, dominant, surgent and venturesome. The low scorer on this dimension is characterized by the opposite set of traits.

Eysenck's psychoticism scales identify the underlying personality traits which at one extreme define psychotic mental disorders. The opposite of psychoticism is normal personality. The high scorer on the psychoticism scale is characterized by Eysenck as being 'cold, impersonal, hostile, lacking in sympathy, unfriendly, distrustful, odd, unemotional, unhelpful, lacking in insight, strange, with paranoid ideas that people were against him'. Eysenck draws particular attention to the characteristic absence of certain emotions from high scorers on the psychoticism scale: 'empathy, feelings of guilt, sensitivity to other people are notions which are strange and unfamiliar to them'. The low scorers are empathic, unselfish, altruistic, warm, peaceful and generally more pleasant, although possibly less socially decisive individuals.

Lie scales were originally introduced into personality inventories to detect the tendency of some respondents to 'fake good' and so to distort the resultant personality scores. The notion of the lie scale has not, however, remained as simple as that, and their continued use has resulted in them being interpreted as a personality measure in their own right. The argument is that, since the internal consistency of a lie scale is quite independent of the motivation to dissimulate the scale must be measuring some underlying personality dimension or set of characteristics. There is considerable controversy, however, regarding the psychological significance of the dimension, which has been variously interpreted as measuring social conformity and lack of self-insight.

Clergy personality

The six studies which have employed Eysenck's model of personality among male clergy and ordinands in England have themselves failed to produce agreement. The first study by Towler and Coxon (1979) among 76 Anglican ordinands suggested that ordinands did not differ from men in general in terms of their profile on extraversion and neuroticism. The contemporary value of this finding is questioned by the fact that the study employed an early form of Eysenck's measures and these measures have subsequently undergone considerable refinement.

A second study by Francis (1991) employed a more recent edition of Eysenck's personality measures among a sample of 252 Anglican ordinands. The major finding of this study concerns the low scores recorded by male ordinands on the extraversion scale. Characteristically, according to this study, male ordinands and clergy are introverts. This finding may have significant implications for the expectations which may be placed on male clergy. Introverts are people who prefer to remain in the background on social occasions. They are shy in company, uneasy in taking social initiatives, uncertain in leadership, unwilling to take risks, uncomfortable with self-assertion, unhappy about meeting new people, reticent on public occasions. They are not people who would naturally choose to lead the dance, to knock on the door, to stand on the soap box, to rally the crowds, or to draw attention to themselves. Characteristically male clergy seem to possess the personality qualities directly opposite to those generally associated with the public and social profile of their occupation. Such incompatibility between personal preferences and public role expectations may lead to frustration, stress and sense of failure. Coping strategies developed to mediate between the requirements of the role and the personal difficulties in meeting these expectations may lead to shaping a public persona unhealthily detached from authentic human responses.

The finding that male clergy tend to be introverts was confirmed in a study among 39 Methodist clergy by Jones and Francis (1992). It was also confirmed in a study among 112 clergy at residential clergy schools by Francis (1992). On the other hand, the finding was not supported by two studies undertaken by Francis and Pearson (1991) and Francis and Thomas (1992) among conference-going clergy. It is however, likely that only the more extraverted clergy may wish to attend such conferences.

Data collection

None of the six studies described above can really be regarded as being based on a representative sample of male Anglican clergy. The aim of the present study was to address this issue by inviting all the full-time stipendiary clergy working within one diocese (Lincoln) to participate in a survey study. All told, 170 male clergy accepted the invitation, from the highly satisfactory response rate of 76 per cent. The respondents included 33 men in their thirties, 47 in their forties, 56 in their fifties, 33 in their sixties and one in his seventies. The instrument used was the short form Revised Eysenck Personality Questionnaire, which proposes twelve item indices of extraversion, neuroticism, psychoticism and the lie scale (Eysenck, Eysenck and Barrett 1985).

Results

In order to provide insight into the personality profile of this sample of male clergy, Table 6.1 presents the proportions of clergy who endorse each of the 48 items incorporated within the personality questionnaire. The extraversion items describe a group of men who enjoy meeting new people (89%) and mixing with people (87%). When with people half of them (49%) do not regard themselves as talkative and two-fifths (39%) consider themselves to be mostly quiet in company. Half of them (52%) admit to keeping in the background on social occasions and three-fifths (59%) feel that they are not the kind of people to get a party going. While professionally at home in social gatherings, a number of clergy clearly display introverted characteristics.

Table 6.1 Responses to the personality scale items

Scale items	Yes %
extraversion	
Are you a talkative person?	51
Are you rather lively?	57
Do you enjoy meeting new people?	89
Can you usually let yourself go and enjoy yourself at a lively party?	58
Do you usually take the initiative in making new friends?	58
Can you easily get some life into a rather dull party?	36
Do you tend to keep in the background on social occasions?*	52
Do you like mixing with people?	87
Do you like plenty of bustle and excitement around you?	41
Are you mostly quiet when you are with other people?*	39
Do other people think of you as being very lively?	57
Can you get a party going?	41
neuroticism	
Does your mood often go up and down?	51
Do you feel 'just miserable' for no reason?	41
Are you an irritable person?	32
Are your feelings easily hurt?	63
Do you often feel 'fed-up'?	39
Would you call yourself a nervous person?	17
Are you a worrier?	52
Would you call yourself tense or 'highly-strung'?	18
Do you worry too long after an embarrassing experience?	51
Do you suffer from 'nerves'?	17
Do you often feel lonely?	21
Are you often troubled about feelings of guilt?	38

psychoticism

Do you take much notice of what people think?*	78
Would being in debt worry you?*	92
Would you take drugs which may have strange or dangerous effects?	3
Do you prefer to go your own way rather than act by the rules?	53
Do good manners and cleanliness matter much to you?*	90
Do you think marriage is old-fashioned and should be done away with?	1
Do you enjoy cooperating with others?*	86
Does it worry you if you know there are mistakes in your work?*	85
Do you think people spend too much time safeguarding their future with savings and insurances?	44
Do you try not to be rude to people?*	93
Would you like other people to be afraid of you?	3
Is it better to follow society's rules than go your own way?*	53

lie scale

If you say you will do something, do you always keep your promise no matter how inconvenient it might be?	72
Were you ever greedy by helping yourself to more than your share of anything?*	56
Have you ever blamed someone for doing something you knew was really your fault?*	41
Are *all* your habits good and desirable ones?	17
Have you ever taken anything (even a pin or button) that belonged to someone else?*	68
Have you ever broken or lost something belonging to someone else?*	80
Have you ever said anything bad or nasty about anyone?*	88
As a child were you ever cheeky to your parents?*	57
Have you ever cheated at a game?*	56
Have you ever taken advantage of someone?*	48
Do you always practice what you preach?	25
Do you sometimes put off until tomorrow what you ought to do today?*	85

Note: * denotes that a negative response counts towards the respective scale score.

The neuroticism items demonstrate that only about one-in-six of the male clergy would describe themselves as a nervous person (17%), as someone who suffers from nerves (17%) or as highly strung (18%). One-in-three (32%) describes himself as an irritable person. Two-in-five often feel fed up (39%) or miserable for no good reason (41%). Half (52%) describe themselves as worriers and nearly two-thirds (63%) find that their feelings are easily hurt. While the majority of male clergy emerge as basically stable, many of them are sensitive individuals who are susceptible to the pressures of their professional experiences.

The psychoticism items describe a group of men who try not to be rude to people (93%), to whom good manners and cleanliness matter (90%) and who enjoy cooperating with others (86%). They are men who would worry if they were in debt (92%) or if they knew there were mistakes in their work (85%).Very few would risk taking drugs which may have strange or dangerous effects (3%). Only 3 per cent would like people to be afraid of them. Only 1 per cent think marriage is old-fashioned or should be done away. Half of them, however, prefer to go their own way rather than act by the rules (53%). While the vast majority of male clergy emerge as basically gentle and tender-minded men, a significant proportion of them are tough-minded enough to reject social convention when it seems appropriate.

The lie scale items describe a group of men who recognize that they are far from perfect in many ways: 88 per cent admit to having said bad or nasty things about people; 85 per cent recognize that they sometimes put off until tomorrow what they ought to do today 80 per cent confess to having broken or lost something belonging to someone else; 75 per cent know that they do not always practice what they preach. On the other hand, many of them claim that they successfully maintain high ethical standards of interpersonal relationships. Thus, nearly three-quarters (72%) claim that, when they say they will do something, they always keep their promise no matter how inconvenient it might be. While basically realistic about their human weaknesses, many male clergy appear to try hard either to avoid certain basic failings or to deny them to themselves. This conclusion is consistent with the findings of Francis, Fulljames and Kay (1992) who demonstrate that the lie scale functions somewhat differently among highly religious samples than among samples for whom religion has no special salience. According to their theory the endorsement of socially desirable but unlikely behaviour patterns by religious subjects may be indicative less of lying than of religiously motivated ethical behaviours.

Conclusion

These new data from the diocese of Lincoln have opened up further insights into the personality characteristics of Anglican clergymen. On the basis of such information clear predictions can be made regarding the specific areas of ministry from which individual clergy may derive special satisfaction or in which they may experience special stress. Individual differences in personality may also contribute significantly to differences in levels of pastoral effectiveness, administrative toughness and professional burnout. Further research is now needed to refine such theories and to establish their predictive value by empirical means. Such research should lead to two key areas of practical benefit. First, recognition of the implications of clergy personality for shaping styles of ministry should enable the more efficient and effective deployment of clergy, with consequent reduction in dissatisfaction, stress and burnout. Second, the informed use of personality theory within programmes of continuing ministerial education should promote healthy personal and professional development, highlighting both areas of strength and weakness.

7

Practical Theology
as a Theological Form
(1996)

Emmanuel Lartey

The pluriformity and ambiguity of practical theology are at once its highest promise and its greatest pitfall. In this paper I wish to keep alive the importance of critical questioning of the methods and models we use in the varied exercises in which we engage in the practice of practical theology. I will be using broad brush-strokes to map out areas of discourse and practice. The aim is to enable practical theologians to locate, or else distance themselves from, specific methods or models in practice today. It is necessary to indicate that this is being done from a particular social context, namely teaching a university course which focuses on an area of practical theology. We all 'inhabit' various social locations and engage in our praxis from specific social contexts. The influences on any person from within, as well as without, their social context are many and varied. This needs to be recognized to minimize the risks of universalizing the particular or, equally heinously, particularizing the universal.

Four main interest groups appear to have been most taken by the possibilities and dangers of practical theology. These are those engaged in the study and practice of (1) ministry; (2) pastoral care and counselling; (3) religious education; and (4) ethics. At times, one or other of these interest groups have sought to claim exclusive rights to the term. Each may legitimately be recognized as engaged in a form of practical theology.

There are a number of ways in which practical theology has been characterized, engaged in, or understood (sometimes by people other than those actually seeking to practice it). In my view these can be categorized into three distinctively different streams, although at times they flow into each other and exert relative influence upon each other. What is common to all three is a concern to relate faith (or doctrine) with practice (or life) and to do so in ways that are relevant and useful.

The branch approach

The first I would like to call the *branch* approach. Here practical theology is seen as a branch of theological science (or art). One of the clearest exponents of this view was

Friedrich Schleiermacher, who used the image of a tree with philosophical theology being the roots, historical theology the trunk and practical theology being the branches (Burkhart 1983a). The emphasis is upon content of a discipline and the method adopted is one of applicationism. Practical theology has to do with 'church government', or else the 'church's action' and is derived by applying doctrinal (philosophical and/or biblical) and historical formulations to the task of church management (Duke and Stone 1988).

The process approach

The second could be termed a *process* approach. Here emphasis is laid on method. The main idea is to generate viable and workable methods which will enable practical theologians to deliver their goods. Tillich's method of correlation is an example of this. Here existential questions are correlated with Christian symbols which provide the answers to the existential questions. Tracy's (1975) 'revised correlational method' or 'critical correlation' seeks to refine Tillich's unidirectional question and answer method, yet offers an approach which could also be described as focusing on method (pp.32–36). Groome's 'shared Christian praxis' method of Christian formation (illustrated in Figure 7.2), which draws inspiration from the work of Farley, Whitehead and Browning, together with the various 'Pastoral Cycles' (e.g. Laurie Green's), diagrammatically represented in Figures 7.1 and 7.3, would fall in the same category (Green 1990; Groome 1987).

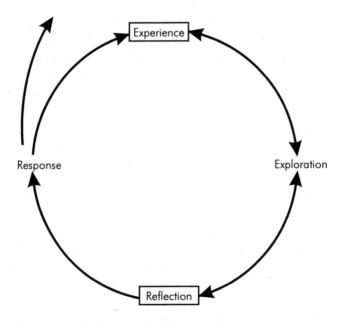

Figure 7.1

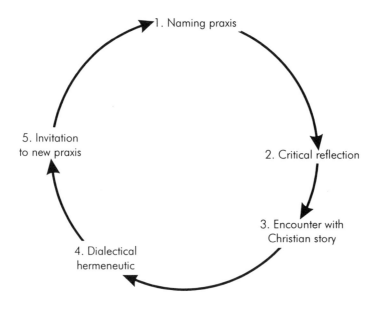

Figure 7.2

The 'way of being and doing' approach

A third approach is one I would describe as a *form* of theological engagement. Here practical theology is understood not primarily as a branch of theological knowledge, nor simply as a method of generating theologically informed action, but rather as offering us *a way of 'doing theology' and being theologians* (Segundo 1976; Green 1990, pp.24–41). This approach attempts to examine the content of faith and practice. It asks questions about what the contents of our faith are, realizing that tradition, context and experience (the 'three elements in the practical theology equation') shape us in such a way that there are very many different forms of equally valid Christian faith (Mudge and Poling 1987, p.xxxii). It seeks to be reflective and thoughtful. It is concerned that faith is made manifest in practice, taking seriously the potentially transformative nature of faith and/or experience. As such it is concerned about what is being done in the name of faith. It is therefore praxis-oriented. It raises methodological questions and realizes that it is important to have and use the right tools for any job. In addition, it asks questions about *who* it is that are engaged in the theological tasks, what the social location of the persons are, *who benefits from what is done*, who is *excluded* by the way things are done and who are *oppressed* by it. It asks contextual and experiential questions and challenges historical formulations in a quest for more inclusive and relevant forms. In doing so, issues of social ethics, spirituality – both personal and corporate – as well as doctrine and teaching are addressed. Moreover, it is a corporate, collaborative endeavour which listens to many different voices. It is a way of being theologians rather than a knowledge of a speciality or sub-discipline in theology. Various forms of liberation theology, such as feminist theologies and black theologies, drawing inspiration from the Latin American experience constitute good examples of this approach. Farley has argued that this approach has historically been marginalized by the overvaluing of rationalism and the quest for scientific scholarship (Farley 1983).

Critique

Each of these approaches has inherent weaknesses. The *branch* approach undervalues the contribution which practical theology might make to the other forms of theology. It also perpetuates the 'second-class' citizenship status of practical theology by making it only and always a derived discipline dependent on knowledge and theory from the other 'more solid' fields of study. The *process* cycles may overvalue method at the expense of content. They run the risk of superficiality and, indeed, scavenging in various disciplines (including theological ones) in the hope of finding appropriate themes for the reflection stage. *The way of being and doing* approaches may become anti-intellectual and thus cut themselves off from an important source of critical life skills. They may overestimate the importance of context and thus end up in a kind of corporate solipsism.

In order to address the question of how practical theology might be engaged in a University Department of Theology, I wish to present my own 'pastoral cycle' suggesting some of the joys and pitfalls involved for me in my current context.

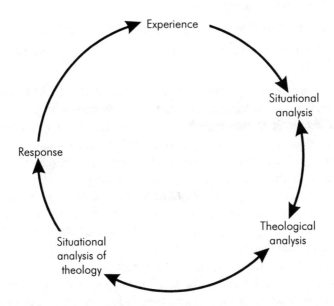

Figure 7.3

There are five phases in the process, as illustrated in Figure 7.3. I seek to point out and demonstrate that the whole process may be seen as theological and not simply the points within it labeled as such. The process normally begins with some form of concrete *experience.* This might be in the form of a placement within a hospital, hostel for homeless people, hospice, community action project, prison or counselling centre. The main point is that it involves an encounter with people in the reality of life's experiences. This phase is incarnational and suggests that practical theology must continually seek to be close to people's real experience of life. It is here that the God and 'Father' of our Lord Jesus Christ is encountered.

My preferred designation for the second phase of the activity is *situational analysis.* This is to indicate that it involves social and psychological analysis but also includes other perspectives on the situation encountered. It is multi-perspectival rather than inter-disciplinary, in that it realizes that it cannot completely encompass the complexity of the various necessary disciplines. What it can and must do is to bring selected perspectives from relevant disciplines to bear on the situation, in the hope of gaining a clearer understanding of what is going on. It is based on the understanding of creation which affirms that the God of all truth can be encountered in various disciplines and glimpsed through different perspectives. It also recognizes that human persons are at best limited in their perceptions but that this should not deter them from the attempt to see clearly. One of the best ways, in theological terms, of gaining clear sight is *collective seeing* or *comparing visions.*

The *third* stage is the point at which faith perspectives are allowed to question the encounter as well as the situational analysis. Here the issues are:

- What questions and analyses arise from my faith concerning what I have experienced and the other analyses of it?

- How has Christian thought approached the issues raised?

- Is there a prophetic insight which may be brought to bear on the situation?

The engagement here is both personal and with the traditions of Christian faith.

In the *fourth* phase it is my faith perspectives that are the subject of questioning by the encounter and the situational analysis. The God of all creation may in reality be 'standing at the door knocking' through what has been encountered (Revelation 3:20). Experience and situational analysis may offer more adequate reformulations of Christian doctrine. In the *fifth* activity I, together with the group within which the whole process is set, explore what response options are available to me in the light of what has gone before and make decisions as to the preferred one. Here the person-in-community recognizes and acts responsibly in the light of the vision and the re-visioning encountered.

What is missing from the cycle, though not from the group activities on the courses each year, are the celebrations, the social and at times sporting events which are often very creative points of engagement. Especially since the groups are always international and multicultural.

Concerning the joys and especially the problems of maintaining a university course of study which reflects this process, in the current national climate, volumes could be written. It is perhaps sufficient to say that what is aimed at in practical theology is a relevant, meaningful, methodologically appropriate and viable form of theological activity which may be personally and socially transformative, while also being uplifting and, above all, great fun.

PART THREE

Practical Theology in Search of Practical Wisdom

8

Pain, sickness and suffering
(1980)

Kenneth Boyd

Pain, sickness and suffering can be ignored or avoided, but only for a time. Susan Sontag (1979) begins her essay on *Illness as Metaphor* thus:

> Illness is the night-side of life, a more onerous citizenship. Everyone who is born holds dual citizenship, in the Kingdom of the well and in the Kingdom of the sick. Although we all prefer to use only the good passport, sooner or later each of us is obliged, at least for a spell, to identify ourselves as citizens of the other place. (p.1)

Pain, sickness and suffering then are part of what it means to be human. But not necessarily for everyone, at least as far as physical pain and suffering are concerned. Professor Thomas McKeown (1976), the epidemiologist, has pointed out that 'with the provision of sufficient food and control of hazards in the past few centuries, many people have completed their lives without severe or prolonged physical discomfort'. Modern medicine, he adds, 'can contribute largely to the relief of such suffering when it occurs' (p.170). That may seem rather optimistic, but clearly not everyone experiences pain, sickness and suffering in the same way, or with equal intensity or for an equal length of time. Nor does everyone respond to these experiences in the same way. For some, they are the making of character; for others its destruction. Some reach for aspirin, others turn to prayer. Pain, sickness and suffering thus raise questions both about how we should understand them and about how we should respond to them. These questions about meaning and action are often quite closely inter-related.

One way of illustrating these questions and how they are inter-related is by considering the medical view of pain and sickness. The medical view of course is only part of the story; pain, sickness and suffering raise questions in the realm of meaning as well as medicine. But before considering these other questions, I suggest that we look first at the medical view. It is too familiar to ignore, and it has practical implications for other people than doctors.

From the medical point of view, pain obviously represents a cry for help, but for the doctor or nurse to concentrate too exclusively on that and to act solely to eliminate the pain can be a serious mistake, since the pain may also be the warning signal of an underlying condition whose nature and treatment have yet to be determined. Under certain circumstances, of course, when the pain is particularly acute or severe, or when the person suffering it is dying, immediate action in response to the cry for help must take precedence, but even then, in order to relieve it, the character of the pain involved has to be understood. In medicine then, things are not quite as simple as in Blake's (1961) remark:

> Can I see another's woe
> And not be in sorrow too? (p.63).

Sorrow or sympathy may well be an incentive, but in order to seek for kind relief, understanding (and trained understanding at that) is also needed.

Pain calls for compassion, but also intelligence and thus a measure of detachment. This is true not only in medicine, but also in everyday experience. There are times, for example, when someone close to you, in a black mood after a bad day, clearly needs more than anything else a good night's sleep or a holiday in order to see things in proportion. Under circumstances like that, intelligent compassion recognizes that the unconscious mind, the body's own recuperative powers, the daily, weekly, monthly and seasonal rhythms, even the accidents and contingencies of life, all may have a part to play in the relief of suffering and the restoration of well-being. Sometimes, of course, these ends cannot be achieved without medical intervention, and sometimes they demand the kind of social, economic or political action which cannot be taken simply in relation to the individual sufferer and whose results may not be apparent in his or her lifetime.

Here obviously there are dangers, not least that the measure of detachment necessary to determine appropriate action may pass into a settled mood, as we harden our hearts against the demands of compassion and sympathy. Intelligent compassion may reveal the need, for example, for fundamental biomedical research or radical political action, only to find no guarantee that either activity will actually relieve suffering, and only to remember that both, at their worst (in Nazi Germany, for example) have served ends neither intelligent nor compassionate. Such risks are real enough, just as, on the domestic level, attributing a wife or husband's unhappiness to the time of the month or the state of office politics may be a means of avoiding painful questions. Nevertheless, the fact remains that, without some detachment, sympathy and compassion can be misdirected and even harmful.

There is also the danger that our action in relation to the sufferings of others may owe less to compassion than to guilt and self-justification. What this possibility of course brings to mind is the fact that a measure of detachment is nowhere more necessary than when the suffering individual is myself. The need to relax, even when the only justification is the fragile one that 'something will turn up', is often the precondition of a breakthrough from suffering to relief or from problem to resolution. The Catholic tradition, which teaches the virtue of self-abandonment to divine providence (Caussade 1959), here has something significant to teach Protestant and other activists; as has the argument, of G.K. Chesterton (1961, pp.157ff) and Harry Williams (1976, p.110) that the universal form of the vision of conflicts resolved is laughter. In seeking to understand and respond to others' suffering and our own, we may learn also from those moralists who argue that among our other duties are those of pleasure and the pursuit of happiness. In a world where there is so much pain and suffering, it may seem frivolous to include gardening, stamp-collecting, listening to music or some comparable activity among our human duties, but if we have the ability to appreciate such activities, and if 'we try to achieve a balance between self-realization and helping others', there is probably something perverse, something of a refusal, in insisting that 'the needs of others (should), always, in every situation, over-ride cultural aims' (Ward 1976, p.26). Against the unnatural pride which underlies such an insistence, the ancient rabbinic saying is salutary:

> On judgment day, a man will have to give account for every good thing which his eye saw and he did not enjoy. (Rabbi Rav)

Action and understanding in response to suffering then, have to be seen in the context of action and understanding in response to other aspects of human experience. In this respect medicine's view of pain is a special case within our general view of suffering, and the ideal doctor, we might say, is the one who not only exercises intelligent compassion, but who also achieves intellectual pleasure from problem-solving in both the clinical and the research context. Such intellectual pleasure, we might add, should not be achieved at the expense of making the patient a means rather than an end, or by diverting to research resources which are needed for care. The ideal doctor, being compassionate and probably just, as well as intelligent, would presumably, however, be aware of this.

In the context of the real, rather than the ideal, the need for understanding as well as action can also be illustrated in relation to medicine's view of sickness. Sickness, Marshall Marinker (1975) has suggested, is one of three different modes of unhealth with which the doctor is confronted. The first mode is disease, the objective pathological process, which the doctor can see, touch, measure, smell, and which is central to the medical view. The second mode, central to the patient's view, is illness:

> Illness is a feeling, an experience of unhealth which is entirely personal, interior to the person of the patient. Often it accompanies disease, but the disease may be undeclared, as in the early stages of cancer or tuberculosis or diabetes. Sometimes illness exists where no disease can be found. (p.82)

When this happens, Marinker suggests, doctors may gain 'the rhetoric (if not the conviction) of clinical common sense' by translating the illness into 'the semantic overtones of personal abuse' (p.82) provided by psychiatric language. Illness then is 'an interior and personal mode for the patient'. The third mode of unhealth, by contrast, is 'external and public':

> Sickness is a social role, a status, a negotiated position in the world, a bargain struck between the person hence-forward called 'sick' and a society which is prepared to recognize and sustain him. (p.83)

Security in this sick role, Marinker comments, is greater for those with a disease, preferably acute and surgical, than for those whose sick status is simply based on illness or even some psychiatric condition. In making this comment, Marinker seems to have the attitudes of his fellow doctors primarily in mind. But the negotiable status of sickness is familiar enough in families and among friends or colleagues, particularly in the winter months when our strengths and weaknesses, our kind-heartedness and intolerance are betrayed by persuasive statements about the need to be fully recovered before resuming work, or the dangers of spreading infection, or, contrariwise, the benefits of fresh air and a return to routine.

In the specifically medical context Marinker goes on to make a similar point: 'the act of communicating is what medicine is all about'. Medicine, he suggests, 'should be regarded neither as an art nor as a science in itself, but as special kind of relationship between two persons, a doctor and a patient' (p.83). This relationship becomes a sort of 'mutual investment company' often surviving the worst either party can do, often continuing – particularly in the case of patients who come for repeat prescriptions – when the patient 'had no demonstrable disease ... no longer complained of an illness and ... rarely seemed to occupy the role and status of a sick person' (p.84). The act of consulting, Marinker comments, 'seemed to constitute its own reason'. And he concludes:

> It is possible for a person to experience unhealth, to have a disease, to feel ill, to be sick, without becoming a patient. To become a patient is to establish a healing relationship with another who activates society's willingness and capability to help. (p.84)

Marinker's view, seen from the vantage point of general practice, of medicine as a special relationship concerned with the act of communicating, is clearly not how all doctors would see it, nor how all patients actually experience it. It is, nevertheless, sufficiently familiar for us to see this medical view of sickness as a special case illuminating our more general view of suffering. Here again, immediate and specific action may be required: in the doctor's case, some action which interprets the symptoms and relieves the patient by confirming or denying his sick status; in the case of family, friend or stranger by the kind of conversation which helps the suffering individual begin to get his or her suffering in some kind of perspective. But here too, the relief of suffering requires something else (in the medical context, the healing doctor–patient relationship, in life generally): friendship. A suffering individual may well find some 'kind relief' in a short, intense experience of unburdening and the sharing of troubles. But an experience of this kind, however helpful, lacks the healing qualities of friendship, which are based on shared experiences of the past and shared hopes for the future.

In relation to suffering, what friendship brings, in other words, is the dimension of those other goals and experiences of life, which, while suffering threatens to swallow them up, are part of the suffering individual's identity. This is one reason why it is so important to visit the sick. Someone who is sick, particularly if he or she is in hospital, is threatened by the loss of part of themselves, partly by the pain and sickness themselves, and partly by the necessarily routine ways in which they are cared for. The medical and nursing ideal, of course, is individualized treatment, and in many respects treatment can be individualized. But never, I think, entirely (at least as long as we wish care to remain professional and thus presumably effective and efficient). The doctor or nurse, clearly, can become a friend, but he or she cannot, in justice to their other patients, share the past and future of this one, or at least only very rarely, perhaps in the case of some rural family doctors. What is required to help the individual whose identity is threatened, is thus not just professional care, but also amateur (the resources of friendship which remind the sufferer that we are more than our suffering, that we have had other experiences than those which now threaten to overwhelm us, that we have other goals than simply recovering). And of course it may well be that those other experiences and goals, mediated through friendship, are decisive factors in our recovery.

Whether or not suffering individuals need professional care then, they will all need friendship. The trouble with friendship, however, is that you cannot be friends with everyone. Friendship needs time. Shared experiences and shared hopes are not achieved overnight. Nor are they achieved without some degree of conflict and reconciliation between friends. All this takes time, and during that time there are always other people who do not have friends. Our friendships are bought at the price of lonely people we pass by, ignore or never even notice. When we reflect on this, it may make us uncomfortable. But it is so, and I do not know any way round it. It is probably why there will always remain a need for professional carers and for 'mutual investment companies', whether medical, social, ecclesiastical or stamp-collecting, in which strangers otherwise, share intensely part but never the whole of their lives.

Friendship is limited in another way also, which again can be illustrated by hospital visiting. Ogden Nash (Nash in Sergeant and Sergeant 1968) has a poem on the subject, part of which goes like this:

> Take the sight of a visitor trying to entertain a
> patient or a patient trying to entertain a visitor.
>
> It would bring joy to the heart of the Grand Inquisitor.
>
> The patient either is too ailing to talk or is panting to get
> back to the chapter where the elderly spinster is just about
> to reveal to the Inspector that she now thinks she can identify
> the second voice in that doom-drenched quarrel,
>
> And the visitor either has never had anything to say to the patient
> anyway or is wondering how soon it would be all right to depart
> for Belmont or Santa Anita or Laurel,
>
> And besides, even if both parties have ordinarily much to discuss
> and are far from conversational mediocrities,

Why, the austere surroundings and the lack of ashtrays
would stunt a dialogue between Madame de Stael and Socrates,

And besides, even if anyone did get to chattering glitteringly and
gaudily

They would soon be interrupted by the arrival of a nurse or an
orderly.

It is a fact that I must chronicle with distress

That the repartee reaches its climax when the visitor spots the
handle on the foot of the bed and cranks the patient's knees up
and down and says, 'That certainly is ingenious', and the patient
answers Yes. (p.94)

Now despite this, I would still argue for the reasons I suggested earlier that it is
important to visit the sick, but I agree with Ogden Nash that it is not always easy.
Moreover, when I reflect on many of the conversations I have had with people in
hospital, I am very conscious of their inadequacy. The real reason for this however, I
think, is deeper and was well put by Simone Weil (1951) in her 'Reflections on the
Right Use of School Studies' where she writes:

Those who are unhappy have no need for anything in this world but people capable
of giving them their attention. The capacity to give one's attention to a sufferer is a
very rare and difficult thing; it is almost a miracle; it is a miracle. Nearly all those who
think they have this capacity do not possess it. Warmth of heart, impulsiveness, pity
are not enough. (p.58)

Simone Weil then goes on to relate the legend in which the Grail belongs to the first
comer who asks its guardian (a king three-quarters paralyzed by the most painful
wound), 'What are you going through?' To which she comments:

The love of our neighbour in all its fullness simply means being able to say
to him: 'What are you going through?' It is a recognition that the sufferer exists, not
only as a unit in a collection, or a specimen from the social category labelled
'unfortunate', but a man, exactly as we are, who was one day stamped with a special
mark by affliction. For this reason it is enough, but it is indispensable, to know how
to look at him in a certain way.

This way of looking is first of all attentive. The soul empties itself of all its own
contents in order to receive into itself the being it is looking at, just as he is, in all his
truth.

Only he who is capable of attention can do this. (p.59)

But this, as Simone Weil says, is a very rare and difficult thing. So in thinking about
visiting the sick, or any comparable activity through which we relate to suffering
individuals, it is important to recognize the point she makes, in another essay, that the

love of our neighbour should not be distinguished from justice. The virtue of justice, Simone Weil writes,

> consists of behaving exactly as through there were equality when one is the stronger in an unequal relationship. Exactly in every respect, including the slightest details of accent and attitude, for a detail may be enough to place the weaker party in the condition of matter which on this occasion naturally belongs to him, just as the slightest shock causes water which has remained liquid below freezing point to solidify. (p.86)

Even this though, is difficult enough, particularly if we, who in this relationship are the stronger in other relationships are the weaker, and all too often, I think, the detail of accent and attitude betray the weakness of the stronger. Recognizing this, however, does not mean that the attempt should not be made, since justice demands it. And in practice the demands of justice can be a social pleasure, especially when the apparently weaker person betrays, by accent or attitude, himself as an equal. Under those circumstances, we can only be grateful, in our own interest, that the distinction between love and justice is false.

Most of this, however, is about our response to suffering in others. But what of the suffering person himself, the person whom no one ever really asks 'What are you going through?' Let me say this, in conclusion, about pain, sickness and suffering.

The dictionary definitions of pain, sickness and suffering include the following. PAIN: punishment, penalty; SICK: spiritually or morally ailing, corrupted through sin or wrongdoing; SUFFER: to have something (painful, distressing or injurious) inflicted upon one. These definitions, I think, indicate something of what the suffering individual, whether or not sick or in physical pain, has to bear: something imposed, something others find distasteful and may even blame him for, something he may blame himself for. Not every suffering individual, all of the time, has to bear these things with equal intensity; and many of us may have only to bear them very lightly or hardly at all. But in so far as the suffering individual – him, her or me – has to bear pain, sickness, blame, guilt, powerlessness, he needs at least three things, which he may or may not receive: medicine, friendship and meaning.

In today's world, medicine – the relief of physical pain – may be the easiest to find, but it may not be enough. The suffering individual may also find friendship, but that too, is often absent or inadequate. Meaning also may be absent, and it simply seems a fact of life that many people fail to find or create it. For many, religion is no help. On behalf of such people, Stevie Smith (1962) asks, about Christ:

> Did he feel pointless, feeble and distrait,
> unwanted by everyone and in the way?

> From his cradle he was purposeful
> His bent strong and his mind full...

> Did he never feel strong
> Pain for being wrong?

He was not wrong, he was right
He suffered from others', not his own spite.

But there *is* no suffering like having made a mistake
Because of being of an inferior make.

He was not inferior
He was superior. (p.6)

Religion, based on a model of Christ like Stevie Smith presents here, clearly cannot
help. Equally clearly, this presentation of Christ is based on how many Christians
have portrayed him. But in the past, and again today, this is not how many others
have seen the ultimate meaning. Another way of expressing this meaning (and if I
express it very obscurely it is because I understand it very obscurely) is in terms of the
belief, as William James (1956) put it, that 'the sweat and blood and tragedy of this
life' means that life is 'a real fight, in which something is eternally gained for the
universe by success'. (p.61) In a similar vein, but based on an understanding of the
experience of human love, W.H. Vanstone (1977) argues 'that the love of God must
be infinitely more costly, more precarious and more exposed than it is commonly
represented to be'. He puts it like this:

> If God is love, and the universe is His creation, then for the being of the universe God
> is totally expended in precarious endeavour, of which the issue, as triumph or
> tragedy, has passed from His hands. For that issue, as triumphant or as tragic, God
> waits upon the response of His creation. He waits as the artist or as the lover waits,
> having given His all. Where the issue is tragedy, there remains only the unbelievable
> power of art or love to discover within itself, through the challenge of the tragic, the
> power which was not there before – the power of yet further endeavour to win back
> and redeem that which was going astray. Where the issue is triumph, there remains
> only the will of love to surrender triumphant self-sufficiency in yet larger, more
> distant, near generous endeavour. Always, for the richness of the creation, God is
> made poor: and for its fullness, God is made empty. Always His helplessness waits
> upon the response of creation. To anyone who does not understand this, or cannot
> accept it, we must answer, 'You have not yet weighed the cost of love, the cost of
> creation'. (p.74)

For the suffering individual, the implication of this is clear: what he makes of his
suffering – whether it becomes a triumph or a tragedy of the human spirit, whether
hope gains, or despair – matters, not just to himself, but to the creation itself. For
everything, as Dostoyevsky's Father Zossima says, 'like the ocean flows and comes
into contact with everything else: touch it in one place and it reverberates at the other
end of the world' (1958, p.376). Whatever anyone may think then, the response of
the suffering individual matters: he is not powerless. But his power is not apparent: its
true measure is relative not to the achievement of others, but to the suffering
individual's own condition – to his genetic, social and cultural inheritance, to the
environment which has shaped his habits and aspirations, to the physical and

psychological constraints which disease or misfortune have imposed upon the possibilities of his existence. Within these constraints, the suffering individual's achievement most of the time will go unnoticed; and understandably so, since frequently enough it can be detected, if at all, only in the 'slightest details of accent and attitude'. In relation to his condition however, the individual's achievement may be heroic, reminiscent of the aged Anglo-Saxon warrior's words to the last remnant of a defeated army:

> Courage shall grow keener, clearer the will.
> the heart fiercer, as our force faileth. (Alexander 1966, p.123)

9

Pastoral Counselling and Psychotherapy
(1985)

Michael Jacobs

Pastoral care and counselling combines the long-standing tradition of pastoral work with the insights of the behavioural sciences. Inevitably this raises questions as to the distinctive nature of pastoral counselling. If, for instance, what is sometimes rather loosely called a non-directive approach is used by the pastoral counsellor, this seems to imply no space for teaching or exhortation about religious concerns, which could be the distinctive contribution of one who has a spiritual outlook.

There is also confusion about the difference, if any, between psychotherapy and counselling, so that if we add that question to the one about the distinctiveness of pastoral counselling, and perhaps even of pastoral psychotherapy (a term used more in American than British literature) the strands of our practice might appear to be inextricably tangled. My own argument of the distinctiveness of the term 'pastoral' necessitates an excursion into both these confusions.

There are some who seem to suggest that the difference between counselling and psychotherapy is to be seen in variation in length and depth, some writers implying that the longer the process the deeper it becomes. While it is possible to draw such distinctions in the case of short-term 'crisis' counselling, and long-term psycho-therapy, the increasing use and validation of brief psychotherapy makes 'length' of treatment invalid as a difference (Malan 1976a; 1976b). Besides, counsellors could point to some of their work where 'depth' had been reached in a fairly brief number of sessions, and psychotherapists could give examples of patients who are in therapy for a long time, but so resistant that very little depth of insight or change is achieved.

Perhaps then we should at once abandon the attempt to make distinctions, and remain content to acknowledge that psychotherapy is a term used more in medical and psychiatric settings, while counselling is the term more likely to be used in non-medical and pastoral settings. C.H. Patterson (Patterson in Arbuckle 1967) suggests that this is the only difference, adding another 'non-essential' difference, that where the level of adjustment of the client is seriously disturbed, the process is called psychotherapy, and as such is more remedial, whereas if the client has problems which are more 'normal' the process is called counselling. Apart from these exceptions he believes that the two processes are in all essentials identical, both in the nature of the therapeutic relationship and the methods and techniques that are used. He sees no essential difference in goals or outcome, since the general objectives of both are to assist individuals towards responsible independence and the development of maximum potential. Patterson does not appear to recognize that psychotherapy is not always suitable with very disturbed people. Supportive and drug therapy are sometimes more appropriate. Psychotherapy may, in fact, be more suitable for the more 'normal'.

Joan Mance, in a lecture to the Guild of Pastoral Psychology, also sees both processes as helping people to grow and change, and to provide conditions which were perhaps lacking in the client's childhood. But she does see some differences, inasmuch as the person who comes for counselling in all probability wants advice, while the person who comes for analysis has already come to accept that he is a considerable part of his own problem. While this is a useful statement about motivation, what she says of the analysis is an ideal, and one which the counsellor would wish to see in his clients too. Advice has a place of course, and Joan Mance conceded that counsellors, like analysts, also see advice only as a temporary support.

O.S. Frank (Frank in Connolly 1978, p.144) similarly distinguishes counselling and psychotherapy, reserving the term 'counselling' for a process that is directive and educative, concerned with problem-solving and with finding new solutions within the existing repertory of the individual. This he contrasts with psychotherapy, where the fundamental aim is intrapsychic modification, or behaviour change. He proceeds, quite correctly, to divide psychotherapy itself into branches.

(1) *Insight psychotherapy*, which is itself further divided into different schools of thought and practice (Freud, Jung, Klein, Object–Relations, etc.). This is concerned to uncover unconscious forces, and so help change from within the individual.

(2) *Behaviour psychotherapy*, which is concerned with the manipulation of the learning process, helping the individual to change response and behaviour.

But Frank has introduced, with this distinction, a confusion between behaviour psychotherapy and his definition of counselling. Behaviour modification is also directive and educative (it is, after all, based upon 'learning theory') and it is also problem-solving, seeking solutions in the existing repertory of the individual, whereas much counselling has its origins in insight psychotherapy, which has also influenced our practice of pastoral care and counselling. Frank does not do justice to the links which exist between these two approaches.

Perhaps Patterson is right after all: no essential differences exist. It seems easier to say what counselling is not, rather than what it is. Yet I believe that it is important to draw out distinctions, which at least feel as if they exist. I wish to do this, not as an academic exercise but because it is important for us to know our goals and also when we are attempting to help those who come to us.

The two main differences between insight psychotherapy and counselling care are, I believe, first by the former more consistently attempts to understand the inter-relationship of past and present in the client who comes for therapy; and second there is more overt use of the transference in psychotherapy that is, the understanding of those projections from significant past and present relationships in which the client is involved, on to the therapist, which enable the therapist to demonstrate to the client those false perceptions which hamper or invalidate his attempts to relate in more mature ways to significant people in the present. Psychotherapy is more likely to draw out the conflicts within the individual, between parts of himself, to give more emphasis to the 'inner world' of the client, than counselling, which will be more likely concerned with the external world of the client.

Such a distinction does not deny that the counsellor also makes use of both of these ideas. Transference, as perceived in the client, may well be used by the counsellor to increase his own understanding of the client, but he tends to share this insight in indirect ways. The distinction is not, however, cut and dried, because the counsellor may be able to show the client how the way he treats him (the counsellor) has similarities to the ways he treats others; and, where unhelpful feelings towards counselling appear to hinder the working relationship, the counsellor may also draw attention to these. But he does not, as does the therapist, seek to use the transference in such an active and open way, not least because active use of the transference needs more training, tact and skill than the training of counsellors prepares them for.

Such distinctions apply especially to counselling and what has come to be called 'brief psychotherapy'. Psychotherapy of longer duration, unlike counselling, brief therapy, or behaviour therapy, is not so limited in its goals or aims. Joan Mance (undated) describes analysis as becoming a 'much more absorbing activity to the client, touching the whole of his being,' and as 'a journey of exploration undertaken for its own sake' so that it is not so much treatment, as an attempt to understand the meaning of life for oneself in relation to others. Such an aim brings us close to the religious goal, though to it the religious person would add 'in relation to God', whatever or whoever he means by that term.

I suggest, therefore, that there are differences between insight psychotherapy, behaviour psychotherapy, and general counselling, though clearly there are many links between them too. We are now in a position to define 'pastoral' counselling, though here too we come up against diverse definitions in the literature, sometimes even in the same author. 'Pastoral' in this book, is, of course, used of counselling and caring in a religious framework, and not, as it has more recently been used in this country, in respect of the work of teachers in secondary education in particular. 'Pastoral' in the field of education is used to distinguish the caring and welfare role of the staff from their teaching function.

One use of 'pastoral', particularly in American practice, is of counselling by ministers and priests. Howard Clinebell (1966), for instance, writes: 'Pastoral counselling is the utilization by a minister of a one-to-one or small group relationships to help people handle their problems of living more adequately, and grow toward fulfilling their potentialities' (p.20).

A rather different view seems to be held by Don Browning (1977), who says that,

> pastoral psychotherapists gain the right to use the word 'pastoral' partially by virtue of the moral context in which they stand. There must be a moral context surrounding the work of the pastoral psychotherapist which has publicly visible continuity with the moral stance of the wider Christian community. (p.18)

Such meanings are not altogether satisfactory. In Britain, for instance, pastoral counselling is not confined to clergy and religious as it tends to be in America. Clinebell draws too strict a line. And since Browning, in the same article (1977, p.18), says that part of the efficacy of the pastoral psychotherapist is the ability to distance himself from the value and norm-upholding role of the minister, we can question whether his use of the word pastoral has any real meaning. More helpful is another phrase of Clinebell's that 'the pastor should be as open to dealing with religious and value problems in counselling as he is to dealing with interpersonal difficulties' (Clinebell 1966, p.20). Or, elsewhere, Clebsch and Jaekle (1964) define pastoral care as consisting of 'helping acts done by representative Christian persons, directed towards the healing, sustaining, guiding and reconciling of troubled persons whose troubles arise in the context of ultimate meanings and concerns' (p.4). There are other definitions, such as 'translating the good news into the "language of relation-ships"' (Clinebell 1966, p.14), but these two are sufficient to help us at this point.

Pastoral counselling can be seen as a speciality in the more general field of counselling, which has parallels with other specialities. Just as there will be some who see their immediate problems as vocational and therefore will approach a careers counsellor, or in sexual terms and approach a sex therapist, or who will approach specialists in family and marriage problems, there will be others who approach the pastoral counsellor because they see their difficulties in religious terms. Thus the uniqueness of pastoral counselling, as distinct from other areas of counselling, might be in the following areas, as outlined by Clinebell:

> the training background of the pastoral counsellor which includes philosophy, theology and ethics, as well as counselling skills.

> the role of the pastoral counsellor as a person likely to attract a religious transference, i.e. a person who stands for feelings about the spiritual nature of man – even though equally some of these feelings may be distorted, and act as a barrier to some people, as much as for others he will be an apparently secure figure.

> the pastoral counsellor is a representative of the quest of the human spirit for more abundant life

> and he/she sees spiritual growth (and, I would add, exploration) as an essential objective in counselling. (1966, pp.49–52)

But if the problem is sometimes expressed in religious terms, this does not mean that the counselling remains bound by the presenting problem. Just as the sex therapist will in all probability be concerned for much more than the obvious sexual problem presented by a client, so the pastoral counsellor, to be effective, should try to 'be tuned simultaneously to the horizontal and vertical dimensions of every human problem' (p.247). The pastoral counsellor cannot reduce human problems either to a religious, or a psychological, interpretation.

The pastoral counsellor is likely to have more than religious problems presented to him. His particular skills and training, and areas of concern mean that he has in mind wider issues which underlie any problem. In reality his long-term goals will always be somewhat idealized, as will be those of most therapists and counsellors, since time is limited, and in counselling it is often difficult to deal with more than immediate issues. There may need to be limited goals. Yet underpinning the work will be views of man, expressed in religious terms. There is of course not one religious view of man, but many, and goals will be expressed in differing ways. Clinebell, for instance, outlines four basic spiritual needs (p.252):

(1) for a meaningful philosophy of life, and a challenging object of self-investment

(2) for a sense of the numinous and the transcendent

(3) for deep experience of trustful relatedness to God, other people, and nature

(4) to fulfil the 'image of God' within oneself by developing one's truest humanity through creativity, awareness and inward freedom.

Victor Frankl (1973) puts it somewhat differently, outlining three kinds of values which man needs: *creative values*, doing something worthwhile; *experiential values*, derived from experiencing the wonder of nature, the joy of relationships, the precious memory, and *attitudinal values*, by which he means a constructive attitude towards even the worst situation.

The danger of all specialist counselling is that, having a limited aim and time, the counsellor tries to reinforce his own values, and fails to guide the client to find his own. There is obviously a place for some 'instruction' in all specialist areas (e.g. knowledge may need to be imparted in career counselling or in sex therapy). The pastoral counsellor, having some such values as those outlined above, may be tempted to 'instruct'. Yet, while these values appear to lend themselves to teaching, the pastoral counsellor holds central to his belief system the uniqueness of the individual. Here again pastoral counselling bears strong resemblance to psychotherapy, and in particular to the Jungian concept of 'the individuation process' (Barnhouse 1979). Given the complexity of 'ultimate concerns', the difficulties of working from the problems of everyday life towards such goals, and the necessarily brief contact the counsellor has compared to the psychotherapist, pastoral counselling is clearly one of the more challenging specialist areas for the counsellor and for the client.

10

Truth or Dare? Sexuality, Liturgy and Pastoral Theology

(1994)

Elaine Graham

The session was all about sex. I didn't actually nod off, though I have heard it before. Marriage gives the OK to sex is the gist of it, but while it is far from being the be all and end all (you can say that again) sex is nevertheless the supreme joy of the married state and a symbol of the relationship between us and God. So, Geoffrey concludes, when we put our money in the plate it is a symbol of everything in our lives we are offering to God and that includes our sex. I could only find 10p. (Bennett 1998, p.30)

Alan Bennett's depiction of the tragic-comic descent into alcoholism of Susan, the vicar's wife, is both precipitated and punctuated by the trivialities and petty obsessions of English parish life. This is nowhere more apparent than in the joylessness and superficiality of parish worship. She finds some of the longed-for passion and spontaneity in the arms of Mr. Ramesh, owner of a grocer-cum-off-licence, whose religion seems to integrate sexuality into the worship and veneration of the gods far more satisfactorily than the faith of Geoffrey, Susan's husband, and his 'fan club' of parish worthies.

To condemn the Church for its inability to celebrate or affirm sexual desire – indeed, to integrate any human experience involving complexity and ambivalence fully within its life, its pastoral practice or its theology – is a familiar pastime of its critics. Much of Bennett's comic effect is achieved through the juxtaposition of liturgical *gravitas* and the sublime absurdity of human sexuality, our knowledge that our grand ambitions about offering our sexuality to God are always tempered by our guilt and uncertainty about the whole business. Despite the solemn assurances of preachers about the joys of sex, the fundamentals of human emotion and bodiliness seem neither worthy nor appropriate avenues to the divine, and so, especially in the context of public worship, any mention, let alone celebration, of human sexuality is virtually taboo.

This is an acute example of the dislocation between liturgy and pastoral care; the former appearing sanitised, esoteric and irrelevant, the latter dealing with the nitty-gritty of human need, the failures and triumphs of our condition. The resulting separation of two essential aspects of the Christian life impoverishes both. It prevents the activities of liturgy – used here to denote any organized act of public Christian worship in word and/or sacrament – from engaging with, and addressing, pastoral need and precludes the private joys and pains of individual experience from finding ritual and theological expression and resolution.

However, such a separation of liturgy and pastoral care is being resisted with renewed vigour, and not only by pastoral theologians. Liturgical scholarship is increasingly aware of its image in some sections of the Church as rarefied and anachronistic, emerging from its ivory tower only to impose exotic and irrelevant products on unwilling and uncomprehending congregations. Yet such a parody is a denial of the concern that has always existed, which is being recovered anew within the present generation to place pastoral criteria at the heart of liturgical reform. The finest and most enduring liturgies of the Church were never developed in abstraction or isolation, but actually emerged from periods or pastoral renewal. Through the rites of baptism and initiation, and in eucharistic patterns that mirror the worshipping community's expressions or its common lire, liturgical reformers have sought the language and actions appropriate to express the essentials of the Christian faith in the context of its day. 'The language of liturgy is not just a matter of words but, rather, involves every action, every gesture of our common liturgical life' (Holeton 1990, p.320).

Such an essential connection between human experience and liturgy is echoed within pastoral and anthropological literature. Thus we have studies of liturgy as models of 'rites of passage', expressing and resolving the points of transition and change endemic to human life, individual and corporate (Gennep 1960; Grainger 1988). Other pastoral theologians have examined the pastoral significance of liturgy: the power of sacrament and ritual to affirm us in times of need, often counteracting the 'privatised' tendencies of pastoral counselling, towards a recognition of the public and corporate context within which Christian care takes place (Ramshaw 1987; Willimon 1979).

However, although such an emphasis on the pastoral applications of liturgy, and the liturgical expressions of pastoral care, does highlight the importance of liturgy for articulating and resolving areas of human need and pastoral care, it also falls short of its fullest potential, which is one of liturgy as practical theology. It is no less than the integration of human experience – including sexuality – with liturgical practice in such a way as to generate and appropriate theological discourse. At its best, Christian worship can simultaneously embrace and affirm the human condition and offer the whole of human life to God in such a way to transfigure that experience into something redemptive and transcendent. I want to argue that, far from being an obstacle to this process of pastoral praxis, an acknowledgement of human sexuality – even supposedly transgressive sexuality – provides us with a model of how that might be achieved.

Sexuality and theology

Theology cannot presume to look down upon sexuality from some unaffected Olympian standpoint. Every theological perception contains some elements and perceptions conditioned by sexual experience, and every sexual experience is perceived and interpreted through religious lenses of some kind (Nelson 1992, p.116). Nelson's characterization of the 'Olympian' tendencies of theological pronouncements and Church policy on sexuality emphasizes how theology has frequently been forged in isolation and abstraction from human experience. Whilst in reality experience and pragmatism temper Church teaching and doctrine, personal stories and human experience are generally peripheral or secondary to the true substance of theology, which is deductively and theoretically, rather than experientially, derived. Church pronouncements begin with principles and are applied to human situations, with the result that theological discourse and pastoral situations are necessarily dislocated.

An example of this in recent theological reflection on human sexuality may be found in the Church of England House of Bishops' Report, *Issues in Human Sexuality* (1991). It is a good example of a time-honoured procedure of Anglican social and pastoral thought, emerging from the reasoned consideration of 'expert' evidence on a particular issue, distilled into theological pronouncements and certain general pragmatic principles. Such a method expresses faith in the importance of what R.H. Preston (1991) termed 'Christian competence'; the commitment to careful and rigorous enquiry as an essential dimension of Christian faithfulness in the world. However, it is not, in the main, this care and attention to 'the facts of the matter' that should cause us to question. It is more the implicit assumptions it conveys about the nature of authoritative experience and the relationship between human experience and theological discourse. Here, it is one of expertise, objectivity and hierarchy; but, fatally, there is little attempt to integrate the authentic or considered testimony of those who actually have experience of same-sex relationships.

This is an example of the 'Olympian' approach to human sexuality; an avoidance of real, lived experience enables the House of Bishops' Report to evade ambivalence, doubt and above all, difference. Those whom the Report rather quaintly terms 'homophiles' remain a shadowy, voiceless group, void of experience, integrity, or Christian commitment. Experiences of same-sex love remain stigmatized and marginal; medicalized and objectified phenomena. The House of Bishops seems less concerned with the exploration of the human and theological depth of sexual behaviour than with debating a condition. David Jenkins (Byrne and Jenkins 1994) conveys some of the contradictions of such a process, and questions the authenticity of such a partial view:

> I was at a meeting of the House of Bishops some little time ago, when we were earnestly discussing matters of sexuality. I suddenly gazed up at all these elderly gents, and I thought to myself, 'This is totally absurd.' ... Here we were, this collection of the middle-aged and elderly, including me, getting ready to pontificate

about sex, which many of us were past and many of us regretted. There was something simply inhuman and stupid about it, that authority should be thought to reside in such a gathering in that way ... the message is belied by the deprived humanity of the messengers. (p.123)

The work of the French social theorist and philosopher Michel Foucault (1977; 1978) has contributed much to our understanding of the ways in which human cultures come to terms with the complexity and perversity of human nature. Foucault's historical studies were much informed by the confessional practices of the medieval Church, and led him to argue that, especially at times of social upheaval, the ruling classes will develop an interest in a particular human condition in order to contain and control it. The emergence of sexology in the early twentieth century was superficially permissive; but the medicalization of sexuality, especially male homosexuality, took place in order the better to pathologize and discipline. For Foucault, social enquiry into a particular human condition, be it in areas of criminology, sexuality or mental illness, is a necessary prerequisite to legislation and coercion. The delineation of a particular characteristic or state of being is often the first time it is identified as a discrete phenomenon in its own right; but only the better to establish it as either socially acceptable or dangerously pathological. It is tempting to apply such an analysis to *Issues in Human Sexuality*, and conclude that the House of Bishops was more concerned with establishing normative sexual behaviour in order to reiterate a particular form of pastoral discipline than with generating insights by which, in dialogue with traditional truth-claims, faithful Christians of all sexual persuasions might seek to order their lives.

Sexuality in gay and lesbian experience

Depriving people of language with which to make sense of their experience is a particularly effective way of keeping them silent and disempowered. (Stuart 1992, p.10)

Contrast such a model of theologizing on human sexuality with the collection of prayers and meditations which celebrate gay and lesbian relationships, *Daring to Speak Love's Name* (Stuart 1992). The circumstances of its publication are probably well known: it provoked controversy after the original commissioning body, SPCK, decided not to publish following intervention by members of its governing body. I suspect its most culpable offence lay not so much in its implied advocacy of gay and lesbian relationships, as in its attempt to achieve what the House of Bishops' Report eschewed: to speak from experience, to tell stories and to give an apologia for sexualities that could be articulated in terms of commitments, values and relationships, and not merely a condition to be 'explained' or legislated about. However, such intentions were, I believe, rendered more unacceptable because *Daring to Speak* used the vehicle of liturgy and worship to do this. By so doing, it dared to denote same-sex love holy and worthy of bringing into the presence of God.

In giving a voice to those who traditionally have had minimal access to a language through which they might make sense of their spiritual and sexual identities (and a language which attempts to integrate those identities, rather than as seeing them at odds), *Daring to Speak* encouraged people to affirm the reality of their sexual integrity. For lesbians and gay men to name the truth about their sexualities in the context of worship is both a release from silence and invisibility, and an affirmation of the possibilities of encountering the love of God at the very heart of such relationships. In this respect, such a process of self-realization is akin to an experience of resurrection:

> We unwind the grave clothes of socialization and of church teaching recognizing them for what they are, bonds to keep us dead, to keep us lying down, to keep us out of the way and powerless. And our 'angels', our friends and lovers, help us to roll away the stone of fear and we burst out of the tomb of self-hatred into new life. (Stuart 1992, p.92)

What is more, the commitments, values and experiences of same-sex love were portrayed as potential places for theological disclosure. New and old images and symbols were used to talk about lives which just happened to be characterized by particular patterns of sexual preference, and finding there something of the Divine:

> In coming together Christians remind themselves and others that we are part of a community, that salvation is not an individual matter but a community experience. We are reminded of how we belong to one another and repent of our failure to live this out in practice ... Through the use of words and, more importantly, symbols, which manage to express realities which words cannot articulate, as individuals and community we experience God's grace the healing, transforming, liberating un-conditional love that so many encountered in the person of Jesus of Nazareth. Liturgy offers us the time and space and inspiration to connect our lives and history with that of other lives and God's life. For the liturgy to be effective it needs to articulate and speak to the experience of those who take part in it, in word and symbol. (pp.10–11)

And ultimately, all this was being offered as a gift to the whole Church: the contributors were making a gift of themselves, and their insights into the meaning of loving and being loved, in the hope that all Christians might learn more about human experience and about the God who brings all things into being. Whatever next?

This is of wider significance. It represents a theology of sexuality that starts from experience, but which has been articulated in a particular way: arising out of pastoral need (the occasions and rites of passage encountered in the course of human lives) and enacted liturgically and practically, thereby generating new ways of talking theologically. The experiences of human love and human need engage with traditional and innovative Christian practices and theological formulations of religious language, in order to produce forms of Christian practice which might speak and embody apprehensions of God at work in the world.

Liturgy as pastoral theology

Other communities within the Christian Church are following similar paths to the contributors to *Daring to Speak*, and using the vehicle of liturgy to express their deepest ambitions and aspirations; liturgy as a vantage-point for the reclamation of self-esteem and the articulation of hitherto unacknowledged needs and experiences. For example, some of the most exciting and creative work within feminist theology has its origins in forms of feminist liturgy and women-church (Graham and Halsey 1993, pp.180–191). They begin with the lived experience of women, but often ones which have been neglected or demonized by patriarchal theology: female sexuality, embodiment, puberty, childbirth, sexual violence and ageing (Dodson Gray 1988; Ruether 1985; St. Hilda Community 1991). Yet gradually, new forms of ritual and liturgy are enabling groups of Christian women and men to reappropriate such areas of life, and to make specific pastoral response via rituals of affirmation, healing and rites of passage. And in the process, such liturgies are apprehending and naming God in these experiences: of seeking forgiveness and reconciliation in the suffering of the Cross; of finding the beauty and integrity of creation in women's power to conceive and nurture; and of discovering healing communities in which new life can be brought to bear.

Such liturgies give a new shape to these experiences as well as providing theological shape: women can bring their lives into the presence of God, and find them holy. As with the authors of *Daring to Speak*, such rituals dare to find God in the midst of such experiences, and offer metaphors and vehicles through which to apprehend the Divine. Instead of relating to theology as primarily a body of intellectual propositions, therefore, such a practical theology sees the truth-claims of the Christian tradition as emerging from, and resting in, pastoral practices – in this case, concrete collective acts of worship.

At its best, therefore, liturgy is a focal point for people to encounter God. This is the essence of all pastoral activity: because Christianity is an incarnational faith, Christians must necessarily ground and direct that divine apprehension in human relationship and activity. So liturgy is pastoral because it can respond to, and express in ritual form, a myriad of human needs. The experience of many women and men in the churches is that the vocabulary of Christian ritual regarding human needs and rites of passage has been over-narrow and impoverished; but attention to hidden needs and life-experiences, especially of women, helps to enhance the range of liturgical expressions for everyone.

The study of liturgy is therefore a welcome and essential aspect of contemporary pastoral studies and practical theology. It is essentially a means by which communities of faith can usher human experience into the presence of God. Truly liberative liturgy will not be exclusive, seeking to encompass all human experience and community life as worthy and redemptive. Christian worship, at its most inclusive and honest, is thus one of the practical embodiments, in word and deed, of the primary values and truth-claims of the Christian faith; an authentic vehicle by which Christian communities seek to embrace and express the fullness of the Gospel:

'Christians are formed by the way in which they pray and the way they choose to pray expresses what they are' (Ramshaw 1987, p.15).

So the study of liturgy via its texts, its traditions and its practitioners, is a valuable dimension of practical/pastoral theology. It enables us to explore, from the practical vantage-point of word and sacrament, how the actions of Christians in the world might speak of their understanding of God.

> The self-understanding of Christian worship and sacramental practice must remain at heart a theological one ... Our vision of the future reign of God, our ideal of Christian community and social justice, and our image of personal fulfillment through 'sanctification' are all aspects of the theological world view which alone can adequately norm our worship. (p.15)

11

Friendship in Community
Creating a Space for Love (1997)

John Swinton

Theology, doctrine and tradition can be truly beautiful things. Theologians can be as creative and innovative as the most elegant of artists, weaving and painting wonderful experiences, explanations and offering understandings of humanity and creation which excite, tempt, tantalize and amaze. Theology can root us in a reality which opens up new possibilities for love and community which are so often hidden from our individualistic, Western eyes.

But doctrine and tradition also have a shadow side. Misused or misunderstood, they have the propensity to entangle individuals and communities in an inextricable and often dangerous mass of confusion, binding them so tightly to words and laws, that it is impossible for them to find a space within their exclusive confines for love.

The purpose of this article is to highlight some of the dangers inherent within the shadow side of the church's practice and thinking, and to offer some pointers towards ways in which the church could go about fulfilling its undoubted potential as an inclusive community. Three examples will help to highlight some of the difficulties that engage the church in its dealings with intellectually disabled people.

At a Church Advisorate on Special Educational Needs conference called to discuss intellectual disability and the church, I spoke with a gentleman whose daughter has Down syndrome. She is a very keen member of the Church of Scotland, and a regular attender and participant in worship at their local church. He told me that, whilst in Aberdeen five years previously, he, his wife and his daughter, had gone to a city centre Church of Scotland for communion. The cup was passed round, but when it reached the visiting man's daughter, the minister who was administering the sacrament, refused, in a very public and embarrassing way, to allow her to participate, his reason being that he did not consider that she had the intellectual capability to understand and meaningfully participate in the sacrament. From this minister's theological standpoint, the girl's participation would risk demeaning or even invalidating the sacrament. It is easy to imagine the humiliation and exclusion which that family must have felt at that time.

Of course, this type of exclusionary attitude is not confined to the clergy. Peter Birchenall, writing from a nursing perspective, suggests that:

People with a profound mental handicap possess a limited ability to reason at the complex level, and are therefore not able to work through any doubts and develop any sort of faith. (Birchenall and Birchenall 1986, p.150)

Severely mentally handicapped people are denied the very substance of a rational productive existence, and are confined to a life of almost total dependence on others for even their most basic needs. Such an existence gives no real opportunity for inner spiritual growth, or the nourishment of the human spirit, both of which are important when coming to terms with the meaning of Christianity. It gives no real opportunity to experience the joy of seeking a lifetime relationship with the Almighty, because the concepts involved are complicated and require a level of awareness which the profoundly mentally handicapped do not have. (Birchenall and Birchenall in Parish 1987, p.75)

It is important to note that quite apart from the more than dubious suggestion that a person's ability to love God and to be loved by Him is somehow dependant on their intellectual capabilities, what this quotation shows very clearly is that, for some, the church is not an open, inclusive community, but one which has firm, fixed boundaries, which are essentially defined by human beings according to a person's intellectual abilities. This seems to me a far cry from the open, inclusive community of love and acceptance which we find revealed and lived out in the ministry of Jesus. Although the church may seek to understand itself as an inclusive community, the reality for many people with a learning disability is that it is not.

In stark contrast to this exclusionary attitude stands the official report of the sixth assembly of the World Council of Churches, which met in Vancouver, Canada in 1983. The following extracts offer a very different understanding of sacrament, faith and community. Section three states that 'all churches should examine with their congregation, the factors which hinder the integration and participation of persons with disabilities, and take concrete steps to remove them' (Monteith 1987, p.81). The report continues with this theme in section eight, stating that, 'we are convinced that disabled people can also have a spiritual understanding of the sacrament, and that they are able to participate in their own way in the spiritual life of the church and the congregation' (p.82).

We can see from these two contrasting examples of Christian responses to intellectually disabled people, that there is a definite need for the clarification and redefinition of their position within the Christian community, in order that such polarization can be overcome and the church can minister effectively. The church can only truly call itself a community when it reveals inclusive love, and it can only reveal inclusive love when it realizes the limitations of its human-made boundaries, and strives to build a space for love; a space in the midst of the complexities of theology and tradition; a space which is not dependent on a person's intellect for access; a space in which *all* persons can be enabled to be themselves in the company of others.

But how does the church go about beginning to build this space for love? The crux of the matter revolves around the issue of community.

In order to overcome the difficulties highlighted by the above polarities, we must seriously consider what kind of community the church is aiming to create, and how it might seek to live, and to enable others to live fruitfully within it. It is to the question of *life in community* that we must turn to find an answer to our dilemma.

If the church is serious in its desire to initiate genuine, compassionate and unpatronizing relationships with intellectually disabled persons, then perhaps the place to begin is by examining its own attitudes and motivations. To achieve this, the first thing it must do is learn to distinguish between *compassion* and *pity*.

Compassion has to do with life orientation. It is an all embracing, proactive emotion which genuinely reaches out to encompass its recipient with active love and acceptance. *Pity* on the other hand is a more static term indicating an attitude of sadness; a feeling of sorrow for another person's suffering, with no necessary corollary of action. Pity has a tendency to engender feelings of sentimentality and often thoughtless kindness. Well-intentioned remarks about 'such people' always being happy and loving, or even to suggest, as Klinkenbeard (1984) does, that mentally handicapped [sic] people are somehow sin-free; 'above the fall' can have the effect of denying the intellectually disabled person's individuality and their rightful place within the Christian community. By suggesting that they are not truly part of fallen humanity, somehow specially blessed and set apart from the rest of humanity, what may be the disabled person's most attractive aspects, loving trust, openness, innocence, are downgraded as merely 'part of their condition' rather than positive attributes which could serve to teach and enhance the entire community.

Contrary to the negative understandings outlined above, I would suggest that the Bible states very clearly that faith and love are not intellectual entities, but are ways of living, or to be more precise, *ways of loving*. We can only understand what it means to love and be loved if we first experience love, and we can only understand what it means to be accepted by God if we are first accepted by his people; by His *community*. A person's spirituality has nothing to do with *what* they may or may not know. It has everything to do with *who* they know and how they relate to them. This being so, one of the primary means of our meeting with God is through personal, temporal encounters. The authenticity of the Christian community is a vital starting point for the communication of the gospel to all people including those with intellectual disabilities.

In terms of community, *acceptance* and *belonging* are key motifs. For many people with intellectual disabilities, their life experience is marked by *powerlessness* and *exclusion*, by feelings of *worthlessness*, helplessly alienated from a world bound by false values and expectations. It is therefore essential that rather than striving simply to do things *for* the intellectually disabled, we begin to learn what it might mean to genuinely *be* with them. It is through everyday life in community, through God's accepting, incarnated love, that intellectually disabled people can begin to discover that they have value, that they are loved, and that they in themselves are essentially loveable. The Christian community must become what Martin Buber (Buber in Vanier 1982, p.8) calls *the place of Theophany;* the place where God reveals Himself and His love. It must become a place of belonging; a place of love and acceptance; a place of caring. Above all it must become *a place of friendship.*

Friendship is of vital importance for our involvement with intellectually disabled people who are more often than not seen as objects of charity rather than as potential friends. Friendship is the perfect counter to the impersonality of contemporary Western society. Jurgen Moltmann (1978) puts it thus:

> Friendship unites affection with respect. In friendship we experience ourselves for what we are, respected and accepted in our own freedom. Through friendship we respect and accept people as people and as individual personalities. (p.115)

Friendship permeates our community and helps keep it human. True Christian friendship is the physical manifestation of God's love, exemplified by Jesus' sacrificial, all embracing friendship. It is through loving, meaningful friendships that intellectually disabled people can come to understand the meaning of Jesus as their friend. Within the context of community, friendship means equality, acceptance and genuine valuing. Friendship is not an intellectual matter. Friendship is a matter of the heart.

There are, however, three important points that must be acknowledged if we are genuinely to seek to develop friendships with intellectually disabled people.

First, friendship is dependent on *freedom* and *mutuality.* Any true friendship *must* be desired by both participants if it is to have any worthwhile meaning. There can be no guarantee that our desire to accept and befriend the disabled individual will be met with similar acceptance. If we are sincerely to befriend intellectually disabled people, then we must be prepared for rejection. As with all of us, the disabled person has the right to reject an offer of friendship. There may, however, be many reasons for such rejection, and it is of paramount importance that we ensure that a person's rejection of another does not become the source of their own rejection. There is a danger within the Christian community, as elsewhere, that individuals appearing less than friendly, or frequently rejecting help, and friendship, will be labelled as 'unfriendly', 'antagonistic' or 'trouble makers', and consequently excluded or avoided. There can however, be no limit to love in genuine community, and it is the responsibility of all to deal with rejection in the same spirit of love and forgiveness that is revealed to us in the gospel story. It is the responsibility of the whole Christian community to work with the individual to ensure that they find and are enabled to maintain genuine friendships.

Second, and related to the previous point, our friendships must be based on a genuine commitment to the individual. Although constantly changing as new members enter, and their gifts and differences alter the shape and texture of the community, the bonds of love and commitment which bind the Christian community together remain unchanged. Our friendships must not be borne out of pity or duty but out of a genuine desire to get to know the individual, and to share in their lives and allow them to share in ours. Only authentic, sacrificial friendship will allow us truly to enter into the lives of others and allow them entry into our own lives.

Authentic friendship also means a transference and sharing of *authority* and *power*. Our friendships must be based on the concept of mutuality and the enablement of self-advocacy. We must move away from the conception that somehow 'we know best' and concentrate on developing ways of supporting the disabled individual as they struggle for their independence, even if this entails times of sadness, disappointment and defeat. Growth and maturity for all of us is often the consequence of ongoing struggles and failures. Genuine relationship demands that we take risks. It is through such acceptance and mutual sharing of responsibility, that the transforming love of God can be made manifest to the intellectually disabled person, and can become a source of enhancement for the entire Christian community.

Finally, friendship, acceptance and equality in community, must also go hand in hand with the preservation of the disabled person's individual identity. None of us wants to be treated equally, if that means we lose our distinctiveness. Intellectually disabled people, irrespective of the severity of their disability, are individuals with their own personalities, aims, hopes and ambitions, and as such demand recognition and acknowledgement of identity in their own right. Any true friend must bear this firmly in mind. Friendship, acceptance, and belonging does not mean the disabled person striving to reach as close an approximation to societies norms as possible. Friendship, acceptance, and belonging are born out of the valuing of differences, and the acknowledgement that differences should not be 'negativized' into difficulties. In this way, we can allow people with learning disabilities and the fresh perspective which they bring to us, to call us towards a community of individuality and diversity where our similarities and our differences help each other to flourish together as a unified people respected, loved and accepted by God and by each other. A community where each person is valued for what they are and given their own space from within which they can begin to experience the inclusive and limitless love of God and contribute to the development of His church.

PART FOUR

Practical Theology
in Critical Dialogue

12

Objections to a National Pastoral Organization

(1971)

Robert Lambourne

It is proposed that an organization be set up that will be concerned to delineate a hierarchy of standards for pastoral counselling. The organization will be concerned with the accreditation of persons and institutions. The objection is against this specific proposal at this particular time and not against any form of national organization concerned with pastoral care.

Introduction

The importance of increasing the range and depth of the Church's and the Christian's sensitivity is not disputed. Nor is the role of the social and behavioural sciences in this task denied. Nor is it disputed that interview techniques, group work, case work, organizational theory and other skills associated with pastoral counselling are of importance. Nor is it disputed that pastoral counselling might play a more important part in the daily life of Christian ministry or that more counselling centres are required. But it is argued that the concepts and structures for this kind of work are already present and gaining strength and that the support of these is now only a secondary matter. The long-term strategy outlined below suggests, however, that the proposed National Pastoral Organization is already out of date and that something else is required. This strategy depends on the following propositions:

(1) That the Church, though it has a professional leadership, is unlike its medical and social work counterparts in that it is in its pastoral work:

   (a) Lay, voluntary and diffuse in the community. (Not agency or institution based.)

   (b) Motivated as much by a struggle for corporate excellence as a struggle against defects.

(2) That therefore, while there may be good tactical reasons for supporting training in pastoral counselling concerned with the prevention or

eradication of defects in the individual, both the distinctive nature of the Church and the necessity to balance the medical and social work institutions and their concepts require that the strategy be towards a pastoral care regarded as the science and art of building groups of 'normal' people who seek health as a chosen way of excellence. For them health and the pastoral care which is concerned with it is seen primarily as a pattern of corporate responsible sensitive acts motivated by a compelling vision. Only a minor part of that vision and only a minor number of those acts are concerned with disease or problem prevention and removal. The long-term strategy is deliberately designed to prevent this minor part controlling the shape of the concepts and practices of the Church in pastoral care.

(3) Therefore to promote at this time a National Pastoral Organization concerned to set up standards which are based upon concepts and practices almost entirely derived from lessons learned in the counselling of problem-motivated individuals is to neglect and frustrate that strategic priority.

(A national organization concerned primarily in promoting communication between the various bodies concerned in pastoralia and which regarded 'deep' counselling of 'patients' or 'clients' as the least normative model, and a healthy congregation as the most normative model might be another matter.)

Main argument

To oppose the setting up of standards of pastoral counselling (or whatever it will be called) with a hierarchy of accreditations is to swim against the tide. The advantages of the introduction of standardization, accreditation, specialization and professionalization in pastoral counselling seem compelling. The good work that can be done in the prevention and care of diseases and problems seems so worthy a cause. The possibility of improved interprofessional relationships, of increased self-respect and sense of competence in the minister of religion, of stimulus to theological thought and of meeting the call for the Church to be a servant all seem irresistible reasons for its adoption. My thesis, however, is that the pastoral counselling called for in this country during the next twenty years cannot be built around a practice and conceptual framework derived from professional problem-solving and prevention of breakdown.

That practice and conceptual framework is based upon the clinical, medical and psychoanalytical models of the USA of twenty years ago, and it has proved inadequate. To copy it, even with many modifications, as a model for tomorrow would be a disaster, because not only is it not what is wanted but also because it will be an obstacle to what is wanted. An accredited hierarchical pastoral movement will be professional, problem solving or problem preventing, standardized and defined.

What is required is pastoral care which is lay, corporate, adventurous, variegated and diffuse. The first-mentioned concepts and practices, though far from being universal, still dominate the field of pastoral care through secular services of psychiatry and mental health, social work, general practice, pastoral counselling, etc. The Church will serve these best not by following them but by providing a supplement and a corrective within the second set of concepts and practices.

Here then follows some of the arguments for a different kind of initiative in the pastoral field, but against the proposed actions based as they are predominantly on a scheme of regularization and accreditation:

(1) If the local fellowship of Christians, whether gathered and definable or dispersed and indistinguishable from new personal centres of better life in society, is the heart of the redemptive activity of God in Christ, then the lay enabler of such gathered or dispersed centres of new health is the pastoral 'priest' of the second half of the twentieth century. Therefore anything which 'downgrades' these persons and the centres of excellence in which they discover themselves as 'priests' must be regarded with suspicion. New institutions we set up affect the concepts that come to life in them. Thus, for example, we cannot separate the spiritual-secular conceptual problem from questions about where and how we train and ordain ministers of religion. Similarly we cannot produce a lay, communal, life-experimental, variegated pastoral theology and practice from a professional, problem-orientated, standardized, accredited pastoral theology and practice. Even from the point of view of the local professional ordained ministry the progressive accreditation of only one of the skills required for such ministry seems dubious. For such ministry, amongst other things, preaching, business administration, praying, theological flexibility, counselling, liturgical sensitivity, teaching ability, and organizational skill are all important. But then why has one of these become the focus of a national network of training, standardization and accreditation, implicitly downgrading the others? What are our psychological, sociological and theological reflections upon this trend? Are there not Christian theological reasons for questioning it? I think there are. I believe that the pastoral counselling movement, most highly developed in the USA, must be seen as part of a too general assumption by society, epitomized by the medical profession, that we come to the good life by delineating problems and then either avoiding them (prevention) or solving them. Pastoral theology has been over-influenced by the puzzle-solving view of human progress – a 'hang up' theology which fits only too closely with the medical clinical professional identity.

   Is it not anomalous that at a time when even the psychiatric profession's approach to mental health, and the social worker's understanding of his task is becoming more interested in the lay and communal aspects, that pastoral counselling should still adopt a training based substantially on experiences gained outside the common field of life and given in training centres, and that it should still be so very much concerned with the one-to-one prevention and cure of illness? Excellence in pastoral skill is to be accredited to individuals who have spent the largest number of hours in improving their skill through such experiences. But too much experience of this kind necessarily structures thought towards a model of health which, because it portrays it as the result of individuals bringing their badness to skilled others, is now seen in other disciplines to be not merely unbalanced or inadequate but a main obstacle to health. Mental health is best seen within the Church's strategy of pastoral care during a time of rapid social changes as the capacity of groups to discover and adopt distinctive contemporary and fitting ways of being healthy, of being human. Not the prevention of illness, nor the removal of illness, but a corporate vision and excitement which enables the participant people to responsibly accept and transform a super-normal level of mutual anxiety into the stuff of health and freedom is the concept of pastoral care and mental health we now need to press. The responsible corporate ethical act vicariously undertaken and not the moment of insight into individual pathology becomes the ground of the theological and psychological work upon which such pastoral living flowers.

Before we embark on a programme of standardization, accreditation, etc., we need to make a theological, psychological and sociological analysis of the pastoral counselling movement. From this we can at least move forward to a strategy even if it should turn out not to be identical with that which I have suggested. It is not enough to change our concepts of pastoral counselling to bring them up to date with those of the USA pastoral counselling organizations, which though sophisticated and enlightened are trapped in their history of having been formed, and having flourished, under the pressure of clinical psychotherapy in a highly individualistic society. A model of healthy interpersonal life, of communal life as requiring mutual confrontation and mutual confirmation around the matter of values, is essential for pastoral care.

A concept and practice of pastoral care which is lay, communal, variegated, adventurous and diffuse should be the aim of those concerned with shaping pastoral care in Great Britain today. This will in no way disparage the work of those who feel the need for pastoral theology to thrust towards increasing experience in the applied behavioural sciences and towards multiplying and supporting educational efforts in pastoral care, but it will require that we test each proposed move by asking whether or not it will promote or destroy the lay, communal, adventurous, variegated and diffuse aspects of this work.

(2) The analogy of the social work scene should be borne in mind. The model of the psychiatric social worker as the archetype of the social worker, based in its turn on the psychoanalyst in contract with a private client, was defeated twenty years ago and replaced by the generic model of the social

worker in contract with an institution or agency. Now this model in turn is under pressure by community, and community action and voluntary service concepts. If this shift in emphasis is taking place in social work, how much more important it is for pastoral care if those images of the Church which picture it as a salt diffused in 'normal' society are given preference within a strategy. Individual counselling as conceived of in the last thirty years has, of course, its place, and instruction in it on a wide scale may even be a tactical move (though I think this highly dangerous) but it must be so envisaged and taught that it serves the strategy and does not obstruct it.

(3) Highly specialized or advanced courses in pastoral counselling are particularly dangerous because they produce a hierarchy of specialists who owe their accreditation to their proximity during training to the experience and concepts of top people in analogous clinical and case-work occupations. Since top people in medicine and social work are still not general practitioners, voluntary workers, health visitors, community workers, etc., and usually have little competence in those other sides of personal development which enable the local Christian person to be effective, such as preaching, organizing a civil protest or celebrating a liturgy, the top people in pastoral counselling will be defective examples. So the criteria of accreditation must be carefully examined with this in mind.

(4) There is no proof that an army of doctors, social workers and priests reduce the incidence in the West of symptoms of being stressed. This unreduced incidence is often blamed on the fact that society is becoming more stressful but there are many other possible explanations, including the possibility that the general population's capacity for turning stress into community health is reduced by the present concepts and practices of medical, social work and other helping professions. A community of high morale which takes pleasure in each other and which is skilled in discovering pleasurable activities and tasks embodying values provides the context in which anxiety is not reduced but carried creatively.

(5) There seems to be good reasons for delaying for as long as possible the regularization of national programmes of training in pastoralia. Once programmes are standardized and tied to qualifications, especially if social work and medical organizations are involved, it may be extremely hard to change concepts and practices or to introduce variety. A pastoral theology which takes account of the psychological and social sciences is very new in this country and has not reached the maturity and balance where institutionalization is reasonably safe. Rapid expansion in numbers of personnel in the social work and mental health professions has made experiment and change relatively easy because recently trained men and

women outnumber the old hands and keep things on the move. In the next twenty years this advantage is unlikely to be available to the Church and to the ordained ministry especially, so flexibility in concepts of pastoral care is a precious thing. Moreover, Great Britain is a more homogeneous society than the USA, allowing less freedom for experiment. Accreditation of students leads to accreditation of supervisors and accreditation of training institutions. This may be valuable or even vital for producing professional technicians yet be more harmful than helpful for the strategy of pastoral care outlined above, which stresses lay, variegated, communal and experimental models to balance the weight of professional secular 'pastoral' care. Now the more we see pastoral care as the optimization of responsible loving living in the daily life of groups of healthy men and women the more difficult it becomes to provide supervised, assessed, standardized, controlled learning situations for students. But the drive for hierarchical accreditation leads to a drive to find just such controlled and measurable situations for teaching, supervision and assessment of students. But such controlled situations are outside the daily life of the 'strong' and from them come decontextualized concepts of pastoral care based upon the cure of the sick, dependent and weak, outside their daily world and outside the daily polymorphous life of the Church. Consider the training of the medical student and note how hard it is for medicine, in which top people are hospital people, to provide substantial learning experiences away from the hospital. This demonstrates the dangers of institutionalizing pastoral training around special centres. What is required is not more standardized courses organized to national grades but a greater number and diversity of training courses for the laity. Inspiring such work, supporting it and facilitating inter-communication of the lessons learned should be the purpose of a national pastoral organization. When it feels certain it knows enough about what pastoral care is to standardize such courses the time will have come for it to disband. The forces for standardization and accreditation are powerful enough already. They can be left to triumph as they almost certainly will.

(6) It is commonly argued that standards are absolutely necessary so that other professional (sic) workers like doctors and social workers can refer patients (sic) and clients (sic) to ministers (sic) they know to be trained and trustworthy. Now the dangers of making this a goal for a national pastoral organization have already been mentioned. In any case where psychotherapy and allied work is concerned it is not technical ability but ethical standards and attitudes which a professional accreditation may reasonably be hoped to secure. Of course if pastoral counselling and psychotherapy is a curative work analogous to the curative work of surgery

and internal medicine then in principle the efficacy of a practitioner could be measured and then if it were adequate he could then be accredited. Thus he could be authorized because of his technical ability and not for his ethical standards and attitudes. But I do not think those conditions can be met in psychotherapy and counselling today. So authorization and accreditation must necessarily be related to trust in the person's ethical standards and behaviour. But cannot these be secured, in so far as they can be secured, by other social arrangements and not be tied to the alleged attainment of advanced technical competence?

(7) The context in which learning takes place determines the available key hero figures by identification with whom the student's new identity is established. This identification in its turn is strongly determinative of the place and type of work eventually chosen by the trainee. Thus, for example, training a medical student in a hospital for general practice raises not just technical problems but professional identity confusion. Similarly, learning advanced pastoral skills outside the location where most pastoral skills need to be practiced is especially dangerous at a time of loss of theological nerve and loss of confidence in any worthwhile priestly role. The capacity to do appropriate work in an appropriate way and to stay in situations different from that where the counselling identity was established may thus not be increased but diminished. Promotion is to teaching pastoral care and moves the promoted person out of the parish towards campus, hospital, or other specialized agency to become one of the main formers of pastoral identities and concepts. A circular process is established.

(8) The dangers of stereotyping the role of ordained ministers of religion appointed to various institutions and agencies by choosing them because of their suitability as supervisors in that one concept of pastoral care dominant in the theory and structures fashionable at the time must be noted. In my opinion, in the USA for two decades the too close identification of the hospital chaplain with clinical pastoral care of a counselling-orientated type was a grave weakness. It produced a stereotype, robbed the hospital of theological prophecy and contributed to the notable failure of the USA health-care-deliverance system. It constitutes now the gravest threat to hospital chaplaincy in developing countries. Hospital chaplaincy needs also to be lay, experimental, variegated and communal and the same is true for other institutions and agencies. If a national pastoral organization is set up with the objectives stated to date, it will hinder rather than help this variety and balance.

(9) In conclusion I do not think a national pastoral organization set up with the goals stated so far is a good thing. I believe it to be harmful. Whether a National Pastoral Organization should be set up with different goals is

quite another matter. If it is, then it will need to be very differently constituted. The basic challenge in my view is not the lack of standards for various bodies involved in pastoral care but the lack of communication between them. Setting up standards now will cut off just those bodies which because they are weak, diffuse, lay, experimental and variegated may most easily fail to communicate with each other and with the 'advanced' institutes at a time when all, and especially the 'advanced', have a need of each other.

13

Religion and Psychotherapy
Friends or Foes? (1978)

Irene Bloomfield

In talking about religion and psychotherapy it is important to recognize that there are many schools of thought in both fields. All try to explain the nature of man, and his relationship to the world around him. Whatever I may say, therefore, about either religion or psychotherapy, can be contradicted. All we can do is to look at what appear to be broad areas of agreement, of conflict, and of ways in which each can learn from the other.

It may be that I shall raise more questions than I can answer, but I hope that these questions will give an opportunity for dialogue. Although I am involved in both, I have no wish to gloss over differences which may exist, but would prefer to look at ways in which conflicts may be reconciled, or acknowledge that there may be some fundamental differences. In talking of religion I am primarily looking at Judaeo-Christian concepts since I have not had enough experience of other faiths.

Joint concerns

Both religion and psychotherapy are concerned with growth and wholeness, with people's attitudes, feelings and behaviour. Both require self-understanding. Both formulate theories about the general nature of man and the determinants of his behaviour.

Differences

Although there are these joint concerns, there are differences in what we mean by wholeness and growth and the ways in which these may be achieved. Religion does, on the whole, pay far more attention to a specification of norms and standards for behaviour. These are thought to be derived from divine revelation embodied in written and moral law. This means that in the past there has been relatively little ambiguity for the religious person regarding conduct which was considered right or wrong.

Solomon Schimmel, in a recent paper on *Judaism and Contemporary Psychology* (reference untraceable), states that

> Jewish law spells out in great detail how the individual is expected to behave in almost any situation, whether towards parents, spouse, children, neighbours, strangers, employers or employees. Nothing is left to chance. Guidelines for behaviour are quite definite, and are meant for the lay person as much as for the Rabbi. No individual, therefore, can plead ignorance.

Psychology, on the other hand, does not, on the whole, specify how the individual is to behave in any particular situation. Instead, the therapist tends to think in terms of 'realization of potential', 'better adjustment', 'individuation', 'self-actualization' and 'wholeness'. Some therapies include in their aims something about values and meaning, but the nature of these values and meaning may differ from one individual to the next. Other therapies do not take account of any existential dimension and in that differ fundamentally from theological thinking.

Religion tends to start with an image of the ideal to be achieved, of where the individual ought to be or get to. Therapy tends to start with where the individual is at this moment and tries to help him unfold and develop whatever unique qualities he has within.

Wholeness in religion is often equated with holiness, with being 'perfect as the Lord is perfect', with upholding certain values, standards, traditions and religious laws as well as with having a good relationship with God. For the therapist, wholeness means an acknowledgement and acceptance of all aspects of ourselves, including the dark side of our nature, such as anger, bitterness, envy, jealousy, and hate. The acceptance of this dark side is necessary, not in order to act on these feelings, but because keeping them out of consciousness means that they exercise power over us which is unpredictable and uncontrollable. Many religious people believe that to own their bad feelings would mean that they are not as perfect as they ought to be, and therefore they need to work even harder to push such feelings underground where they become inaccessible. The individual who has to deny so much of himself cannot be a really authentic or whole person, and authenticity is one of the aims of therapy.

Differences in the concept of man

Freedom of will. According to the biblical view of man, he is made in the image of God, and therefore has free will to behave in accordance with religious law, and to live the good life, or he can turn away from God and behave sinfully and wickedly. The assumption is that nothing but his weakness or his badness prevents him from becoming whole or holy, and further, that the sinner brings injury upon himself.

It seems to me that such teaching addresses itself almost entirely to the conscious, adult part of the individual which can make such choices – leaving out of account the more primitive, child-self which is an inevitable and important part of all of us throughout our lives.

Most schools of psychotherapy would agree that there comes a point in all our lives where we have to take responsibility for what we are and wish to become. Psychotherapists do not accept the notion that we can simply make decisions about desirable or unacceptable behaviour. They take the view that man's behaviour and attitudes are, partially at least, determined by a combination of hereditary and environmental factors. They believe that patterns of response are laid down early on in life as a result of childhood experience, and frequently continue relatively unchanged into adult situations, where they are no longer appropriate. But because the origins of such patterns go back such a long way, to the time before we could apply our logical minds, they are very deeply ingrained, often hard to understand, and very difficult to change. I would like to give an example.

Jennifer could not comprehend why she always became anxious and depressed when she was enjoying herself and things were going well, until she recalled how mother had always warned her; 'you are laughing now, but you will cry before the day is out'. Only after making this connection did she begin to enjoy her successes without guilt.

So much of our behaviour, our attitudes and our perceptions of the world are determined by childhood experiences. Our first relationships largely determine how we experience relationships with subsequent people and with God.

Injunctions

One of the injunctions that comes to mind is the one about honouring your father and your mother. There are people whose experience of parental cruelty, neglect and rejection makes it impossible for them to honour or respect their parents, but for the religious person the failure to do so is just one more piece of evidence that he is now well launched on the way to perdition.

As a therapist I have seen a number of people who were able to forgive their parents' cruelty and neglect when they could understand them better and recognize that the parents too had suffered from their respective backgrounds, and perhaps this understanding and forgiveness is the first step towards 'honouring' parents, but I do not think that people can just make a positive decision to do so until they feel understood, accepted and 'honoured' themselves.

You may say that this happens through confession or spiritual guidance, but frequently that is not how the penitent perceives what happens in the confessional. Acceptance has to be based on real, genuine understanding. It has to be more than outer form. I am not in a position to speak from my own experience, but I am speaking about the way in which many of my patients or counsellees experience confession and spiritual guidance.

As I said earlier, theologians generally act on the presumption that man has the freedom to be good if only he tries hard enough. They do not, therefore, take into consideration the unconscious mechanisms which often give rise to incomprehensible behaviour and irrational emotions, the areas with which the psychotherapist is primarily concerned. I would like to give another example.

Valerie was determined to end her life. Three serious suicide attempts had put her into hospital three times in the year before she came for therapy. She felt badly about being so depressed. It made no sense because, as she herself remarked, 'I was terrified on my birthday when I was surrounded by people I loved and who loved me. I had everything going for me at that point, a new job, a home, good friends, and yet all I could think of was how to find a fool-proof method of dying and to stop the pain of living. It is all wrong that I should feel like that.'

Valerie could not see until she came into therapy that her fears, resentment, bitterness and hatred of the parents by whom she felt totally rejected was getting in the way of living, and having been brought up in a strict Baptist home the recognition of such terrifying feelings was in conflict with the injunction about honouring your father and your mother. She was trapped by these contradictory emotions. Her parents, now getting older, needed her and she wanted to do her duty by them, but her bitter resentment got in the way.

Much religious teaching is concerned with the way people *ought* to feel, like loving your neighbour as yourself (Leviticus 19:19; Matthew 19:18), but how can you make yourself love either yourself or your neighbour when you have never experienced love? I gather there are the few who are able to feel loved by God, even though they have not experienced the love of man in the shape of parents or parent substitutes, but I must confess that such people have not come my way, even among clergy and religious. The religious person may say that the individual's self-hatred can be transformed through the love of God, but in my experience he cannot feel the love of God if he has not felt the love of man. Perhaps St. John recognized this when he said 'Anyone who says I love God and hates his brother is a liar, since a man who does not love the brother that he can see cannot love God whom he has never seen' (1 John 4:21).

This is a truth the therapist comes up against constantly. The child who has never experienced parental love, affection and acceptance cannot feel loving towards other people, or towards God. It is very difficult to enable such a child to receive love from anyone because either he does not trust it or he simply cannot feel it. The prognosis is more hopeful where there has been someone at some point in the child's life who gave him love. This does not have to be a parent. It may be a granny, a foster parent, an older sibling or a nanny. So long as he has experienced love from someone, it is possible to help him find it again in later life, whether in a marriage partner, a friend, a priest, or a therapist. I have to say here of course, that the therapist may get a somewhat distorted view of mankind because on the whole he sees only those people whose development has been arrested or blocked, thus preventing growth – the clergyman's experience of people may be different. I would like to give a further example.

Jim illustrated these issues very vividly for me. He was a minister of religion in his early 30s. He came for therapy because of a truly dark depression which had landed him in psychiatric hospitals three times during the previous two years. He had tried to end his life twice, and had almost succeeded.

He thought of himself as a 'loathsome creature, no better than a poisonous insect which should be trodden under foot'. He told me at the start that women could not stand him and invariably turned away from him, and that I was sure to do the same. He looked unkempt and slovenly, almost as if he was carrying a banner, saying: 'This is Jim the loathsome, he is poisonous, so keep away.' He could see the point of this when I pointed it out and actually smiled, but said that he felt so bad he could not make the effort to tidy himself up.

He was terribly envious of all the young men he saw around him who seemed to have all the things he lacked, like good looks, money, cars, girls and respect. He felt quite murderous towards these mostly unknown young 'princes', and this shocked as well as frightened him, because it was such an unseemly emotion in a priest, and it added to his feeling of being a loathsome, sinful creature who did not deserve to be a priest. It all began in childhood where he was the only one of the four boys in the family who was academically bright and did well at school. He was clumsy and hated games and wore glasses and wet the bed until he was twelve. All of this did not endear him to his working-class parents or his brothers, who bullied and teased him. His father said angrily: 'This boy will never amount to anything. He has always got his nose stuck in a book instead of kicking a football around or tinkering with a motor bike as any proper boy would.'

The others went to watch football with father and had something to share with him. Joseph had nothing he could share with him. Father and the brothers were contemptuous of his bookishness and thought of him as dirty because of the bed-wetting and a sissy because he did not like sports. The young men in the street whom he envied so much were his 'brothers' who, he imagined, had respect, acceptance and acknowledgement which Joseph would never get.

He tried hard to make me turn away as well, but when I refused and helped him to see how much he had actually achieved (he had two degrees, plus Ordination), and that there were many good things about him, his feelings about himself began to change. He took more care of his appearance, which made people look at him differently, and as he was getting more from people he no longer felt so envious of others. My acceptance of him with his good and his bad characteristics made it possible for Joseph to like himself a little better. This acceptance, however, did not mean that he was not expected to change and grow. Towards the end of his eight months with me he had acquired a girlfriend and was offered a good living in another town.

It is four years now since I last saw Jim, but I recently had a letter from him in which he said, 'although my experiences at the time of our sessions were extremely painful, I now view them as some of the most valuable time I have ever spent. I am not saying that they were magical, but I am not the same person that you first met. I don't detest myself any more, nor do I constantly look at others and see myself in a negative light by comparison. The old problems do emerge from time to time, but are becoming increasingly rare. Life has a quietness, a gentleness and a contentment which I would never have dreamed possible.'

The moral of this story is what I said at the beginning, that people can only love and accept their neighbour if they feel loved and accepted by someone. I do not know how far the religious dimension is present in this kind of therapy, but I have no difficulty in accepting that whatever we offer another person is something of God within ourselves.

Authenticity

Much religious teaching and perhaps especially Christianity, does not encourage honesty with ourselves. For the recognition that we are not able to meet the most important requirement, that of loving, may be a devastating one.

The question arises; can religion or psychotherapy do anything about this impasse? As I said earlier, one important difference between the two approaches is that religion emphasizes what we *ought* to be, think, feel and do. Psychotherapy stresses the importance of recognizing what we *are*, think and feel at this moment in time. Once we have identified and acknowledged the dark side of our nature, that is, the unacceptable emotions and impulses, they can be modified or transformed; but all the time that they have to be pushed underground because it is too painful and frightening to face them, they remain as a permanent cancer within.

The religious person may deny that much religious teaching encourages us to be dishonest with ourselves and point to confession as an attempt at honestly facing undesirable aspects of ourselves, but the penitent can only face what he knows about. He has no way of getting in touch with those powerful forces within which he has gone to great lengths to push underground and deny to himself. Religious teaching has, in the past, fostered repression of all those apparently unacceptable feelings, like anger, envy, hatred, bitterness, violence and jealousy, as well as sexuality, because they have not fitted in with the image of the good person, the good Christian, or the good Jew.

This is not to say that psychotherapy encourages people to act on these emotions or impulses. Rather the reverse. Through acknowledging their existence we gain greater control over them. We know what we are fighting. When, on the other hand, impulses are forced underground they are experienced like an underground battalion of assassins who threaten our carefully built citadel or conscience. Much mis-understood psychology has given rise to ideas of permissiveness, laxity of morals and encouragement of violence or sexual acting out. This is far from the truth. It is not the aim of therapy to allow people to act on their impulses. There is instead encouragement to take responsibility for bad feelings as well as good ones, and to substitute inner discipline for external threats. The childhood system of reward and punishment may then give way to internal authority.

Most of the people who come to a psychiatric department have not strayed very obviously from the straight and narrow. They are more likely to turn aggression against themselves rather than against others and to accuse themselves of acts of omission or commission. They are not, on the whole, the people who have committed unlawful acts, but are more likely to be casualties of their own harsh judgement on themselves. A severely depressed person so often is the person who cannot allow himself to express the rage they feel about some hurt which they experienced in the past. The hurt may be one done to them by another person or it may be experienced as having been done by the Almighty, but since they cannot let themselves feel angry with parents or God, they believe that they must themselves be bad and worthless. I would like to give a final example.

Veronica's mother died shortly after her birth. She was brought up by her father's two unmarried sisters who were unused to children and unable to respond to the needs of a little girl. They believed that their strictness would make her into a good God-fearing Christian girl. Father remarried and started another family, but his new wife would not take Veronica and so she stayed with the aunts who were quite elderly and did not really want to be bothered with her. Veronica felt unloved and unwanted. When she had enquired about her mother the aunts told her that mother had wanted to go to Jesus. Veronica did not understand. How could it be that mother preferred to go to Jesus rather than to stay with her? 'There must be something terribly wrong with me' she argued. The only explanation she could think of was that she was so bad that no one could love her or want her. The fact that her daddy, to whom she was devoted, would not have her either confirmed it. She could not imagine what this terrible thing was that was wrong with her. She just 'knew' that it was something unimaginably bad.

There was not much in her life to disprove this notion. As she got older the aunts became more severe in their admonitions and never having experienced sexual satisfaction themselves, they issued dire warnings and threats about the dangers of lust, and contact with members of the opposite sex. Almost everything Veronica might have wanted to do seemed to be sinful. About the only thing that was not was eating, so she stuffed herself and became huge. She weighed 19 stones when she first came for therapy. She felt extremely guilty about her overeating and every now and then she made resolutions to stop it. But the compulsion got the better of her and whenever she went on a strict diet she became acutely depressed, unable to work and feeling suicidal.

To her God was a fierce punishing figure who sent his thunderbolts down to earth to express his wrath. Veronica was terrified of thunder, and every thunderstorm sent her into such a state of panic that she almost stopped breathing and was in danger of dying in an asthma attack.

She had never had a sexual relationship, but had fantasies of being tied up and beaten by the priest of her church. These fantasies added to her feeling that she was sinful and doomed. She had tried to confess what to her were abominations, but that had made it worse. She did not feel forgiven, and certainly she could not forgive herself and could not conceive of the possibility of God being able to forgive her. The priest felt himself to be out of his depth with Veronica. In any case, he was not sympathetic towards her. He believed that it only required a bit of will power to go on a diet. He had done so, so why couldn't she?

It was not will power that Veronica was short of. It was a re-evaluation of her experiences and the religious teaching she had absorbed as a child. Her image of God and her fear of him only changed when she began to feel more accepting of the little girl within who had had so many disappointments, and so few satisfactions in her life. She had been *told* about forgiveness, but no one had *modelled* it for her until she came into therapy, and it is not just what we say to people that brings about change, but much more how we feel and how we behave towards them.

It is obvious that psychotherapists can be as caring or as uncaring as priests. This depends on the individual rather than on his profession.

Is the thought as bad as the act?

Veronica made me think of another, to me, fundamental difference between the two approaches. She felt damned because of her fantasies and her occasional wish for revenge against her mother who preferred to go to Jesus, her father who abandoned her, her aunts who did not understand her, and the priest who was impatient with her.

This reminded me of Matthew 5:28, 'You have learned as it was said: You must not commit adultery, but I say this to you, if a man looks at a woman lustfully, he has already committed adultery with her in his heart.' As a therapist I cannot accept that the thought is as bad as the act. I spend much of my time trying to persuade people that their murderous, vengeful *thoughts*, or their lustful sexual ones, are fundamentally different from the *act* of murder or adultery.

The individual who can accept sexual impulses as natural and normal can deal with them more adequately than the one who has to deny them or push them underground. When they are pushed underground they are more likely to erupt in inexplicable and excessive forms. As we gain in tolerance of our own sexuality we can also be more understanding and tolerant of it in others.

The same goes for all our potentially dangerous or unacceptable feelings and impulses. The more we can identify and acknowledge them, the easier it becomes to deal with them. Much religious teaching, however, encourages repression and denial of impulses which seem too hot to handle. Yet although this may seem a fundamental difference in approach between the two disciplines, I have found it in practice to be negligible, among the more progressive and open members of both disciplines.

Conclusion

(1) I believe that psychotherapy and religion are concerned with the same basic human truths and that both aim at the development and growth of the individual and society.

(2) Some psychotherapy emphasizes the importance of ethical values, but the non-religious psychotherapist might believe that only his skill, expertise and personal qualities are necessary to achieve wholeness. Most religious people, on the other hand, would believe that wholeness and healing are only partially due to the therapist's personality and skills, and rely heavily on the grace of God and the relationship with him.

(3) Most therapists believe that although man has to take responsibility for his behaviour his attitudes and his feelings, he is not entirely free to choose how he wants to feel or behave. According to them, feelings and behaviour are largely determined by heredity and childhood experiences, frequently forgotten and not readily available to consciousness. The concept of the unconscious which is vital in psychotherapy does not appear to come much into theological thinking, and religion therefore makes little allowance for unconscious motivation, although individual priests may do so.

(4) Where distortion of perceptions have occurred, due to childhood experiences, and the world, its inhabitants, and God are perceived as dangerous, persecutory and punitive, the individual is not able to change these perceptions just because he wants to or because he is told that they are false. Psychotherapy or counselling may be necessary before a real understanding of religious concepts becomes possible.

(5) It may be a misinterpreted and simplistic theory, but there is frequently the idea among people with a religious background that God is the equivalent of the father who hands out rewards and punishments for good or bad behaviour. This can prevent the individual from becoming an independent adult with authority within himself.

(6) Religion often encourages splitting into good and evil, black and white, heaven and hell. Therapy should encourage integration of conflicting tendencies within ourselves and acknowledge the existence of good and evil tendencies. It should attempt to help people towards wholeness by owning all of themselves, including the dark side of their natures. According to psychotherapists only when this dark side is owned can it be transformed.

(7) Religion may foster a permanent sense of guilt and unworthiness because of the notion that we are born sinners, whereas most psychotherapies try to reduce inappropriate or excessive guilt. This does not, of course, always work out and psychotherapists may also induce guilt by telling people that they are resistant to therapy, acting-out, or whatever the respective ideological misdemeanour may be.

(8) It is accepted in most religious teaching that an uncharitable thought is as bad as the uncharitable act. Psychotherapy sees the thought and the act as fundamentally different.

(9) There is little to differentiate the enlightened practitioner in both fields and indeed there is more common ground between the open-minded therapist and cleric than between the progressives and the more rigid fundamentalists in each discipline. I have tried to identify differences and similarities in our respective approaches and may have exaggerated some of the differences or not properly understood some of the religious approach, but we can only have reconciliation if we have conflict first.

I would like to end with a quotation from Lucien Bouet (reference untraceable):

Anxiety finds its sustenance in the painful events of the past, its occasion in some physical weakness in the present, and its specificity in fears of the unknown. It is the job of the psychological technique to explore the past, that of the physical technique to rectify the present, and that of faith to illuminate the future.

Our task as representatives of religion or psychotherapy is to know which is appropriate when.

14

The Theology of
Pastoral Counselling
(1980)[1]

Frank Lake

Pastoral Counselling is somewhat like the rescue of someone who has fallen into tidal waters and become trapped in some half-sunken wreckage. There is the task for the counsellor-rescuer of the diving in and swimming to the wreckage. Then begins the task of freeing the entangled individual. This is not the time nor the place either would have chosen to be doing anything so complicated. But, easy or difficult in itself, the success of the rescue may well depend on whether the tide is coming in, rapidly submerging the wreck and those now entangled in it, actually, by misfortune, or virtually, by the counsellor's own choice to stay by the entangled one until they are free to swim away for themselves, or whether the tide is going out. If the dangerous waters are receding, both time and place would seem to be favourable. Others will come to help and the entangled one's ability to swim away may not be tested. He can walk away, without testing a function he or she hasn't had much practice in or ever learned, to swim, over fathoms of water which is the Kierkegaardian image for faith.

In theology there are tides rising and falling, some helpful to pastoral counselling, some a serious hindrance. It is one thing to affirm, as ascetical theology has always done, that in the Dark Nights of Sense and Spirit, *God seems to be dead*, to have gone absent, and quite another to proclaim that *God is dead*. In the Dark Nights, God seems to have abandoned the soul to darkness, in abhorrence of its miserable state. However, ascetical theology affirms at the same time that this dark night will pass and will give place to an unprecedented dawning sense of God's nearness and unfailing love. He has been there all along, imperceptible and impalpable.

If the tide of this sound teaching were to rise, about *how to expect,* when maturing in faith, *God's seeming deadness* and how to cope by waiting, our task in dealing with Christians in mid-life crises would be much simplified. It would often not have been necessary to intervene. They would be prepared for the mysterious fact that these frightening waters are 'a severe mercy', not rising to drown us, but to compel us to realize that what we have been hanging on to is bound to go under with every high tide. It teaches that our task is to let go, and accept help if necessary in loosening the ties we have ourselves made, earlier in life's day. We thought, when we began to cling, that the old grounded ship would save us, so we tied ourselves to its mast, as if to life itself. For a while it served and we called it 'God', clinging to it with an energy charged by inner dreads and forgotten fears. Now the tide of the love of God is rising, to save us most effectively from ourselves and our clinging just at the moment where it seems most effectively to be drowning us. The divine wisdom, which the pastoral counsellor may have to teach in a hurry to a person in no mood for being taught, being in a state of panic, is to let go of these solid but relatively sinking objects, and let God teach the unfamiliar art of swimming away.

God is not to be identified with anything we can cling to. Faith teaches us how to swim, which we never learned to do while the tide stayed out. God the Father in charge of our spiritual growth and of our transitions towards maturity, has no alternative but *to seem to be dead indeed to be dead* to our mistimed and misplaced attempts to cling on to objects and persons propositions and social structures, even to the sound timbers of old church hulks. They will still be there when the tide goes out, but our relationship to them, and the nature of our dependence on them, will have changed. God will be all in all, not tied to things that can be clung to, not even counsellors.

As school-boys we took training in life-saving in the water. The first move when you reached the drowning person was to expect that they would cling to you so hard as to stop you swimming. You would both drown together. How to free yourself from the clinging of a drowning person was the first skill to be learned in rescuing. It is much the same in counselling. Clinging is crippling, and to permit it is a double cruelty, for both of you will perish.

There was that tide in theology a few years ago which announced, in quite another sense, the *Death of God*. Tom Oden, in the name of a sounder-based theology of pastoral counselling, trounced it recently in his *Agenda for Theology* (1979). It seemed to me to be a manifestation of a familiar sickness, the schizoid intellectualist defence against history, concreteness and the body, combined with the 'progressivist illusion' that to label something 'new' ought to sell it. In fact we know that in the depths of every schizoid personality there has been a distress so prolonged and so severe that hope and trust, faith and love, which longed for and waited for 'God', died a terrible death. 'God' has died in them. What follows is built, shakily often, on that rocky foundation. How should it not find its way into their philosophical theology, and from there infect Christian theology. It is a branch of the perennial tree of gnosticism.

Oden perceives the tide of modernity in theology as basically hostile to the interests of pastoral care. His propensity for hard hitting almost gets out of hand, but in the main, his description of the tides of modernity that are, in his view, as hostile to mainstream Christian counselling as they have been hailed by secular counselling as progressive and helpful tides, match my own experience of them. Oden writes:

The philosophical center of modernity is no dark secret. It is an easily recognized, thoroughly narcissistic hedonism that assumes that moral value is reducible to cash value and sensory experience. It views human existence essentially as spiritless body, sex as depersonalized vaginal ingress, psychology as amoral data gathering, and politics as the manipulation of power. It systematically ignores the human capacity for self-transcendence, moral reasoning, covenant commitment, and self-sacrificial agape. These axiomatic assumptions prevail among the intellectual elite that has of late become the apple of many a parson's eye. While the religious leadership should have been giving them what it distinctively has to give – namely, firm, critical resistance rooted in an historical perspective that modernity could find instructive – instead the religious leadership withheld its gift and whored after each successive stage of modernity's journey. While its lusty affair with modernity has been going on for about two centuries, it has not been until the last quarter century that there has been a wholesale devaluation of the currency of Christian language, symbolism, teaching, and witness.

Young people in ministry are beginning to be vaguely aware of the depth of the sellout, the urgency to redirect the momentum and the fatefulness of their calling to ministry at this nexus of history. The collusions are intricate. A fair amount of courage is required even to face the problem. (pp.41–42)

Again he writes:

These are the axial assumptions of later-stage modernity: contempt for premodern wisdoms, the absolutizing of the values of autonomous individualism, awed deference to reductionistic naturalism and scientific empiricism as the final court of appeal in truth questions, the adolescent refusal of parenting, an optimistic evolutionary historical progressivism linked uncomfortably with the most unabashed forms of narcissistic hedonism.

Unfolding modern history is embarrassing precisely these axioms. Not some theory, but actual modern *history*. We need only mention Auschwitz, My-Lai, Solzhenitsyn's Gulag Archipelago, Screw magazine, the assault statistics in public schools, the juvenile suicide rate, or the heroin epidemic to point to the depth of the failure of modern consciousness. While modernity continues blandly to teach us that we are moving ever upward and onward, the actual history of late modernity is increasingly brutal, barbarian, and malignant. (p.40)

The tides of fashion in academic theology as I have observed them, as a reader rather than as one attempting to swim in them as a participant, over the past forty years, have been such as to warrant Oden's strictures:

When a theologian forgets the distinction between heterodoxy and orthodoxy it is roughly equivalent to a physician forgetting the difference between disease and health, axe and scalpel, or a lawyer forgetting the difference between criminality and corpus juris. Yet it is just this distinction that theology has over the past two centuries of alleged progress systematically forgotten how to make. A long chain of regrettable results has followed for pastoral care, biblical studies, preaching, Christian ethics, and the mission of the church. (p.48)

So little of the theological product has been of use to us as counsellors of Christians. Their effort has been, in effect, to demonstrate how little is trustworthy in the historic records of the faith. To expect the same men to be enthusiastic in showing how a robust faith could be built on these primitive remains would be too much, since their critical faculties seem still to be busily engaged in nibbling away at what is left. The basic assumption of Descartes that truth is approached by postulating our sole certainty as deriving from the thinking subject, and his way forward into more truth as pursuit governed by methodological doubt, has led us away from the main body of Christian experience, which takes more risks and is open to input in many more dimensions than the merely intellectual.

I am far from wishing that professional theology should become a shop window to ecclesiastical orthodoxy or a supermarket for counsellors out shopping. It could, without loss of integrity or dignity, attempt to stock on its shelves more of the writing that comes from the heart of a man who knows that God has spoken, that his logos is powerful, sharper than an two-edged sword, cutting, more like a scalpel than a sword, into the delicate tissues where soul and spirit, body and mind, meet and influence each other.

It is this need that sends me back time and again to P.T. Forsyth, who wrote more relevant theology for the 1980s, in the last decade of the nineteenth century and the first two of this, than any theologian since his day. With Sebastian Moore's *The Crucified is no Stranger* (1977) and Rowan Williams' *The Wound of Knowledge* (1979), I sense the dawn of a new and vitally relevant handling of tradition, a theo-logos that speaks deep into the whereabouts of our hidden dilemmas.

Tom Oden heralds the rise of what he terms postmodern orthodoxy. He writes:

Some of these postmoderns have happened on classical Christianity and experienced themselves as having been suddenly lifted out of these quicksands onto firmer ground. They have then sought to understand the incredible energy and delivering power of Christianity, and, in the process of returning to the classical texts of ancient Christian tradition and scripture, they have begun to discover that the orthodox core of classical Christianity constitutes a powerful, wide-ranging, viable critique of modern consciousness. Who are the postmodern orthodox? These hardy pilgrims who have set their feet on the path of reappropriating classical Christianity have been through the rigors and hazards of the modern consciousness. Many of my students have set out on this pilgrimage. They are now inviting their theological teachers to join them.

It is useful here to make a basic distinction between two types of orthodoxy: *pre*- and *post*modern. Both are schooled in the same scriptural and patristic texts, and both celebrate and embody the same Christ, but one has journeyed through and dwelled in modernity, while the other has not. Postmodern orthodoxy is distinctive not in its essential doctrine, but in its historical experience. It has been deeply impacted by the modern sociology, physics, psychology, and, more so, by modern history, which premodern orthodoxy has either avoided or by historical accident never had a chance to meet. Postmodern orthodoxy by definition must have undergone a deep immersion in modernity, worked for it, hoped with it, clung to it, and been thoroughly instructed by it, yet finally has turned away from it in disillusionment, only to come upon classical Christianity as surprisingly more wise, realistic, resourceful, and creative than modernity itself. (Oden 1979, pp.49–50)

It is characteristic of these postmodern orthodox students Oden speaks of (I wish I had met more of them) that they are seeking a Christianity with a better contact with its Jewish roots. They have found in the biblical anthropology, Jewish-Christian rather than Greek, a refreshing sanity and humanity. 'They have plunged,' he writes

to the depths of psychoanalysis, behavior modification, structuralist sociology, relativity theory, and quantum physics, existential ethics, marxist politics, and alleged sexual 'liberations' of every kind, and yet have come away from modernity more demoralized, only belatedly to discover that the classical Jewish-Christian tradition is wiser and better, more realistic and humane. (p.52)

Asking why neo-orthodoxy failed us, Oden writes of Barth, Brunner, Tillich, Gogarten and Bultmann that they all

thought of themselves as programmatic theologians, essentially out to alter the tradition rather than sustain, cultivate and nurture it. Furthermore, neo-orthodoxy on the whole was enormously bored by liturgy, sacrament, pastoral care and concrete tasks of ministry – all issues with which we are now deeply engrossed. (p.54)

The para-modern solution

For myself and for most of the men and women who have been my colleagues in the Clinical Theology Association, our history is such that we do not fall into either of Tom Oden's categories. We are neither 'pre-modern' nor 'post-modern'. We are essentially 'para-moderns.' We have responded to modernity but always with reservations, because alongside its flux we have been abiding in Christ, who is not just today but tomorrow, who links us to past, present and future.

One or other of us may for a while have heeded one of its seductions or fallen for its blandishments, because we have been close to those who have been thoroughly taken up with it. We have never willingly moved from our grounding in the Gospel. The faith once for all delivered to the saints has sustained us. Searching out its gracious ramifications in the predicaments of pastoral counselling has been, and is, our enthusiasm.

We have been aware of the strength of tides, particularly in our close work with Roman Catholic 'religious'. Anglicanism has seemed relatively tideless. I cannot discern yet, any movement among us so sound in depth that I could wish to see it grow to tidal proportions. The charismatic Renewal has seen hands raised in true praise. To praise God, now that maturation is required, which is 'the achievement of ambivalence', as at home with grief as with joy, some hands must be occupied with digging. There are subterranean waters to be tapped in the Gospel – under the ground where we are today. I would rather see, gushing forth, these streams in the desert, than look out to see and pray for a wonderful tide, tomorrow.

Do we just need tide tables, and bide our time till the flux of theological fashion changes, hopefully in time for our clients to benefit? Or must we as pastoral counsellors, study these tides mainly to know when we shall have to swim against them, or use them with canny precaution lest they use us. Could we even envisage creating tides, or asking questions and doing our own thing in the obedience of faith so persistently that we might conceivably help to create a tide?

A trickle of 'postmodern orthodoxy'

The tide of a defunct modernity turns, giving place to a trickle of 'postmodern orthodoxy'. Could it become a tide?

Tom Oden (1979), looking out like Elijah's servant from the top of Carmel sees a little cloud like a man's hand rising up out of the sea of sterile modernity. He sees a rain cloud which he hopes, as I do, will water our souls with the whole counsel of God, the Gospel once for all and daily entrusted to his Church. He writes of the 'embryonic profile' (p.60) of this movement. He sees its students as 'digging deeply into the patristic and medieval texts that Roman Catholics and Eastern Orthodox have always found edifying' (p.61); 'The sons and daughters of modernity are re-discovering the neglected beauty of classical Christian teaching' (p.3); They want 'the chance to experience the power of authentic Christian consciousness in the presence of a community of living faith, without heavy distortions by modern assumptions about what Christianity has recently been assumed to be' (p.4); 'The boredom of theology ends the moment it takes up advocacy of the classical Christian understanding of God within the context of modern hopes and disillusionments' (p.16).

The living tradition of pastoral care is tidal

Oden asks: 'Where did we get the twisted misconception that orthodoxy is essentially a set of ideas rather than a living tradition of social experience? Our stereotype of orthodoxy is that of frozen dogma, rather than a warm continuity of human experience' (p.90).

It has been a particular joy to me, over the past seven years, to teach at St. John's College Bramcote, a short course on the History of Pastoral Care. My own basic text has been W.A. Clebsch and C.R. Jaekle's *Pastoral Care in Historical Perspective* (1964). I do sense a 'warm continuity of human experience' linking pastoral care-givers throughout the Christian ages. But even more amazing to me is the discontinuity due to the rise and fall of the tides of emphasis. Some elements and functions, predominant in one century, fall completely out of sight in the next. These authors delineate eight epochs in the history of Christian pastoring, showing that for periods of up to a hundred years or more one of the four main functions has been so dominant as to eclipse the others. In the first, primitive era, and again during the pitfalls of the 'Enlightenment', *sustaining* souls was the foremost function.

Under the persecutions, with the tasks of receiving back or rejecting those who had given in, and again at the Reformation, *reconciling* was dominant. After Constantine the pastoral task of *guiding* came to the fore, and again in the 'Dark Ages'. *Healing* became 'the rage' in the High Middle Ages, the Sacraments used for the healing of diseases.

Yet when they come to our own Post-Christendom Era, the authors are unable to designate any dominant function as tidal. Indeed, my own experience of pastoral counselling has included the whole New Testament gamut of Reconciling, Sustaining, Guiding and Healing, and I would be hard put to say which tide has run highest. It genuinely is one, as Christ, their source is one.

Some readers will remember a four-sided Dynamic Cycle which was the basic model for our Clinical Theology Seminars on pastoral care and counselling. These four functions are identical with, or dynamically related to the four we first introduced, as the theological basis of all we wished to teach about pastoral and secular counselling. Introduced in 1958, they have made good sense in terms of both disciplines and provided a dynamic bridge between them.

(1) *The way in* indicates the move into the life-giving relationship. It presupposes the outgoing willingness of the source person to grant *acceptance*. Since breaches have occurred in the *relationship,* here we must speak of the grounds of *reconciliation,* restoration to fellowship, or *justification* (which must be a gift not a reward, or all dynamic soundness is lost).

(2) The second phase has to do with the raising of 'being' to 'well-being'. This is the phase of *sustaining,* satisfying, filling with the character of the resource person. On any level this is a kind of *sanctification,* where 'holiness' is the infused gift from the Source Person, reproducing his qualities in the recipient who 'sits and eats'.

(3) This is the movement from dependency to a grateful *autonomy.* Filled with the life and good-life of its source, the overflow is available for others. Awareness of personal *status,* self-esteem and a joyful motivatedness are matched by a grateful sense that they have all first been given. 'As I have loved you, love one another'. The dynamics of grace mean that *inclination and obligation flow together.* It is as profoundly important that this should be the dynamic order of events in the secular relationships of counselling as in the practice of spiritual direction and the right ordering of ethical priorities. It is here that people may need *guidance.* Not all that we have an individual dynamic urge to express may be compatible with our responsibility to others. The dynamic outflow instinctively uses the model

of its originator, Christ, so that it is his character the Holy Spirit reproduces, in those who have responded to the experience of (a) acceptance and (b) sustenance.

(4)   The fourth phase is one in which the dynamic input of phase two *oscillates with* a dynamic *output*. Bruce Reed of the Grubb Institute sees this oscillation as the basic dynamic of the Church, the ground of its offer to society. The *achievement* of a satisfactory sustaining relationship is to enable the beneficiary of that resource to be, in his or her turn, as satisfactory a *sustainer* of others. Since acting in Christ-like fashion is risky in a world like this, and those who are more faithful tend to get most hurt, the function of *healing* must figure here.

My point is that this theologically-based cycle, worked out from St. John's Gospel, as a dynamic two-way flow present in the dynamic interchange between the father and the Son, and manifestly applicable to the 'Law of the Spirit of Life in Christ Jesus', has proved to be a most sensible model for all the basic relationships of human beings from the womb, and the cradle to the grave. Counselling needs a norm, so that it can recognize deflections from it and know where in the circuit a fuse has blown so as to mend it. This theological norm has enabled us to see more clearly the definitions, i.e. limits and wise boundaries, and the directions of flow in our own and many other people's secular counselling.

I should be happy if, in a hundred years time, students of our age could say that such pastoral care and counselling as there was available kept four-square to the New Testament norm, without surging tides of energy excessively devoted to any one special function, for we and our counsellors certainly need all four.

Oden describes his and others' turning back to the classical Catholic texts as a revelation of Christian resources. Having been brought up an Augustine, St. John of the Cross, de Caussade, Pere Grou and von Hugel, with excursions into Marmion, Josef Goldbrunner, Urs von Balthazar and André Louf, I think I have always been with the best of thorn. Many disappoint me. Cassian, on accidie or depression is phenomenologically interesting, but no adequate guide to the pastoral care of depressed Christians nowadays. St. Bernard is full of treasure but his handling of transference and use of emotional pressuring do not inspire emulation. In respect of 'normal' Christian living we learn from them all, just because they are grappling with the task of expressing Christ in ages so different from our own. However, as Tom Torrance showed many years ago, the doctrines of grace suffered badly at the hands of some of the sub-apostolic Fathers. Yet Ignatius, writing of 'the Passion of my God' and Irenaeus opposing the Gnostics and striving for a union with the Cross deeper than 'saving information', remain tap roots for us as pastoral counsellors.

It is in the area of depth pastoral care, where medicine is needed for the sick soul, that I have looked most persistently and been most disappointed. The rot started, from the depth counsellor's point of view, when a Gnostic mysticism crept in with its 'theology of glory', thrusting aside the centrality of the 'Word of God from the

Cross'. All the deepest problems of mental pain such as I have spent a lifetime exploring, were then evaded by trying to get above them, in a kind of 'Christian Buddhist' fashion. The Cross is deprived of its force and finality. A spirituality is espoused which is rich in imagery, like Jungian archetypal dream material, or high on tranquillity of a kind, as in Transcendental Meditation, both of which provide an exit from pain. But neither fully claims it nor explores the bodily roots of pain in order to be reconciled to it. For this reason, some of the ancient spirituality of the Catholic Church is not helpful in dealing, for instance, with Catholic charismatic Christians now. The Holy Spirit is directing us deeper into an indebtedness to the Incarnation, the Passion and Resurrection of Christ, to give us strength to 'arm ourselves with the same intention' and by suffering with him *in the flesh,* to be more fully reconciled with the anguished primal experiences of our inner child of the past.

The Wounded Physician

The master image of the Cross of Christ is capable, as the Holy Spirit applies its truth, of transforming the ruined archaeology of the self, with patience removing the ivy of our defences against the pain of exposure of old and jagged wounds, and with the salve of God's own loving and willing woundedness, of so richly using those primal occasions of anguish that they become the deepened foundations of our power to praise him. What we then build stands firm, free of the lop-sided structures erected by our former fears and faulty perceptions. This living reality is the heart-land of the Theology of Pastoral Counselling.

Editorial Note

1. This chapter comprises of two extracts that form the concluding remarks to a longer piece of work by Frank Lake under the same title.

15

Pastors or Counsellors?

(1992)

Alan Billings

Counselling is a growth industry. This has been apparent for sometime, but when one of my children jokingly suggested he be given counselling for 'post-dental trauma' (he went to have a filling but had to have an extraction) I realized just how far things have now gone. No wonder the ordinands I teach want to develop 'counselling skills' rather than read the New Testament!

In fact, whenever I advertise options for courses in Pastoral Studies, those that have 'counselling' in their title are always oversubscribed. This probably reflects three inter-related factors:

(1)   the continuing and possibly increasing need for the ordained to be able to make sense of the caring role in ways which are acceptable to the wider, secular community

(2)   the burgeoning of counselling in our society and the esteem which is now accorded it: only a few years ago stigma attached to receiving 'psychological' help; now people in almost any kind of distress demand it as a right

(3)   the fact that, superficially, counselling appears to be not unlike traditional forms of pastoral care – a cross between auricular confession and the confidential interview.

But I want to suggest that theological colleges should reconsider their attitudes towards counselling and return to more traditional ways of understanding pastoral care. I do so for these reasons:

(1)   the theory and practice of counselling understood as 'psychological healing' or therapy is fundamentally flawed

(2)   the values implicit in counselling are often antithetical to Christianity

(3)   counselling tends towards coerciveness

(4)   'non-directive' counselling is the very antithesis of what Christian pastoral ministry is about with the result that distinctive features of that ministry are overlooked.

I will seek to justify these bold statements, turning first to the question of counselling and the concept of 'psychological healing'.

Counselling as therapy

One way of understanding pastoral counselling is to see it as 'psychological healing', drawing on the theories of one or more of the various schools of psychotherapy. The work of the counsellor is seen as analogous to that of the doctor: the doctor 'cures' by using medicine or surgery, the counsellor by using 'talk'. Counselling is therefore held to be therapeutic. This understanding of pastoral counselling has been un-wittingly boosted by the influential concept of the pastor as 'the wounded healer' (Campbell 1986; Nouwen 1974). There are, however, three principal reasons why Christians (and others) ought to be suspicious of the claims made for both psychotherapy and counselling regarded as psychological healing which cumula-tively make the whole enterprise look dubious.

No agreed theory or testable techniques.

It seems clear that whatever is claimed by practitioners, there is in fact no underlying, empirically-based theory of psychotherapy or counselling. Nor are there agreed techniques which can be learnt and applied. On the contrary, there are many different 'schools' and they are often bewilderingly contradictory in their approach. So, for example, some therapies are concerned only with what the client is experiencing in the here-and-now (Gestalt), while others hold that significant past events hold the key and must be re-experienced (such as birth trauma therapy). Then again, while most counselling is one-to-one between counsellor and client, 'Family Therapy' starts from the assumption that individuals can only really be helped effectively if therapy is undertaken in the context of and involving the whole family.

In the face of so many different theories and therapies many counsellors are simply eclectic (Pattison 1986). But on what basis do they pick and choose? And how would one decide between one approach and another?

In the widely-used *A Dictionary of Pastoral Care*, Michael Jacobs attempts to find common ground between the various therapies by suggesting that they all share 'similar basic techniques for listening to the client' (Jacobs 1987, p.55). These listening techniques consist largely of encouraging the client to talk, presenting back to the client what has been said, putting the onus for making decisions back on the client and not being judgemental about what has been revealed. Leaving aside for the moment the claim of being non-judgemental, I would make two brief comments on this. The first is that these 'listening skills' are no more than those we all employ all the time in day-to-day living. They describe what every parent, friend or good neighbour does. Of course, some people do it better than others: they are 'born listeners'.

This raises the question of how far such 'skills' can be learnt. My experience with ordinands suggests that poor listeners do not become good listeners as a result of counselling courses – any more than poor teachers become good teachers as a result of 'further training'. If it really were possible to make bad teachers good ones with extra training then there would be no excuse for the government not to do it. Good pastors need a combination of qualities, not only an ability to listen: understanding, warmth, kindness and so on. The implications for training are that good pastors, like good teachers, need to be identified at selection: the pastorally inept and insensitive are not going to improve significantly in training.

In the second place, it is not enough to say that 'talking cures'. We know that talking can help people who are emotionally or psychologically upset. Who doubts the truth of the adage that a problem shared is a problem halved? This is not the issue. The claim made for counselling is not that talking cures – that is not in dispute – but that talk of a particular, learnt kind, brings about changes of a specifiable nature. This is because we could only claim to have a counselling *technique* and that it worked if we were able to say (a) what it was, (b) when it was being applied, (c) what it would be for the aims of the counselling to be achieved, so that (d) it could be repeated in similar circumstances in the future. But this is just what counselling theories fail to do.

This becomes all too clear when one considers some remarks of the British psychologist Dorothy Rowe. She claims that any and every technique works! At least each works to some extent: 'As I am often wont to say, "All therapies work, but no therapy works perfectly"'. She goes on to make the astonishing and I would have thought ultimately self-defeating claim:

> You can take a ward full of patients of whatever diagnosis, age and sex and you can give them all a new drug, or a new kind of therapy, or simply a change in their routine, and a third of them will get better, a third will stay the same, and a third will get worse, give or take a few each way. (Rowe cited in Masson 1990, p.20)

If this is true – and I must take her at her word – then the cheapest 'method' of treatment (and a method that is no less effective than any other) would seem to be to get rid of the psychotherapists and counsellors altogether and rely on changing the patients' routines on a regular basis, discharging those who got better! The serious point, however, is that what Dorothy Rowe says demolishes all claims for technique or method. 'Cures' are simply hit-and-miss, lacking any empirical basis. We could only claim there was some method or technique here if we could specify in advance which patients would get better, which would stay the same and which would get worse as a result of any proposed treatment. This is the very thing that cannot be done. We are forced to conclude that there is no theoretical basis for psychotherapy or counselling and that claims made about method and technique are therefore largely bogus.

Basic contradictions

Second, we should be suspicious of counselling because claims are often made for it which are simply contradictory. These incompatible claims are that counselling is (a) therapeutic and (b) non-directive. These claims cannot both be true (Graham 1990).

I have already said that where counselling is called therapy or 'psychological healing' it is because it is seen as analogous to the work of the medical practitioner. The doctor 'cures' by using appropriate medicines, the counsellor by using appropriate 'talk'. For the analogy to be properly applicable the counsellor would have to know what would count as 'healing' just as the doctor does. But the analogy breaks down almost completely. The doctor knows the difference between a healthy organ and a diseased one: healing consists of the application of medicine or surgery to the organ so that it functions appropriately again. In an analogous way there is probably a narrow range of psychological conditions where it is appropriate to talk about 'cure'. These are where people's behaviour has no *rational* basis. Anorexia would be a case in point. We know what it would be to return the anorexic to normal, healthy behaviour, and there would be a measure of agreement amongst us. But when we turn to the enormously varied types of situation which come before the counsellor, the idea of 'cure' is inappropriate. People may need help, but hardly 'cure'. Their behaviour is not irrational and they are not ill – though they are unhappy. (Sometimes, of course, the distinction is not easy to make.) The trouble with psychotherapy and counselling conceived as psychological healing is that they constantly confuse the two. But in the case of those who have rational reasons for being emotionally or psychologically upset, there is no agreement amongst us as to what the appropriate behaviour is or ought to be in the face of bereavement or marital breakdown or redundancy or involvement in a major disaster. Until we have some clarity about that we cannot know what our therapy should be seeking to bring about. We are, then, inevitably involved in a consideration of the aims of our counselling and, as a consequence, questions of value.

For example, when faced with people whose marriage is breaking up, should the primary aim of the counsellor be to keep the marriage intact or to ease the pain of the breakup? Much depends on the value the counsellor attaches to the married relationship. If marriage is regarded as a contract there may be less incentive to seek its maintenance than if it is understood as sacramental. Similar considerations of aims and values enter into almost every other counselling situation. If, therefore, we are to claim that counselling is therapeutic we need to have some idea of what normal or healthy or appropriate behaviour is if we are to help bring about desired change or to recognize it when it has happened. As Gordon Graham observes, 'We cannot say in general when "desired" changes have been brought about until we are told what changes are desired' (Graham 1990, p.43). But it is precisely at this point that we encounter the concept of 'non-directive' counselling.

Non-directive or client-centred counselling is particularly associated with the American psychologist Carl Rogers. It has been very influential in this country. Robert Harper has described the therapy and the basis of its popularity in this way:

The client-centered way appeals to the young, insecure, inexperienced, prospective therapist as, at least superficially, the 'easy way'. It is unnecessary for the therapist to have any great knowledge of personality diagnosis or dynamics, and he takes no real responsibility for guidance of the disturbed client. He simply encourages the client to be more fully himself, he provides warmth and acceptance as the means whereby the client can achieve self-realization. Any permissive, warmly loving person can readily become a therapist via the client-centered system. (Harper cited in Masson 1990, p.240)

I will come back to what Harper might mean by 'permissive'; but one can see why ordained ministers, with little formal knowledge of psychoanalytic theory and with limited time at their disposal, have particularly warmed to the Rogerian approach. The basis tenets can be mastered in a few hours! In theory, then, non-directive counsellors set aside any views they may have and seek to help their clients choose their own values and goals. But I have already suggested that, logically, no counsellor could even begin to help a client unless the counsellor knew what the end or aim of the counselling should be. In other words, if counsellors claim to be acting in a non-directive way, they must in fact be mistaken.

Why do Counsellors think they are 'non-directive'? This comes about in three principal ways.

First, they may not realize how judgemental they actually are until their own values are seriously challenged – as they would be in extreme cases. For instance, what would a non-directive counsellor do in the face of a client who wanted help to overcome the guilt he felt about having a sexual relationship with his daughter? (The examples can be multiplied.) If the counsellor is really 'non-directive' he or she will set aside moral judgements and consider how to help relieve the client of this burden of guilt. I suspect that at this point many counsellors would discover just how non non-directive they really were!

Second, counsellors rarely recognize just how judgemental and directive they are because they unconsciously operate with the prevailing utilitarian values of a liberal society which they assume to be uncontroversial. (I think this is what Harper means by 'permissive' values.) So in the case of marriage breakdown the utilitarian ethic would suggest that the overriding aim should be the happiness of the maximum number of individuals: this would be regarded as more important than the preser-vation of marriages. But to conduct counselling on that assumption is not to do so in a 'value-free' or 'non-directive' way; it is to do so on the basis of utilitarian ethics.

The third way in which counsellors deceive themselves into thinking that they are acting in a non-directive way comes about through believing that concentration on the client's 'feelings' is somehow value-free in a way that concentrating on their beliefs and opinions would not be. But in calling feelings 'appropriate' or 'inap-propriate', 'positive' or 'negative', we are only talking about what are and are not rational responses to situations – and this at once plunges us back into the discussion of ends and values.

To sum up. Counselling cannot be both therapeutic and non-directive: that is a contradiction. My own view is that what purports to be non-judgemental and non-directive in fact assumes the prevailing utilitarian values of a liberal and secular society. This is a serious matter for those who are Christians, especially those who are the ordained representatives of the Christian faith.

Counselling tends to be coercive

The third objection to counselling understood as psychological healing is that it has a tendency to be coercive because it is always confusing those situations where it is appropriate to talk of 'cure' with those where help is needed but not cure. What I mean is this.

One of Freud's most celebrated cases was his analysis of the young woman Dora (Ida Bauer). She was sent to Freud as a teenager by her parents because she was depressed. She told Freud that her depression was the result of a cluster of external factors: she discovered her father was syphilitic and having an affair with Frau K whose husband, Herr K, had in turn made sexual advances towards her, Dora. Moreover, her father dismissed her allegations about Herr K as fantasy. Freud set this explanation aside and attributed her depression variously to being in love with, amongst others, Frau K, to childhood masturbation and the suppressed memory of earlier sexual seduction. What is of interest, however, is not so much the analyst's explanations as the fact that he discounted hers.

Commenting on this, James Masson has said of Freud that he 'treated her like a patient not like a human' (Masson 1990, p.96). In other words, her emotional and psychological difficulties were not to be relieved through rational talk (conversation) but by using talk to unmask underlying causes which only the analyst could diagnose. Freud discounted her explanation – that her depression was an understandable reaction of a normal person to terrible external factors – preferring his own interpretation which located the problem in her – her alleged suppressed homosexual love and buried memory of seduction. This is to treat a person as a less than autonomous human being. It is to treat them coercively. And this is always the temptation where psychotherapy and counselling are conceived as psychological healing.

Pastors not counsellors

It must be clear by now that I think (a) the concept of 'psychological healing' is disastrous and (b) Christians should not confuse non-directive counselling with Christian pastoral care. I have explained why I believe that no counselling can be 'non-directive' and how so-called 'non-directive' counselling usually reflects the unexamined utilitarian ethics of a liberal and secular culture. But even if 'non-directive' counselling were possible, Christian pastors cannot be non-directive for if Christianity is true we can hardly be said to be offering Christian pastoral care if we do not pass on to people that truth about the human condition and human destiny which is given us in our Christian faith – but is no part of the values of a secular society. There is nothing coercive about this: no one is compelled to accept the Christian account. In fact, in my experience, people are often disappointed when the clergy are unable or unwilling to bring the Christian tradition to bear in moments of ethical dilemma or emotional trauma. It is not more counselling courses that we want for ordinands and clergy but a greater knowledge of the Christian faith and greater skill and courage in using it to illuminate contemporary situations. In short, we need pastors again, not counsellors.

16

Where is the Theology
of British Pastoral Counselling?
(1996)

Gordon Lynch

This year marks the thirtieth anniversary of the publication of Frank Lake's *Clinical Theology* (1966). In this article I want to advance the claim that since the publication of *Clinical Theology* there has been no substantial theological reflection within the field of British pastoral counselling either within the academies of pastoral theology or within the major pastoral counselling organizations. It would clearly be absurd to deny that there has been any theological reflection undertaken by those involved in pastoral counselling. My claim, rather, is that such reflection has not been substantial, in the sense of offering either a theological critique of entire therapeutic theories or of providing constructive theological work upon which pastoral counselling might be based.

Academic pastoral theology and pastoral counselling

In the period since 1966, no British writers based in the academies of pastoral theology (i.e. theological colleges, university departments of theology) have written texts which offer a substantial theological engagement with the field of pastoral counselling. Writers such as Alastair Campbell (1986) and Stephen Pattison (1988) have produced books which provide theological reflection which is relevant for pastoral counsellors. David Lyall's *Counselling in the Pastoral and Spiritual Context* (1995) also offers a very useful discussion of this field, but has to cover too much material within a short space to give either a detailed critique of particular therapeutic models or a substantial constructive theological basis for pastoral counsellors.

Where British publications since 1966 have addressed specifically the field of pastoral counselling, these have usually been written by people working outside of the academies of pastoral theology. Typically these have provided the reader with useful material about therapeutic practice, but have offered no theological reflection on pastoral counselling. This is true of books such as R.S. Lee's *Principles of Pastoral Counselling* (1968), Peter Liddell's *A Handbook of Pastoral Counselling* (1983) and Michael Jacobs' *Still Small Voice* (1982). Roger Hurding (1985) has attempted to offer some theological basis for the practice of Christian pastoral counselling, but his work, whilst useful for an Evangelical market, lacks the breadth and depth that would be expected of work from the academies of pastoral theology.

The one exception to the lack of substantial academic theological engagement with pastoral counselling in Britain is Emmanuel Lartey's book *Pastoral Counselling in Inter-Cultural Perspective* (1987). Lartey is very conscious of the influence of one's culture upon theological reflection, and he offers a Ghanaian Christian critique of two models of therapy, Gestalt and Family Systems therapy. This study indicates Western cultural assumptions that are present in these models and points to the value of allowing insights from African culture to speak as we reflect upon pastoral care and counselling. Lartey's work stands as an invitation for British pastoral theologians to engage in a culturally-conscious way with existing models of therapy. As yet this invitation has not been seriously taken up.

If there has been no substantial engagement with pastoral counselling from the academies of pastoral theology, then why might this be so? There are possibly two related reasons for this. First, although the status of pastoral theology within theological colleges has grown since the 1960s, it still has to compete on the syllabus with a range of other theological disciplines. Detailed theological teaching in the field of pastoral counselling is therefore difficult given the constraints of time and resources within which pastoral studies are taught and is also hard to justify, given that few theological students would see themselves as training to become pastoral counsellors. Second, although there has been a phenomenal growth of interest in counselling since the 1960s, there has not been a corresponding growth of interest in pastoral theology. At a seminar in Birmingham last year, a leading pastoral theologian lamented the fact that there had not been the growth of interest in the subject that he had hoped for. Certainly the only postgraduate university courses in pastoral studies currently on offer are those which were established back in the late 1960s.

It can be argued that, as a consequence of these two factors, academic pastoral theology in Britain has lacked the resources to engage substantially with the field of pastoral counselling. For academics to produce detailed work in this field would take many years, and perhaps there is some wariness of focusing too much on therapeutic models of pastoral care.

Pastoral counselling organizations

In addition to the lack of substantial theological engagement with pastoral coun-selling from the academies of pastoral theology, there has also been no substantial theological reflection within the main pastoral counselling organizations. For a variety of reasons neither the Westminster Pastoral Foundation, the Association for Pastoral Care and Counselling nor the Clinical Theology Association have, since 1966, offered detailed critiques of existing therapeutic models or sought to develop a theological basis for pastoral counselling.

The Westminster Pastoral Foundation (WPF) was founded by Bill Kyle in September 1969, and began its life at Central Hall, Westminster (Black 1991). Kyle had previously set up a counselling centre in Highgate, and subsequently developed the idea of a 'church-cum-centre' which would primarily offer a specialist ministry of pastoral counselling, as well as training courses in counselling and healing services. From the outset, however, theological reflection occupied only a small place in the WPF's main training course. In the first full-time training course offered by the Foundation in 1978, the study of theology and pastoral ministry occupied less than a seventh of the curriculum. The strong emphasis on psychodynamic psychology within the Foundation led to increasing tension between Kyle and administrators of Central Hall, who felt that he was moving away from 'deep Christian Spiritual Counselling' (Black 1991, p.54). This tension ultimately led to a clear split, with the Westminster Pastoral Foundation leaving Central Hall and moving to new premises in Kensington in 1978.

As the WPF continued to grow, the 'pastoral' content of the Foundation's work was seen in increasingly vague terms. The prevailing view that developed within the organization was that 'pastoral' care was a form of care in which an individual was approached with awe, love and well-informed understanding. A symbolic shift away from the 'pastoral' took place when, in 1988, the Foundation changed the name of its graduate institute from the Institute of Pastoral Education and Counselling to the Institute of Psychotherapy and Counselling.

It is remarkable that an organization originally envisaged as a 'church-cum-centre' should fail to offer substantial theological reflection on its work and, over time, play down its connection with its pastoral roots. Three reasons can be identified for this. First, Kyle himself was enthusiastic about the contribution of the human sciences to pastoral care and counselling, but he never subjected these resources to a rigorous theological critique. This enthusiasm led, over time, to the conflict with Central Hall, and the eventual split from Central Hall made it harder for the Foundation's work to exist in the creative dialogue with the Free Church tradition that Kyle had originally hoped for. Second, an increasing number of people with no church connection undertook the WPF training. For such people, detailed theological reflection on their work in relation to the Christian tradition was not relevant. Third, those training at the WPF were primarily concerned with gaining a qualification which would be credible amongst other professionals. For these students it was more pressing to undertake substantial study of psychodynamic theory than to engage in theological reflection. For a range of reasons, therefore, theological reflection played a decreasing role in the work of the Westminster Pastoral Foundation and as a consequence no substantial theological work in relation to counselling has emerged from this organization.

Unlike the Westminster Pastoral Foundation, the Association for Pastoral Care and Counselling (APCC) did not arise out of the vision of one person, but was an umbrella organization which included representatives from pastoral counselling organizations (e.g. Frank Lake, Bill Kyle), diocesan directors of pastoral care (Leslie

Virgo, Derek Blows) and pastoral theologians (James Blackie, Alastair Campbell). The APCC was formed in 1972, in a climate of discussion about the need for the accreditation of properly trained counsellors and psychotherapists. Its original aims were both to increase awareness of the contribution of the human sciences to pastoral work and also to advocate the value of pastoral work within the context of professional multidisciplinary settings. The APCC went on to make a significant contribution to the counselling scene in Britain through becoming a founder member of the British Association for Counselling, now the leading counselling organization in Britain.

Within the APCC's *Constitutional Papers* (1974), theological reflection has an ambivalent status. Even given this ambivalence, it may still be seen as somewhat disappointing that members of the APCC have not offered substantial theological discussions of pastoral counselling. Of the leading figures within the APCC, John Foskett (1994) has published creative pastoral theology, but this has not engaged in a detailed way with pastoral counselling. Michael Jacobs (1985a) has also written valuable texts in relation to psychodynamic theory, but I am not aware of anything in his writing, particularly in relation to pastoral counselling, which suggests that psychodynamic theory should be subject to some form of theological critique.

Given the leading role of the Association for Pastoral Care and Counselling in the field of pastoral counselling in Britain, how might we account for the lack of substantial theological reflection on counselling within its membership? First, it is important to recognize that most members of the APCC are therapists rather than professional theologians, and that as such they would be less likely to have the resources, in terms of time and research material, to do substantial theological work. Second, much time and energy appears to have been expended within the APCC on structural and professional issues, such as accreditation procedures for counsellors and supervisors. Such efforts have arguably proved beneficial for the wider counselling community in Britain, but have inevitably less left energy within the organization for detailed theological work. Third, some members of the APCC may feel an ambivalence towards the churches of which they are members. John Foskett (1985, p.103) has commented that churches often do not welcome the difficult questions that pastoral counsellors raise about church teaching and practice on the basis of their counselling experience. Similarly, pastoral counsellors, who have seen some of the harmful effects of Church life and teaching on their clients can find their connection with the Church difficult. Given this ambivalence, it is perhaps not surprising that some pastoral counsellors do not feel motivated to engage in detailed theological work, especially in a way that would be considered orthodox within the Church.

The British pastoral counselling organization which has shown the most consistent commitment to theological reflection is the Clinical Theology Association (CTA). Such theological engagement is evident in the CTA's seminar programme, in its annual conference, in its newsletter and in the Lingdale Papers that it publishes. In 1993, this commitment to theological reflection was demonstrated by the organization's invitation to Professor Tom Oden to speak at its annual conference; an event shared with the APCC and the Acorn Christian Healing Trust. Oden's contribution, although perhaps too theologically technical for his audience at times, represented a powerful plea for the role of theological reflection in relation to pastoral care and counselling. As Oden put it, every effort should be made to focus on the 'Theos' within Clinical Theology.

Whilst this commitment to theological reflection is to be very much welcomed, it is also evident that since the publication of *Clinical Theology*, there have been no detailed critiques of existing therapeutic models or constructive theological models for pastoral counselling emerging from the CTA. Again the issue of limited resources is undoubtedly a factor behind this. It is also reasonable to suggest that, for a variety of reasons, the work of Frank Lake has been so pre-eminent within the CTA that it has been difficult for alternative models to emerge within that organization.

If there has been a lack of substantial theological work emerging from the major pastoral counselling organizations since 1966, then this is also true of the Christian counselling organizations which have developed since the 1980s out of the Evangelical constituency within the Church. Crusade for World Revival (CWR), based at Waverley Abbey, is a good example of such an organization, which has sought to train counsellors in a model which seems consistent with Evangelical theological beliefs. CWR's model of counselling is essentially a theological rendering of cognitive-behavioural therapy. The literature supporting this model is typically written by American clinical psychologists such as Larry Crabb (1985) and Gary Collins (1980), who claim biblical support for their approach, but who do not offer a detailed theological discussion of their ideas. Christian counselling organizations in Britain have not yet provided a substantial theological rationale for their work, nor have their approaches come under serious theological scrutiny from people outside of those organizations.

Some dangers and questions

It is important that we recognize the lack of substantial theological engagement in this country in the field of pastoral counselling. In making this case, however, I want to recognize that there are certain dangers and questions in relation to it that need to be addressed.

First, this article runs the serious risk of setting a negative tone for the history of British pastoral counselling over the past thirty years. Whilst I believe that this has been a disappointing period in terms of theological reflection, it is also important to recognize the positive achievements that have been made. Foremost amongst these, I believe, is the contribution of the pastoral counselling movement in Britain to the setting up and management of the British Association Counselling. It seems clear to me that the wider counselling movement in this country does owe a great debt to the pioneering work of the pastoral counselling organizations, and one which is generally unacknowledged.

Another danger with this article is that, in emphasizing the need for detailed theological work, it neglects the need for more empirical research in the field of pastoral counselling. There is an urgent need for field research which establishes where pastoral counselling is being practiced in Britain. Valuable research could also be conducted into how pastoral counsellors understand their work, and also into the outcomes of pastoral counselling. Similar research also needs to be conducted within the realm of Christian counselling. The focus on theological reflection within this article should not therefore be seen as neglecting the need for other forms of research in the area of pastoral counselling.

The central claim made within this article, concerning the lack of substantial theological engagement with pastoral counselling over the past thirty years, does also beg the question, 'if this is true, then does it actually matter?' It is reasonable to argue that theological reflection does have some place in relation to pastoral counselling, if one accepts that pastoral counselling is conducted on the basis of some kind of relationship to a religious tradition. It is perhaps less clear that substantial theological reflection, as I have defined it in this article, is of genuine use to pastoral counsellors. Given the complexity of therapeutic work, there is a danger that substantial theological constructions in relation to pastoral counselling may prove to be impressive theoretical edifices which have little practical value. Theological reflection which is limited and diverse might be seen as better fitting our fragmented postmodern culture than monolithic theories which claim (implicitly or explicitly) to be universally true.

Whilst acknowledging these issues, I would want to suggest that there is scope for more substantial theological reflection in relation to pastoral counselling. Whilst not prejudging the usefulness of the process. I believe that there should be a fuller critical interplay between therapeutic theory and theology in this country than has been seen over the past thirty years. The growing use of the metaphor of narrative in both theology and therapy is a good example of an area in which a fruitful integration of theological and therapeutic insights could occur (Epston and White 1990; Hauerwas 1981).

In this article, I have argued that since the publication of *Clinical Theology* there has been a lack of substantial theological reflection within the field of British pastoral counselling. As we look forward to the next thirty years of the pastoral counselling movement, I would suggest that one of the many challenges facing it is whether the theological resources that it bears can be brought into a substantial and creative dialogue with the therapeutic wisdom that it has developed.

PART FIVE

*Practical Theology
and Social Action*

17

A Healthy Society?

(1976)

James Mathers

The question mark in the title is important because a healthy society is a visionary concept, a work of the imagination, far removed from current realities. I do not intend to describe my personal utopia: if I were to do so the result would be a static image which I would be ready to discard tomorrow. The vision I want to share with you is that of a dynamic and evolving society whose glory, if ever we glimpse it, is iridescent, changing, continually new and unpredictable. It seems to recede further into the future with each new discovery we make about the world we live in. It is constantly being altered and (we hope) corrected by fresh experience.

The vision of a healthy society is perhaps the one aim or goal that all men, everywhere and in all ages, have in common, however much they differ as to the path by which it may be approached, or disagree as to whether it can be realized in time or only in eternity. Since all life is movement, our activities gain their significance by leading us either more or less towards our vision, or more or less away from it. It gives us a compass-bearing, a sense of direction. It gives us a dimension along which we can evaluate our lives and actions. We try to give it form and plausibility by seeking to endow it with a harmony of optimum values rather than average ones: it is a vision of what ought to be attainable, not of what we currently know to be attainable. Although it is a creature of the imagination, it is a vision which each man wants to share with others, for only when it is shared is there hope of progress towards its realization. Perhaps we should be glad that such a vision seems to recede as our experience grows, for nothing is so fatal to human endeavour as actually to reach one's ultimate objective. The zest for living depends upon all realizable goals being recognized as only provisional. Neither wealth nor health are more than dust and ashes unless you know what to do with them when you have them.

The healthy society will include everyone

Until recently, it was always possible to conceive of any society, small or large, as being an area of ordered existence surrounded by chaos. In such a context, a healthy society could be conceived as one from which disorderly elements could be extruded or exiled. The deviant who could not or would not abide by the rules could go into the wilderness or be transported to a penal colony or become a tramp. But our twentieth-century electric and jet-propelled communications technology has now so enlarged the perceived boundaries of all societies that there is no wilderness left into which the deviant can be exiled. The wilderness of yesterday has become our neighbour's garden, and he will protest if we try to throw our rubbish over the hedge. We live in a global village. There is no future in any attempt we may make henceforth to regard our neighbours as non-human denizens of the wilderness. In future we have to consume our own smoke, to discover some way of dealing with deviant members of society to our mutual benefit.

We still tend to think of such problems as if they were matters of ethics, areas in which we feel it appropriate to make moral choices or decisions. But biological considerations may be more compelling than moral ones. From the immensely long span of evolutionary history we learn that any species of organism multiplies until it fills every ecological niche to which it can adapt. If it is a successful species, as ours is, these niches may vary quite considerably. Subsequently, through the slow but inevitable changes of the natural world, such niches may become so separated, in space or in kind, that the organisms in question can no longer move easily from one to another. The inhabitants of each niche then become, over generations, specialized; first in habit, so that fairly quickly their differing patterns of mating behaviour ensure that there will be no interbreeding between them even though mating would be physically possible for the few who are still able to visit from one niche to another; and then, more slowly, they specialize in structure, as mutation occurs and their specialization becomes written into their genetic inheritance. Thus do new species arise. Darwin's finches in the Galapagos Islands, of which fourteen species are known all stemming from one South American ancestor, are perhaps the best known example.

Now the interesting thing is that – alone among the species known to us – mankind has avoided this biological trap, of becoming so well adapted to a specialized niche that he can no longer breed with his erstwhile fellows. And human curiosity and adaptability being what it is, it is inconceivable that he will ever be thus constrained by his environment in the future, at least on this planet. For better or worse, the whole of mankind will almost certainly henceforth always share a common gene pool, and thus remain one species. And if one applies relevant Darwinian principles analogously to cultural evolution, the conclusion seems even more certain; because each human society not only refreshes its genetic make-up by physical intercourse with members of other societies, but more importantly, it communicates with, and learns new ideas from, even those societies to which it is most hostile. Even when we build an 'iron curtain' we employ soldiers and agents to keep us informed about what happens on the other side. We are thus committed not only to a single shared gene pool, but to a single shared idea pool as well.

Thus we are biologically as well as ethically committed to recognizing mankind as one society. There is no place outside society to which we can consign elements or members whom we choose to label deviant or disordered. Since this situation has never occurred before in evolutionary history, its consequences are unpredictable. I suppose it is possible that humanity may find a temporary escape from the problem by colonizing other planets, but the discovery of humanity as essentially one species, committed to coping with its own disorder as an internal problem, will henceforward be a fact of life to be reckoned with. It is not an easy idea. It is a fundamental fact of our experience that health depends upon the excretory apparatus functioning properly; but for the future the social organism, society, must learn to live with, and reinterpret the significance of, its own waste products.

Diversity or conformity?

Evolution shows us that a species only survives so long as there is sufficient variability among its members to withstand the changing environmental pressures which constitute the process of natural selection. The law is quite fundamental, and will apply as much to mankind in the future as it has to all other species in history. Since all natural environments are themselves evolving and changing, a species whose members all conformed to the same constitution would be doomed to extinction when change occurred. The generation and maintenance of a pool of variability is a biological imperative. Since we can now rely on the transmission of ideas through the generations as well as genes, our capacity for variation is multiplied enormously. It is safe to say that the human race has sufficient potential variation to be adequately armed against almost any imaginable environmental change on the planet; but there is a warning implied in the word 'potential'. Rene Dubos (reference untraceable) has said 'the cultivation of diversity is essential, not only for the growth of society, but even for its survival'. But it does have to be cultivated.

Perhaps because of our evolutionary history, we have a vestigial respect for conformity which is likely to be too strong for our future good. Among other species, to distinguish between members of the same species and those of other kinds had survival value. The distinction between 'us', who conform to our pattern, and 'them', who don't, is still common among human beings. But this would not obtain in the hypothetical world-wide society, for a moment's reflection will convince you that you would not regard yourself as healthy in a society which did not recognize and value you for those aspects of yourself which are unique and belong to you alone. Your differences from other men will have a greater significance for your sense of well-being than will your similarity to them.

For the time being we have to live with this inherited tendency to draw lines between ourselves and some of our fellows, and we must learn to keep it under control. Erik Erikson (1968) speaks of our tendency to distinguish *pseudo*species: our tribe, class, nation or religious association is seen as the only one – all others are lumped together as outsiders. And to preserve this illusion of the oneness of our own special pseudospecies, we demand from one another a great deal of conformity to custom and law, and only tolerate diversity within narrow limits. In fact, our inherited nature is such that we actually need the cultural invention of the pseudospecies in order to develop a sense of identity. When you first meet a stranger, he identifies himself to you by saying what groups he is a member of: his place of origin, his occupation, and so on. Each of us needs a sense of individual identity to be healthy, but it is always a social as well as an individual creation. My affirmation of who I think I am has to be confirmed by my fellows if I am not to fall prey to crippling self-doubts or feelings of alienation. So my sense of identity is constantly developing and maturing as I grow up into wider and wider social environments.

Erikson shows that from infancy onwards there are times when we respond to stress by making a kind of 'total' restructuring of our experience, usually of a transitory nature. We can all recall childhood occasions when, following an angry encounter with someone, we said 'all right; that settles it; I'll never speak to you again'. Thus for the moment we restructure our experience, which till then would have had a healthily variegated patterning of light and shade, into a sharp distinction of black and white. At such a time the boundary of the sense of self becomes rigidly inclusive and exclusive, contrasting with its open and fluid nature at more normal times. Whereas in infancy such a temporary shift from 'wholeness' to 'totality' is usually individuocentric, in adolescence this kind of experience tends to be group-centred, and is often associated with what Konrad Lorenz describes as 'militant enthusiasm' – for some cause which claims our allegiance and with which we identify ourselves. Adult groups in later life may show similar patterns, particularly when they feel threatened. Parallel features can be found in W.R. Bion's (1961) descriptions of the way groups unconsciously organize themselves for 'fight or flight'.

The shift from wholeness to totality may therefore have survival value in that it sharpens our sense of identity when it is threatened. But, like bodily emergency defence mechanisms, it is only for emergency use. It is more primitive, less complex and differentiated than the best of our potential, and is less often evoked as we grow into maturity. It increased the value we set on conformity and the negative value we set on variety. Under stress, conformity gains approval; otherwise it is seen as a virtue mainly by those who cherish prejudice.

Technology with a human face

Modern technology needs re-examination in the light of our vision. Unlike nature, it has no built-in, self-adjusting mechanisms. Nature is self-cleansing and has her own rhythms of seasonal change and balance. But mankind has unleashed a kind of technology which doesn't know where to stop. Its speed increases in an ungovernable way, creating pollution faster than nature can deal with it. Technologists work in terms of populations rather than societies. The characteristic of a population is that it is composed of a number of entities which are seen as equivalent to one another, and to be related in a random rather than a systematic fashion. In this sense a population is the antithesis of a society or community – especially a healthy one: for in the latter each component is valued for his uniqueness and difference from others; and the healthy man related to other people systematically rather than at random.

Too often the technologist of today thinks in terms of the mass: mass advertising, production, markets – and even mass education. By ignoring the uniqueness of the people he employs and the people he purports to serve, he depersonalizes and alienates them. Mass technology does not improve the standard of living of the very poor, nor does it make people more comfortable by relieving them of distressful labour. In the world as a whole, the rich get richer while the poor get poorer. The more so-called useful goods it produces, the more useless people feel. The faster the speed of transport, the greater the traffic jams. Not so long ago the psychiatrist was known as an alienist. If alienation means insanity, then mass technology drives people mad. Its complexity is dealt with by the proliferation of specialists, each with his own private language which becomes less and less intelligible to the rest of us. Specialization has become a disastrous caricature of the differentiation and variety which should characterize a healthy society. It leads to the fragmentation of endeavour, to the substitution of proximate and partial goals for the overall goal of society's well-being. As E.F. Schumacher (1973) says, we need a technology which makes machines we can use and govern instead of machines which use and govern us. We need technology with a human face.

The excellence of a whole society depends on its components being 'just good enough'

In a truly healthy society, each man would see himself as partly responsible for the whole of it, rather than wholly responsible for a part of it. Each of us has his special interest, and seeks excellence in his chosen field. But excellence in one field can usually only be achieved at the expense of resources which are needed in neighbouring fields. A healthy society cannot be one which has unlimited resources available to it, for it will inevitably expand until their limits are in sight; and the healthier it is the sooner it will see them. Difficult though it may be, we must come to terms with the idea that the excellence of the part will nearly always have to be subordinated to the good of the whole. So a degree of individual frustration has to be built-in to our vision of the healthy society, we must learn how to tolerate it rather than escape from it. But is this psychologically possible?

We have seen that a man's sense of personal identity matures as he grows up and moves into wider and wider social environments, in each of which other people recognize him anew and confirm his sense of who he now is. Self-interest constrains a man to identify himself with successively more comprehensive groups, even though his commitment to them is only partial. Enlightened self-interest impels me to act for the good of others beside myself. We begin to transcend egocentricity early in life, as we identify successively with our parents in infancy, our heroes in childhood, the social causes to which we commit ourselves in adolescence; and then with those we fall in love with and have children by, and so our family and, in maturity, the community in which we perceive ourselves as living. All such groups are in some sense supra-individual, outside and beyond our egos, though they include them too. We only regress to egocentricity when we are sick or anxious. At our healthiest, then, it is not inconceivable that we might hope to identify ourselves with the whole of society, and by this means transcend the frustrations which we feel as individuals.

Death will be something to look forward to

The healthy society will be one in which its component members will die. I think this unpalatable conclusion is inescapable. To ensure long-term adjustment to environmental change society will need continual replenishment of its reservoirs of variety, both genetically, by the recombination of patterns of genes, and culturally, by recombination of traditions and customs and ideas. This means that children must be born, which in turn means that others must die.

What this teaches us about our present attitude to medical science is problematic. Somehow we have to persuade our doctors, and ourselves, to treat death not as an enemy, but as the person's end not in the sense of his end in time but as the end he has in view. In the healthy society, to make a good end or death will have to become something worth striving for: the reward for, and the fulfilment of, a job of living well done. This will be so important a life goal for everyone in the society – important because inevitable – that we will be at pains to teach our children from their earliest years that death is something they should regard as a privilege, whenever it comes, rather than as something terrifying, to be denied or evaded or ignored. Death education will be as important as sex education is thought to be now: both are basic facts of life. We will teach our children that the pain of bereavement is the price we have to pay for loving; and that, although it is costly, it is not too dear, since the experience of losing what you have loved, and grieving over it, is a challenge to learn more about yourself, to become more mature, more healthy, more truly human.

What I have tried to do in this essay is to affirm my belief that each of us has some kind of a vision of a healthy society, even if it remains unuttered: all of our lives are lived in the faith or hope that our future state will be 'better' in some way than what we experience at present. I have tried to illustrate how a man's vision grows and develops as he modifies fantasy in the light of empirical experience; and conversely, how his vision provides him with a means of evaluating that experience. We mostly prefer to keep our fantasies private; but even a moderately healthy society will only be realized inasmuch as men are able to share a common vision. The healthy society is not a vision of a society for other people: it must include every one of us, those who are currently our enemies as well as our friends. Because we see it from inside, it is useless to seek to define its boundaries; and because it values our differences more highly than our similarities it does not call for quantification or measurement. It is a vision of what it might be like to be truly human. We all of us need such a vision if we are to grow towards maturity. We do well to nurture it, not in the hothouse atmosphere of privacy but in openness of mind, exposed to the wind and rain of critical evaluation by others, sharing it with them as an affirmation of our hope in our common future.

18

The Politics of Pastoral Care
(1979)

Alastair Campbell

Why the politics of pastoral care?

It may seem strange for a theologian (and doubly strange for a Scottish Presbyterian) to take as his text a quotation from Aristotle, but I would suggest that the sense of my title is best explained by the following passage from Aristotle's *Politics*:

> [I]t is evident that the state is a creation of nature, and that man is by nature a political animal ... The proof that the state is a creation of nature and prior to the individual is that the individual, when isolated, is not self-sufficing: and therefore he is like a part in relation to the whole. But he who is unable to live in society, or who has no need because he is sufficient for himself must be either a beast or a God. (Book 1, chapter 2)

The claim of Aristotle that it is impossible to regard man in isolation from his participation in some form of society provides me with the basis for a criticism of the contemporary understanding of pastoral care and for some suggestions for the politicization of pastoral care. First, however, I need to clarify what I mean by the term 'politics'.

According to the *Shorter Oxford English Dictionary*, politics is 'the science and art of government'. But an older meaning is also given by the Dictionary, which suits my theme better: 'that branch of moral philosophy dealing with the state or social organism as a whole'. Just as suited to my theme are the two meanings of the adjective *politic*: '(a) sagacious, prudent, shrewd; (b) (in a more sinister sense) scheming, crafty, cunning'.

'Politics' and 'politic' as I apply them to pastoral care are intended to convey the idea of broadening the context of pastoral care to include the communal aspects of human experience. This excursion into politics inevitably exposes pastoral care to the ambiguity of the shrewd and sagacious versus the crafty and scheming. To speak of the politics of pastoral care means a descent from idealism and a cloistered view of human problems to the harsh realities of life in society. Having quoted Aristotle, I hasten to complement his view with the words of John Knox (1994) in his 'Letter to the Scots Nobility' persuading them to enter the political arena:

The subtell craft of Pharao, many years joyned wyth his bloody cruelty, was not able to destroy the male children of Israeli, nether war the watterisof the Redd Sea, much less the rage of Pharao, able to confound Moses and the cumpany which which he conducted; and that because the one had Goddis promisse that thei should multiplie, and the other had his commandiment to enter into such dangeris. I wold your Wisedomes should considder, that our God remaneth one, and is immutable; and that the Church of Christ Jesus hath the same promeis of protection and defence that Israeli had of multiplicatioun; and farther, that no less caus have ye to enter in your former enterprise, than Moses had to go to the presence of Pharao; for your subjectis, yea, your brethrein ar oppressed, thare bodyis and saules haldin in bondage: and God speaketh to your consciences, (onles ye be dead with the blynd warld,) that yow awght to hasard your awin lyves, (be it against Kingis or Empriouris,) for thare deliverance. (p.137)

This statement by Knox serves to demonstrate that the phrase 'the politics of pastoral care' implies the articulation of a particular theological understanding of the nature of the pastoral task. It rules out rigid distinctions between church and world, between the sacred and the secular and it demands some exploration of how the course of human history coincides with or conflicts with the ends towards which God is leading man. It injects a kind of hard-headedness into pastoral care, but not, I hope, at the expense of that essential sensitivity which lies at its heart.

However, my account of the topic to this point is at too general a level to be either useful or properly comprehensible. I must try to make it much more specific from this point on, first by describing what I would call the 'psychological captivity of pastoral care', and then by offering a number of models of how pastoral care can be politicized. I shall conclude with a sketch of a theological framework for supporting this reorientation of pastoral care theory.

The psychological captivity of pastoral care

The observation that pastoral care has become trapped in psychological categories is by no means a new idea. The late Bob Lambourne (Lambourne 1970) pointed this out in several provocative and hard-hitting papers. The following extract from his essay, entitled 'With love to the USA', provides a good illustration of his spirited attack on the dominance of the psychotherapeutic model:

The first necessity is for all concerned to recognize the extent to which the dialogue between theology and psychotherapy has been a tribalistic one which has concealed implicit value judgments ...The reason for this excessive tribalism lies in the special conditions in which psychoanalysis and counselling skills were developed. These conditions, of which the Jewish professional community of the late nineteenth century and the academics of the mid-western American campus between the wars provide good examples, provided a maximum of openness between the two or more participants within a highly enclosed situation...

Thus began the separation of the theory and the art of loving from the theory and art of justice. Those who practiced psychotherapy and those who learned from them did so in an artificial situation, which protected them from the stings of cultural relativity, poverty, stupidity, unemployment, poor housing, and physical concern. The marks of this are clearly visible after fifty years in the latest writings on the theology of pastoral care. (p.135)

The dangerously close relationship between psychotherapeutic theory and the theology of pastoral care has been particularly obvious in the American literature. Yet there have also been powerful American critics of this alliance. An extreme example is provided by the writings of O.H. Mowrer (1961; 1964), who attempted to eradicate the heresies of Freudianism in pastoral theology, in the name of a new moralism. But the more moderate and balanced critiques are to be found in the works of Howard Clinebell and Thomas Oden. Clinebell, in his widely used textbook, *Basic Types of Pastoral Counselling* (1966), has tried to replace the insight-orientated model of pastoral counselling with a 'revised model' which stresses the healing of relationships and the alteration of behaviour as methods alongside the exploration and reflection of feelings. Elsewhere, Clinebell (1965; Clinebell and Seifort 1969) has described methods of enhancing mental health and of bringing about social change through the use of church resources. At a more rigorously theological level Oden (1967) has exposed the lack of relationship between developments in pastoral care theory and developments in contemporary theology. He summarizes his reflections on the American pastoral literature as follows:

It has been content to derive its 'theological' bearings essentially from psychological case studies and clinical pastoral relationships, the result of which is a derivative or functional theology, in which theology functions now and then to help out in the solution of some practical problem. (p.57)

It is another British writer, however, who brings my theme into sharpest focus. In a remarkably perceptive and prophetic book, *The Faith of the Counsellors,* Paul Halmos (1965) has documented the rise of the counselling professions, corresponding with a fall in the overall numbers of clergy. His book summarizes the faith of this new priesthood in a series of memorable phrases, for example, 'the counsellor's love as therapeutic skill', 'faith in the triumph of love over hatred', 'the fiction of non-directiveness'. Part of Halmos's explanation for the emergence of a faith in counselling methods is what he sees as the 'discrediting of political solutions' among those who are concerned for the betterment of society. He lists seven reasons for this, two of which I find of particular interest. One is a modern tendency to be suspicious of any form of political commitment. Halmos writes:

The contemporary western intellectual has long felt obliged to be dispassionate and objective. He has developed an ideological cramp and can't now make an energetic or determined move in any direction, even the right one. (p.12)

A second reason results from what Halmos calls 'the formalized and exploitive human contacts of political manoeuvre' which tend to attract the more detached, cynical members of a society and to repel those with a genuine interest and concern for the welfare of individuals. Halmos's analysis is obviously in danger at times of over-generalizing in a rather grand manner. But his book can help us to understand why pastoral care theory has been so attracted to counselling and psychotherapy and so neglectful of the social and political aspects of people's needs and problems. The 'faith of the counsellors' seems very close to Christian affirmations not only because it stresses the primacy of love but also because, as Halmos also points out, it rests upon a set of paradoxes – warmth in tension with professional detachment, a focus on feelings in tension with the quest for rationality, non-judgementalism in tension with the desire to intervene, and so on. These paradoxes provide the sort of richness of understanding of the complexity of human problems towards which the Gospel also points. At the same time, the tendency for political movements to be fanatical, exploitative and neglectful of personal values makes them unattractive to those Christians who have already been drawn towards counselling by a dislike of dogmatism.

So the trap opens and springs tight shut. The literature of pastoral care becomes largely a restating of the tenets of good counselling in a religious context; the activities of pastoral carers become narrowed down to the refinement of one-to-one and small group interactions; the development of the individual's capacity for self-determination according to values he chooses for his own life become the epitome of the Gospel hope and promise. Somewhere in the by-going the prophetic edge of Christianity is lost and the pastoral care movement becomes dangerously like a new version of Marx' 'opiate of the people' – only in this case the people are articulate, highly self-conscious, middle-class Westerners.

How then is this 'tenderness trap' to be avoided? Certainly not by throwing aside the important values which have been reaffirmed and restated by the counselling movement. There is no question but that respect for the individuality of others, responsiveness to their feelings and the active encouragement of the autonomy are all worthy goals for pastoral care. Above all the concept of *acceptance* (especially as it has been interpreted by Paul Tillich in his creative dialogue with psychology) is a vital contribution to a contemporary Christian doctrine of man. It is not a matter of supplanting these insights from psychology, but of supplementing them with a different perspective on the meaning of pastoral care. In the section which follows I will suggest three different but related ways in which a new perspective may be gained: (1) we-formation and ethical responsibility; (2) prophecy and ministry to structures: and (3) being and vision.

The politicization of pastoral care

'We-formation' and ethical responsibility.

For my first model for politicization I return to the writings of Bob Lambourne. In his important, though at times obscure, essay, 'Personal reformation and political formation in pastoral care' (1974), Lambourne seeks to re-locate pastoral care 'within the realm of the church'. He is concerned that the pastoral counselling movement has torn pastoral work away from its roots in the Christian *koinonia* and, because of its stress on the development of the individual ('ego-formation'), has perpetuated and increased the split between the individual and the community. The corrective which Lambourne offers to this is a return to the idea that pastoral care is first and foremost a nurturing of the church fellowship ('we-formation') which will prepare it for its task of ministering to the world. In proposing this Lambourne is aware that he is returning to a view of pastoral care which gained emphasis at the Reformation. The Reformers made a conscious move away from the model of pastoral care based on the confessional and on the 'medicine' of the sacrament, which characterized medieval Catholicism. In its place they stressed the idea of the fellowship of believers, each his own priest through the one mediatorship of Jesus Christ. Pastoral care in this view of the Church became a matter of church discipline, the regulation of the fellowship to ensure that each member was both a hearer and a doer of the Word. In Calvin's Geneva all aspects of life were under scrutiny of the church elders. In the churches and sects in this tradition attendance at the Lord's Supper became conditional upon regular prayer and Bible reading and upon either a godly and circumspect life or publicly made repentance for the lack of it.

It is not entirely clear in Lambourne's essay, however, how he wishes to implement this proposed return to the Reformed tradition of pastoral care. It is obvious that he sees the danger of a false pietism in which pastoral care is simply the encouragement of self-righteous, defensive and world-denying religiosity. To counteract this he uses the rather heavy phrase, 'we-formation-in-we-responsibility', by which he means that such pastoral care must produce people who are *more* involved in the world and *more* concerned with justice than they would be without the experience of the *koinonia*. But how is this 'we-responsibility' to be achieved? At this point Lambourne's essay becomes somewhat vague. He writes:

> To do this, such groups must in their meetings find a style of waiting on the Word, a way of feeding an the biblical images to which we have referred, and a style of sacramental celebration, which knows no division between the grace of insight given in the shape of revelation within the we-identity on the one hand and the gift of power to be committed to a responsible decision to act on the other hand. (p. 37)

This seems a good statement of intention, but it is frustrating in its lack of specificity. It is clear from an earlier part of the essay that Lambourne places a lot of importance on Old Testament imagery in which the righteousness of God is stressed, but because he does not attempt any kind of overall theological interpretation of the goals of pastoral care we are left with a set of rather isolated Scripture references and a (perhaps) naive hope that Bible reading and sacrament will produce politically active and ethically alert Christians.

This limitation in Lambourne's programme for politicization can be seen more clearly if we compare it with the account of the theology of pastoral care given by Edward Thurneysen, a German theologian in the Barthian tradition, whose book entitled *A Theology of Pastoral Care* (1962) was clearly a potent influence on the essay I have just summarized. Here is Thurneysen's description of pastoral care:

> pastoral care occurs within the realm of the church. It proceeds from the Word and leads back to the Word. It presupposes membership in the body of Christ, or it has this membership as its purpose. (p.53)

At this point Thurneysen and Lambourne sound similar, but the difference appears in Thurneysen's heavy emphasis on proclamation as the specifically Christian mode of communication. For Thurneysen pastoral care is to be understood as 'a specific communication to the individual message proclaimed in general in the sermon to the congregation' (p.11). Moreover, this proclamation must always be, and is nothing other than, the *word of forgiveness*. No other form of communication deserves the description of Christian pastoral care, however helpful it may be (in a less ultimate sense) to the individual or the group.

The advantage of Thurneysen over against Lambourne is that his clarity and consistency allows one to know without hesitation whether one wants to agree or disagree with him. While Lambourne sketches rather idealistically a programme with which one could scarcely disagree, Thurneysen's tells us uncompromisingly that proclamation of forgiveness is the only true form of pastoral care and that that is all there is to be said regarding the church's task in the world.

It is therefore in dialogue with Thurneysen that I would like to move to my next 'model for politicization'. I do not intend to reject outright the notion of 'we-formation', but I believe we can only see its advantage and limitations if we ask in much more specific terms what such an emphasis intended to produce in terms of political involvement. My next model uses the concepts of prophecy and ministry to structures to illustrate the potential strengths and weaknesses of the proclamation model.

Prophecy and ministry to structures

If you recall the quotation from John Knox which I gave in an earlier section you will gain the atmosphere of the Reformed understanding of the prophetic ministry of the church to the state authorities. Knox had no hesitation in speaking out, be it to the aristocracy or to the sovereign herself, in circumstances in which he saw the state denying the gospel of Christ. This outspokenness of the Calvinist tradition contrasts both with the post-Constantinian Catholic tradition and with the teaching of Luther. In the Catholic tradition there was a tendency toward theocracy, in which all authority both temporal and spiritual resided in the Pope. Luther, on the other hand, made a sharp division between kingdoms – the heavenly and the earthly. In the

Lutheran view the Church leaves the state to manage its own affairs, protesting against it only when freedom of worship is threatened. (This explains Luther's famous instruction to the rulers during the peasants' revolt of 1525 to kill the rebels as they would mad dogs.) The Reformed tradition is in a middle position between medieval Catholic theocracy and the Lutheran separation between temporal and spiritual. In the Reformed view the Church has a duty to point out the errors of the state and to help to guide it in the direction of man's true fulfilment, but it should never allow itself to become an integral part of the state.

Two contemporary illustrations may serve to make this middle position clearer. I take them from national situations of which I have a direct, though extremely brief, knowledge. The first is the situation of the South African churches, especially those in the Reformed tradition. The ambiguity of the Reformed approach to social problems is shown by the fact that the official statements of the Dutch Reformed Church have never questioned the government policy of 'separate development', and indeed have often produced arguments from Scripture in support of it. Yet from that same church have sprung some of the most courageous critics of the system, who have spoken out tirelessly, and at great personal cost, about all the destruction of human values which the government policy creates. (Anyone who has been to South Africa and has visited an African township – as I have – will see at first hand how pastoral care requires a political dimension to meet even the most basic of human needs in such situations.)

My second example is that of the Christians in East Germany. Again there is no escaping the political edge to being a Christian in that country, and again the uncertainty for those who seek a prophetic ministry is almost overwhelming. Yet there is a kind of wise courage among the church leaders in East Germany of which we, in our British complacency, know nothing. The following extract from an address by the principal of a theological college to the Synod of the East German Federation of Protestant Churches is a good example of prophetic speaking in a country in which officially the churches are supposed to keep entirely clear of politics:

> In the light of Christ's promises we shall not cease to care for our society; rather we shall resolutely continue to believe in a socialism that is capable of improvement … The Church … might well provide a critical public, a place of free speech, a place of openness to radical questions and a willingness to learn that is not tinged with fear. That would be an eminently important way of participating responsibly in the life of our society.

To my mind these two examples provide concrete illustration of what it is that Lambourne's and Thurneysen's accounts of pastoral care might mean. The reconciling Word creates agents of reconciliation. The experience of acceptance turns a person outwards to confront a society in which individuals are treated as of no concern, as pawns in a system, or the unimportant victims of a party policy. This is the strength of the Reformed emphasis on the ethical dimension of the Gospel. It creates

– or should create – an uneasiness with the given conditions of all societies, a radical questioning of the values which find embodiment in social conditions. But there are also two potential weaknesses in this approach. The first is a tendency to 'preachiness', and the second is an overstress on guilt and responsibility. I shall discuss the first of these weaknesses immediately, but the second will require an exposition of my third and final model for the politicization of pastoral care.

The most obvious danger in the emphasis on the Word and on proclamation as the medium of communication is that political pastoral care would become merely a kind of verbal exercise. The sins of a system may be decried in the most eloquent terms, but this is always the easiest of moral stances. For, preaching at political systems, though it may have its hazards in a totalitarian state, is basically a way of keeping distance, of not being too involved in the actual changing of things. For this reason I wish to add the phrase, 'ministry to structures' to my description of this model. By this I mean that a prophetic form of pastoral care must mean prophecy in *deeds* as well as words. Membership of a community health council, a housing association, a club for the handicapped, a minority rights group, etc., would be one form of such ministry to structures. Another could be specialized chaplaincies to industry, hospitals, prisons, educational establishments. Another is the use of the parish system to promote community work with young people, the unemployed, the housebound. The details need to be worked out by each person in his situation but the general point remains the same: not to rest content with picking up the casualties of a social system, and not to stay in the easy position of critic of the evils of society, but to become involved in specific ways in changing those things which oppress the humanity of one's neighbour – *acted,* not just spoken prophecy.

Being and vision

Yet when this has been said not all has been said that must be said about the politics of pastoral care. There is still the subtle danger that a conscience-driven activism may dominate our attitudes to our own lives and to the society in which we live. This is a major hazard of Protestantism in particular, and it is one which requires us to balance the prophecy model with a very different approach, one which I describe in the phrase 'being and vision'.

It is not easy to find the words in which to convey the character of this model. I find I have to look to the words of Eastern rather than Western thinkers and to poets rather than formal theologians. Let me begin with a poem by Rabindranath Tagore (1974) which has moved me greatly. Although it is quite long, I must quote most of the poem to convey its gentle force.

> The morning sea of silence broke into ripples of
> bird songs; and the flowers were all merry by the
> roadside; and the wealth of gold was scattered
> through the rift of the clouds while we busily went
> on our way and paid no heed.

We sang no glad songs nor played; we went not to
the village for barter; we spoke not a word nor
smiled; we lingered not on the way. We quickened
our pace more and more as the time sped by.
The sun rose to the mid sky and doves cooed in the
shade. Withered leaves danced and whirled in the
hot air of noon. The shepherd boy drowsed and
dreamed in the shadow of the banyan tree, and I
laid myself down by the water and stretched my
tired limbs on the grass.

My companions laughed at me in scorn;
they held their heads high and hurried on; they never looked
back nor rested; they vanished in the distant blue haze…

The repose of the sun-embroidered gloom slowly
spread over my heart. I forgot for what I had
travelled, and I surrendered my mind without struggle
to the maze of shadows and songs.

At last, when I woke from my slumber and opened
my eyes, I saw thee standing by me, flooding my sleep
with thy smile. How I had feared that the path
was long and wearisome, and the struggle to reach
thee was hard! (p.29)

Tagore is telling us that constant striving and journeying, the activist way, can leave
us with no vision, no meeting with God, no discovery of true being. I fear that
contemporary pastoral care whether in its counselling mode or in its prophetic,
ethically involved mode can miss the simplicity of Tagore's kind of vision all too
easily. The root of the danger lies in the splitting of the self from its natural habitation
in the body, in the community of others, and in nature as a whole. Many forms of
counselling do this by stressing conscious, rational choice as a goal. Equally the
prophetic emphasis on guilt, forgiveness and ethically responsible action places one
part of our being and experience in the limelight to the exclusion of the rest. What I
am looking for is a return to the oneness of human existence, in which politics means
not just activism and changing things but finding a true being in this world which is
ours to receive, to experience, to suffer in and to rejoice in.

A powerful image for this understanding of being and vision is to be found in
Herman Hesse's novel, *Siddhartha* (1978). Siddhartha follows a way in his life which
takes him to the forest as a Samana (a wandering ascetic), and then to the city where
he learns the arts of sexual love and the skill of acquiring wealth and possessions. But
then his journey takes him to a river and a ferryman and there his journey ends, for he
finds in the ever-changing river all that he has been seeking in his restless encounters
with life:

Siddhartha saw the river hasten, made up of himself and his relations and all the people he had ever seen. All the waves and water hastened, suffering, towards goals, many goals, to the waterfall, to the sea, to the current, to the ocean and all goals were reached and each one was succeeded by another. The water changed to vapour and rose, became rain and came down again, became spring, brook and river, changed anew, flowed anew. But the yearning voice had altered. It still echoed sorrowfully, searchingly but other voices accompanied it, voices of pleasure and sorrow, good and evil voices, laughing and lamenting voices, hundreds of voices, thousands of voices.

Siddhartha listened. He could no longer distinguish the different voices – the merry voice from the weeping voice, the childish voice from the manly voice. They all belonged to each other; the lament of those who yearn, the laughter of the wise, the cry of indignation and groan of the dying. They were all interwoven and interlocked, entwined in a thousand ways. And all the voices, all the goals, all the yearnings, all the sorrows, all the pleasures, all the good and evil, all of them together was the world. All of them together was the stream of events, the music of life. (p.106)

Perhaps it seems perverse of me to try to incorporate such material into the *politics* of pastoral care, yet I believe it essential to attempt it. Politics must be about wisdom, not just about manipulation. What point the altering of injustices if all that is given in return is a new and insatiable quest for false security? If politics should encompass a vision of the totality of human life, in pain as well as pleasure, in rest as well as movement, in death as well as the struggle for survival, then such a vision should come somehow from the style of our pastoral care. Christian pastoral care should surely be capable of bringing to society an awareness of finitude, of the uselessness of running from the pain necessary for living and of the oneness of all that God has created. Yet somehow we seem a long way from this at present. I doubt whether either the pastoral counselling movement or the Lambourne idea of 'we-formation' in the worshipping community is equal to the task. The trouble is that both are caught in presuppositions alien to such a vision. Christian worship seems inextricably entwined with a sense of guilt and unworthiness, which although it can motivate to action, creates at the same time an anxiety inimical to the serenity of contemplation. Pastoral counselling, whether in its directive or non-directive forms, can undoubtedly remove all sorts of blocks to growth, but yet leaves us with a set of isolated individuals, adrift in the world, too conscious of themselves, still yearning for something which no counselling relationship, however loving, can give.

To achieve this kind of politicization of pastoral care we need to launch more fearlessly into the unknown, to discover what Alan Watts (1976) has called the 'wisdom of insecurity', to undertake the kind of journey toward the unknown boundaries of the self and the world which Carl Jung documents so graphically in his *Memories, Dreams, Reflections* (1973). I suppose there is too much timidity and traditionalism in most of us to allow us to offer this kind of pastoral care to our contemporaries. It is so much easier to stay with the familiar psychological, ethical and religious categories than to try to see beyond them.

Yet let me offer you one more signpost on the way I wish pastoral care could go in order to serve the end of a new being and vision. It concerns security and freedom and is taken from Khalil Gibran's *The Prophet* (1976):

> Then a mason came forth and said, Speak to us of Houses.
> And he answered and said:
>
> Would that I could gather your houses into my hand, and
> like a sower scatter them in forest and meadow.
>
> Would the valleys were your streets, and the green
> paths your alleys, that you might seek one another
> through vineyards, and come with the fragrance of the
> earth in your garments.
>
> But these things are not yet to be.
>
> In their fear your forefathers gathered you too near
> together. And that fear shall endure a little longer.
> A little longer shall your city walls separate your
> hearths from your fields.
>
> Verily the lust for comfort murders the passion of the
> soul, and then walks grinning in the funeral.
>
> But you, children of space, you restless in rest, you
> shall not be trapped nor tamed.
>
> You shall not dwell in tombs made by the dead for the
> living.
>
> And though of magnificence and splendour, your house
> shall not hold your secret nor shelter your longing.
>
> For that which is boundless in you abides in the
> mansion in the sky, whose door is the morning mist,
> and whose windows are the songs and the silences
> of night. (pp.38ff)

Conclusion: towards a richer theology of pastoral care

I can come to no tidy conclusion to this paper, for, what I have been struggling with are two strands in the Judaeo-Christian religious tradition which do not neatly tie together. On the one hand there is the prophetic strand which stresses the loving righteousness of God and ties Christian obedience to a life of service of others. The parable of the sheep and the goats and the parable of the Good Samaritan are prime examples of this in the New Testament. From the Old Testament we could well take the words of Micah as the motto of a politically involved and morally self-critical pastoral care: 'the Lord has told us what is good. What he requires of us is this to do what is just to show constant love, and to live in humble fellowship with our God' (Micah 6:8). Yet – by no means consistent with this ethical emphasis – there is quite another strand in both Old and New Testaments. This is the theme of the Suffering Servant, which finds its culmination in the life and death of Jesus. Perhaps this theme is best captured in the stark phrase of Jurgen Moltmann (1974): 'the crucified God'. Of course, attempts have been made to integrate these themes in a single theological interpretation – for example, through the penal atonement account of reconciliation in which the suffering of Christ is seen as the price paid for sin to an angry God. But terrible things must be done to the biblical documents in order to make them conform to this, or to any other theological dogma.

I believe that we must stay with the dissonance of these two themes, and, by maintaining them both, try to create a richer theology of pastoral care. After all, *any* theological statement is inevitably a diminution of God, since it dares to confine in words that which is eternal and before all things. Better, then, to keep our theology diverse and untidy than to lose God utterly in our dislike of incoherence.

In this paper I have sought to bring back into prominence what I see as two neglected dimensions in the theology of pastoral care. First, I have argued for a reaffirmation of the need to both speak and act in the world of social action and state policy. At the same time I have presented a contrary theme which changes our understanding of the political. The ethical emphasis is necessary, but not enough, if we are to speak to our society, live fully in it, and try to remain true to the vision of Jesus, the crucified one. I therefore wish to conclude with a final statement of the theme of suffering and wisdom which leads to what I have called 'being and vision'. This simple statement, in the words of an American poet, Richard Shannon (1975), encapsulates an understanding of human potential toward which I hope a richer theology of pastoral care may yet lead our society:

> Wounded oysters build out of gory wounds
> A pearl. And create within the gap of pain
> a jewel.
>
> May we be so wise.

19

Personal Care and Political Action
(1985)

Michael Wilson

Personal care

The well known definition of pastoral care by Clebsch and Jaekle (1964) confines it to personal help by 'representative persons' (p.4) for religious problems in the context of the Church. The notion of helping individuals 'in trouble' is a common understanding of pastoral care. For example, in the monthly newsletter of a local Methodist Church there is a section devoted to 'Pastoral Notes'. Consistently this is devoted to death, illness, operations, accidents, etc. Almost all occasions of joy and celebration find other headings. It is common knowledge that this casual image of pastoral care owes more to secular society than to Christianity, being shaped by Western individualism, the medical model of health and psychology, undergirded by a theology of salvation and healing which neglects a theology of learning and suffering.

   Before I develop a criticism of the basis of this approach to pastoral care, there are two further points I wish to make:

(1)   The term 'pastoral' is now widely used in secular settings, particularly in education. If I go into the bookshop and take a book of pastoral care off the shelf, I may not know until I open it whether it is an educational textbook or a Church-related study. The word 'personal' can get round the ambiguity but has disadvantages because the word is often synonymous with 'individual'. The idea of a person-in-relationship is not always inferred.

(2)   The term pastoral care (Church-related) is used in two distinct but not separate fields of discourse. First, as a word to describe the nurture and training of a Christian congregation for its mission in the world. Bob Lambourne (1974) develops this theme and, firmly placing pastoral care in the context of mission, describes it as a 'servicing function'. The word 'mission' here is an overall term for the action of a Christian congregation in its own local setting, and includes evangelism, prophesy, healing, suffering, worship and service. In this first field of discourse the Christian language of Bible and Sacrament is held in common and therefore explicit.

But in the second field of discourse – personal care and service by Christians and others in a secular context – there may be theological assumptions but they are implicit (e.g. a Christian doing work with the Marriage Guidance Council or Samaritans). This second field of discourse is the normal situation of Christians every day when teachers, mothers and British Leyland workers have to find secular words and actions with which to express their faith and pastoral care for others.

Criticism of pastoral care

I propose now to criticize the commonly held view of pastoral care described above from a stance of political awareness. This may help to tease out the points at which pastoral care has been cut off from political action, doing violence to a true understanding of man, the Church and spirituality. (In passing let no one think that I have set up an Aunt Sally just to knock it down. A form of pastoral care shrunk to pastoral counselling only still spreads around the world.)

I think such a model of pastoral care is inadequate in five ways:

(1) Its particular strength – taking seriously the uniqueness of each individual – may lead to *the privatization of problems and suffering.* I mentioned above the human cost of unemployment. To discover this we need to talk to the Samaritans, Marriage Guidance Counsellors, Probation Officers, Alcoholics Anonymous and nurses in the admission wards of psychiatric hospitals. Here is where the human cost of unemployment is borne, individualized and private but never added up publicly. I have wondered how we would respond to some imaginative act which could organize all the unemployed in the country to demonstrate together – simply walking side by side – on one day: and the first ten minutes of the national BBC television news devoted to photographs without comment from helicopters – just mile after mile after mile of unemployed human beings.

The pastoral approach fails to turn private problems into social issues. I receive so much literature about counselling the unemployed, understanding redundancy in terms of bereavement theory, setting up clubs, job centres, etc. All excellent, *but not enough.*

'You cannot help people fully unless you also do something about the situation which makes them what they are'. Even in such a unique and private sorrow as the care of the dying person the whole context of death in our society, attitudes to it and the uses of technology cry out for a wider public dimension of change. Even ethics can become privatized and specialized so that public and political action are neutered. It is not that the personal approach is wrong: it is not enough. It has become cut off from its context.

(2) We ought therefore to say that *pastoral care is situational* and neglects its context at its peril. Certainly the withdrawn type of psychoanalysis

instituted by Freud, and the similar context-excluding method of counselling instituted by Rogers has given place, though slowly, to more mutual methods of exploring human predicaments and to group work. But to take the situation seriously may lead to unexpected action. To give a sharp example. Dr Berhorst (1974), working as a medical missionary in an Amerindian village in Guatemala, was faced with a number of peasants suffering from tuberculosis. After some research, he spent his money on a scheme to reallocate land to landless peasants. He did not spend his money on drugs for treatment: that is, he actually left patients without treatment (which was how they had always been). For he had discovered that landless peasants were catching tuberculosis when they migrated to the coast for seasonal work, and returned home with it. On receiving land, a peasant may say: 'Now I am a man again.' Something more than curing individuals has been achieved, but Dr Berhorst has been criticized for not treating sick people, perhaps because the land question is always politically sensitive.

This poses certain questions for our understanding of pastoral care as healing. When does pastoral care cease to be 'pastoral' and become 'political' action? (This question opens up the awkward relationship between the so-called Church's ministry of healing (charismatic) and medical missionary healing.)

(3) Methods of pastoral care may also be seen to be based upon false *assumptions about the nature of human beings.* Do we, for example, share the widely accepted Western model of human beings which sees us like marbles in a box? In this view we are certainly related to one another in families, clubs, tribes or blocks of flats, but each of us is a discrete and separate individual like a marble, beginning and ending at our skins, related because of proximity – we are together in one house, place or nation.

Or do we believe that we are inter-related more like the members of a body (1 Corinthians 1:2) – that we co-inhere? Evidence from medicine and group dynamics would support such an idea, and this more corporate model is certainly more common in many parts of Africa, for example the Shona greeting:

'How are you?'

'I am well if you are well.'

I am suggesting that we must not only help individuals but also that both helper and helped are representative persons in whom and through whom symptoms of a wider malaise and compassion are expressed: in whom and through whom even the bystanders are caught up in suffering and change of mind. If we take such a view of the nature of human beings, then a social dimension of pastoral care is inescapable.

(4) Pastoral care of the kind described may spring from a *false spirituality* which traps people in narcissistic self-development. In the English tradition prayer and action belong together. Daniel Berrigan (Berrigan in Leech, undated) wrote:

> The time will shortly be upon us, if it is not already here, when the pursuit of contemplation becomes a strictly subversive activity ... I am convinced that contemplation, including the common worship of the believing, is a political act of the highest value, implying the riskiest of consequence to those taking part.

And Thomas Merton (Merton cited in Leech, undated):

> The monk is essentially someone who takes up a critical attitude towards the contemporary world and its structures ... The great problem for monasticism today is not survival but prophecy.

It is not easy to defend pastoral care against the accusation that the personal approach cuts the nerve of political action. Prayer, however, puts personal problems into the wider context of God's purposes. At a conference in Edinburgh in 1979, Tom Oden accused his fellow Clinical Pastoral Educators of neglecting the Church's tradition of prayer in pastoral care, and this could be one reason why pastoral care may remain narrowly personal without the wider contextual demands which prayer so disturbingly makes.

Much more needs to be said about worship, and I will return to it later.

(5) Last, current models of pastoral care do not take seriously enough *the building of a healthy congregation* (even two or three) or a healthy school or a healthy department of theology in a University. I need not develop a well-known theme in Birmingham that pastoral care is often captive to the medical model of health and finds difficulty in resisting the authority of secular models. Even in our personal tutor system it is more often the student with problems who claims attention – problems and isolates. In the Diploma in Pastoral Studies (DPS), we do try alternative patterns, giving priority to the group as a whole (pastoral care of a group – sometimes a strange concept which many clergy are at a loss how to handle) and its common task of learning together. We take seriously the coherence of the group, its morale, styles of leadership and the use of authority. A course of this kind is bound to be subversive within the life of the University in its approach to educational matters (taking seriously learning by experience, the importance of educating the feeling life, and giving students full responsibility for choices within the course even to making mistakes and having to bear the consequences), to examinations, and to admissions policy (we have openly and consistently opposed the differential scale of fees for overseas students).

I am not myself temperamentally good at confrontation, and I have to take seriously the Ghanaian proverb: 'You will catch more flies with molasses than with vinegar'. But I have no doubt that membership of the DPS course involves an awakening to the corporate dimension of pastoral care.

These five points of criticism indicate an impoverishment of accepted methods of pastoral care as developed in the West since the War. They indicate the existence of a social dimension which has been lopped from pastoral care and whose proper relationship to the personal approach must now be explored.

Personal and political

David Goodacre (1980) records that:

> Towards the end of his life Dag Hammarskjold wrote to Martin Buber to say how much he would like to call on him when he was passing through Jerusalem on one of his peace-making missions. When at last they did meet, they gave most of their evening discussion to the problem of the failure of the spiritual man in politics. (p.32)

In his book *Moral Man and Immoral Society*, Neibuhr (1963) emphasizes how different are the problems of the individual and society. He writes:

> The perennial tragedy of human nature ... that those who cultivate the spiritual elements usually do so by divorcing themselves from or misunderstanding the problems of collective man, where the brutal elements of man are most obvious. (p.54)

Halmos, in his *The Personal and the Political* (1978), similarly discusses the differences:

> It is like the lion and the lamb trying to lie down together. The politician and the personalist are two different types of agent for change. The one who sets out to change society is a reformer, whereas the person who hopes to change an individual is a therapist, and if each tries to do both from their position as a politician or counsellor, they fail because they act inappropriately. Quite apart from the basic opposition of the two to each other, politicians are like dominant genes, all too easily taking over and excluding the personal, while counsellors, and churchmen for that matter, tend to underestimate the problems of politics. (p.21)

Both agreed that this is a Western problem since it is in Western culture that the personal and individual approach (which we have described as moulding Western patterns of pastoral care) has developed. Halmos describes as desirable 'equilibration' between personal and political attitudes in which both can act as critic and inspiration to the other without confusion. Pattison (1982) used such a method in his Ph.D. thesis when he brought insights from liberation theology as critical tools with which to examine psychiatric hospital chaplaincy work.

Campbell, much influenced by his visit to South Africa, has spoken of the 'politicization' of pastoral care and in his Jim Blackie memorial lecture (Campbell 1979) developed the theme of prophecy and ministry to structures, a theme which depends upon both word and action. Here we find an echo of Ghandi's tactics in setting up 'signs of contradiction'. (I see the DPS course in such a light.)

Distinction to the point of difference seems to be the conclusion of most writers when discussing personal and political approaches. Without denying the above arguments I wish to describe an example of synthesis.

Case study

I propose to describe an actual example of a Christian congregation which achieved not only 'equilibration' but, I think, a synthesis of personal and political elements in its mission.

I was brought up in the Potteries in the 1920/30s and my father was vicar of Snyed Church, Burslem, a member of the Catholic Crusade. This order was founded by Conrad Noel and was generally Anglo-Catholic and left wing: there is a direct descent to the more modern Parish and People movement.

The social situation was the Great Hunger and Unemployment of the years between the two Great Wars. I remember the General Strike of 1926 and the collapse of 1929. At the age of fourteen in school holidays I often sold 'Daily Workers' to the dole queue; and saw there cases of chlorosis (green anaemia due to malnutrition in teenage girls) which has since disappeared in Britain. When I was five, I sat in our Church of England primary school next to children barefoot through the winter.

The church, black with soot, was next to Doulton's. On one occasion the keystone of the chancel arch fell out due to mining subsidence underneath. The cross behind the lectern was flanked on one side by the red flag of St. George (the union Jack was regarded as a symbol of brutal conquest and was not displayed). In the vestry there was a fine revolutionary poster depicting Lenin leading the people.

The mission of the church was founded on the Kingdom theology of F.D. Maurice (1837). From its local situation of oppression there evolved an indigenous liberation theology, understood by the congregation because hammered out by them in the weekly Parish Meeting. It was there that pastoral needs were recognized and political actions decided: for example, the pastoral care of an evicted family, the demonstration (they could be very rough) to expose the evils of landlordism, or the public protest by vicar and churchwardens at the AGM of the Church Commissioners over Church investments in Vickers the armament manufacturers (*circa* 1930). The congregation was committed to its task for the Kingdom of God in Burslem, and its worship, the Parish Mass, was made as beautiful as possible because in it we saw a foretaste of the Kingdom to come. Perhaps the centrality of worship would be a distinctive thing in making any comparison with the much later and more academically developed liberation theology of South America. The sharing of funds with the poor and the political activities for justice were simply related to the Mass – if you shared equally the eucharistic bread inside church then you shared bread outside too. At this level the word of God is explosive.

I can best illustrate facets of this case study by some quotations from what are mostly confirmation instructions for new members: remembering that the purpose of this case study is to show that pastoral and political approaches were actually unified within the mission of a local church – in the potteries of the 1920s. (A brief analysis will follow.)

Worship and justice. Unless bread and wine and all they symbolize are produced and used in the right way there will be no Kingdom of God on earth, for the Kingdom includes at least these material blessings. In the Mass a band of comrades produce bread and wine and divide it and share it as God wills, in the spirit of service for common use, and in fellowship and justice. In that bread and wine they see God, not hiding himself but manifest, expressing himself in the material creation, his very body and blood. In the Mass they see the way to the Kingdom and the values of it. To win the world to such a way of life, and to change this present system means struggle and risk and danger. It means the breaking of our bodies and the shedding of our blood.

Service. A worker who can win the respect of his or her mates and perhaps become one recognized as courageous enough to speak out against injustice, who is not afraid to voice the grievances of others, who can keep calm, who consistently talks sense and puts forward a sensible line of action at a Trade Union meeting, and who is known to be a member of a church group which is active in a social way: such a worker is doing excellent work for the cause of Christ's Kingdom. He is acting as leaven in the world.

Care and common life. As members get to know one another, and their different standards of living become apparent the inequality of incomes may lead to some searching of hearts. Some may be led to consider the possibility of income sharing. A common purse for the group, to which those who can afford to contribute do so anonymously, and from which any communicant can draw when in need as a matter of justice, is a valuable help. Such a fund could probably provide help in time of sickness or unemployment and also holiday money for those members of the group who would otherwise have none.

Salvation and justice. But where people urge us to confine the Christian religion to the saving of our souls, to personal salvation, and forbid us to mix religion with politics and economics they are really the deadly enemies of personal salvation for the soul can only become 'sound' or 'saved' when, forgetting self, it is merged in the love of God and the comradeship and service of its fellows in the battle for that new world wherein dwelleth righteousness.

Unity of pastoral and political

It would be folly to try and point in the passages above to personal or political 'bits'. We are in the presence of an overmastering theology which draws both together in word and action.

The centrality of worship. Both personal and political approaches are interwoven in worship. As a whole the parish Mass tried to present a vision of God's social order – beauty, warmth, sharing – with an earthy sense of our worldly situation where sin, starvation and Empire stalked. It was an inspiration, not an escape. And in the light of that vision the Church's work, individually and corporately, was planned in the parish meeting.

If intercessions (for example) are to be lively, then there has to be a *free flow of information* from the weekday situations of the members back into worship – the situations in schools, dole queue, mines and transport homes, etc. – giving both an individual and solidarity-in-polities flavour to the prayers. This keeps prayer and action close to one another and helps to turn private suffering into public and political issues. Otherwise prayer for healing (for example) can get trapped at the level of Mrs Jones' bunions. (It isn't that Mrs Jones' bunions aren't important. She may not be able to walk on a demonstration, but she can sit by a bedside or address envelopes. Bunions or not, she has her task for the Kingdom.) A master purpose which draws upon both personal and political insights and action, and puts one's bunions in a wider context!

Mission in the world. Here I use the word 'mission' (as above) to cover evangelism, service and healing, prophecy and suffering – all aspects of the work for the Kingdom in the local situation. A sense of purpose in a group raises morale and helps to build a healthy community.

Although some mission involves extra effort (visiting the sick, public speaking, attending a demo, trade union work) the key to the situation was each members' understanding that their own place of work was where their mission and ministry lay. For some this could be mainly personal, for others mainly political, and for a few, both. Perhaps one should point to a process of political conscientization flowing from worship and the theology of the Kingdom of God. (It is interesting how the Burslem group decisively rejected pietism and saw it as a threat to their personal/political gospel.)

It may well be that our unbalanced development of pastoral counselling in the West stems in part from a loss of political vision and hence a sense of outgoing mission exciting enough to raise morale and outflank individual problems which loom large when secular humanist models of individual self-development predominate in society. Perhaps we can only achieve individual wholeness when we are caught up in a corporate cause that is greater than our individual wholeness. Exploration and mountaineering have a great deal to teach us.

The Body (1 Corinthians 12). If we have had difficulty reconciling personal and political approaches, there may lie behind that the polarity between 'individual' and 'corporate' often discussed by the DPS and highlighted by Bob Lambourne's (Lambourne 1983, p.190) well-known diagram with arrows between various polarities in theology. However, I think we must also speak of *membership* as a word which encompasses both individuality and belongingness. Membership is a concept of a higher explanatory order (Gregory Bateson's terminology). For the Burslem group, membership was highly important, with its admission, training and mutual responsibilities.

Gifts (1 Corinthians 12). The aggression and insight necessary for prophecy, confrontation and politics are different gifts from the empathy and gentleness of the personal pastor. (Not that confrontation is absent from pastoral care nor gentleness from politics.) But I do accept the weight of argument for the differences which Halmos and Niebuhr have described. The different gifts, however, are unified within the Body. A strong doctrine of gifts seems essential to unite both personal and political involvement. Pattison's (1980) criticism of hospital chaplaincy suggests the need for a multiplicity of gifts which must be rare in an individual, but a very possible combination when the ministry (and mission) is viewed in terms of the laity.

Ecological view of the world. If the world is viewed as God's day-by-day ongoing creation, then an ecological view of the world follows: the world in one inter-dependent developing whole. The writings emerging from the new physics (Capra 1982) give us exciting parallel insights into the interdependent nature of matter. The Burslem congregation found their mission exciting because it fitted into the pattern of growth, struggle and change towards their vision of a whole earth – it was worth suffering for.

Personal and political approaches become separated and polarized when we lack some higher understanding in which both are synthesized. I suggest that the unifying concept may be found in an understanding of membership of the Body of Christ engaged in a mission to bring God's Kingdom into being in the world. This particular theology can synthesize personal and political approaches, but other theologies reject political involvement altogether. It depends upon your under-standing of God's relationship with the world; of how spirit and matter are related in the Body of Jesus, or bread, or you or me.

PART SIX

Practical Theology as Story

20

Telling Tales

The Narrative Dimension of
Pastoral Care and Counselling (1998)[1]

Gordon Lynch and David Willows

Finding ourselves in God's story

DAVID: To sum up our discussion thus far, it appears that stories are an indispensable part of what it means to be human. They are part of the bedrock of our lives, from which is hewn a sense of self in relation to others and our environment. Stories create order and meaning out of the scattered fragments of human existence. They provide spaces in which to remember our past and rehearse our future. In short, as is beautifully illustrated by a story I came across once in the writings of Martin Buber (1963), stories are agents of transformation.

> An old rabbi sat on a chair among his friends in the shadow of the great temple. Wearied by his age and infirmity, the fraternity were well used to passing their time in discussion and debate. On this particular day, however, the rabbi chose not to entertain those around him with fine rhetoric and sophisticated logic. He chose, rather, to tell a story about his teacher; about how he used to jump up and down when he was praying. Hour after hour the story continued, and the longer it went on the more the rabbi was carried away by what he was saying. Indeed, all of a sudden the rabbi altogether forgot his infirmity, stood up and began to jump and dance, just as his master had done. From that moment on, or so the story goes, the rabbi was healed. The story had transformed him. (p.71)

I like this story because of the way in which it helps us to understand the power of story in our lives. The question that keeps nagging at the back of my mind, however, is whether the stories that we tell are true. Or maybe the question of truth is simply not appropriate at this point.

GORDON: In our previous conversation, I recall that you raised this issue by contrasting those who see stories purely as a defense against anxiety (Cupitt 1991) with those who regard stories as having some transcendent point of reference outside themselves (Frankl 1964). On a practical level – thinking for a moment about the story that you wrote about you and your unborn child – it therefore seems important to ask whether your image of Christ 'fashioning that which is broken and frail into icons of divine love' actually bears any relation to the way things are. Might it not simply be the case that this poetic language provides a superficial resolution to your experience that was not otherwise possible? After all, we all want to be 'mastered', says Loughlin (1996), 'or written into a narrative that is larger, longer, and stronger than our own' (p.8).

DAVID: The question that you are posing is certainly challenging and I have often considered whether my story is less true because of the way in which it resolves itself so neatly. Part of me realizes that my story is a defence in the face of deep existential anxiety. Yet another part of me also wants to affirm its truth; to declare that the structure of existence that is present in the biblical narrative interposes meaning upon my experience and helps me locate myself in relation to some transcendent reality. Indeed, it is for this reason that I tend to react against the textualist slogans of so-called postmodern thought that seem to relegate the question of 'ultimate truth' to the theological scrapheap. Can it not be the case that some stories go all the way down to the way things really are?

GORDON: In other words, you believe that some stories are set apart as somehow having universal significance for the way we live our lives.

DAVID: Precisely. They are stories we can live by; stories that make an imperialistic claim upon us. As Erich Auerbach (1953), one of the earliest so-called 'narrative theologians', once explained with reference to the distinctiveness of scripture: 'Far from seeking, like Homer, merely to make us forget our own reality for a few hours, it [i.e. the biblical story] seeks to overcome our reality. We are to fit our own life into its world, feel ourselves to be elements in its structure of universal history' (p.15). Of course, this is a long way from the Enlightenment legacy of individual autonomy whereby each of us become our own masters and weave our own narratives into the events of history. For me, however, this tendency to assert human independence and self-sufficiency, even to the exclusion of divine revelation, is itself open to question.

GORDON: How do you mean, exactly?

DAVID: What I mean is that the modern emphasis upon human autonomy is not necessarily beyond dispute. Indeed, if you look closely at the philosophical ideas which arose during the Enlightenment, it is possible to discern a common narrative theme which goes all the way back to the classical age: a story in which man (*sic*) is portrayed as emerging from the darkness of his cave and learning to live in the light of his innate powers of reason. To be sure, the story is compelling. Yet we have to ask ourselves whether this myth of human ascent is truly commensurate with Christian faith.

GORDON: The way you describe these God-given stories as making 'imperialistic' claims upon us and 'overcoming our reality' makes me feel a little uneasy; for is there not a shadow side to the theological view that you are advocating? Is it not equally true that stories from scripture or religious tradition can often be imposed on people's experience in a way that denies them an authentic voice? For me, the way that the story of the destruction of Sodom and Gomorrah has been used to pathologize homosexuality, or the way that Old Testament stories about the development of different tribes has been used to sustain racist practices such as apartheid, illustrates how the imposition of religious stories on human experience has the potential to cause tremendous suffering and injustice. I am therefore unsure how it is possible to give religious stories the authority that you do without risking such harm being caused to people. Whilst you may not be convinced by the Enlightenment emphasis on narrating our individual experience, it does seem to me that there it does at least capture an important principle of authenticity – i.e. of being true to oneself – which we somehow need to hold on to. Just supposing, however, that I were to accept your way of reading the significance of scripture, it would seem that the theological task is to make God's story fit with the story of our lives.

DAVID: Not exactly. At least, I would put it the other way round and suggest that the theological task is to find ourselves narrated into God's story (Kierkegaard 1941, p.232). That is to say, we do not affirm the meaningfulness of scripture on the basis of its ability to cohere with our own story. No, narrative theology argues that God's story is logically prior: a consuming text that transforms our misshapen outlook upon reality and enables us to view ourselves and the world from a radically different outlook. When we talk of being incorporated into God's story, in other words, perhaps what we are really saying is that we have learned to see the world, and thereby tell our own story, in a certain way: from the point of view of one already caught up in the divine drama.

GORDON: I must say that I am beginning to feel that these theological distinctions are nothing more than semantic games. Perhaps you would like to illustrate your point?

DAVID: The distinction I am trying to make was recently embodied for me in the life of a woman named Jean. Jean has a long history of institutional psychiatric care. Faced with deteriorating health, she asked to see a chaplain in order to – as she herself puts it – 'find God and be forgiven'. As she began, week by week, to tell me the tragic tale of her life, Jean would often ask herself where God was throughout all the pain and heartache but answers were always difficult to come by. Indeed, it often appeared that God was absent from her story. Until, one day, I told her story back to her and asked her to respond in whatever way she felt that she wanted. Somewhat to my amazement, she replied:

> You know who's story that is, don't you? I mean, I know it is me, but it is not just me. It is the story of Mary Magdalene. I am Mary Magdalene, although not so lucky as she. But Mary Magdalene was Jesus' friend.

Jean still struggles to come to terms with her story. In this sudden moment of realization, however, it was clear that she had found her 'narrative home'. That is to say, she had begun to locate her place in God's story and, in solidarity with Mary

Magdalene, was able to view the scattered fragments of her past from some more central region.

GORDON: Okay, so our stories are transformed inasmuch as we learn to see that we are participants in a wider story, i.e. God's story. But what does this mean in practice? Are we merely to assume, for instance, that a story is true simply because it uses the language of God and faith more explicitly? If so, then sadly we would have to admit that some of the most destructive and misleading stories of our time – stories shot through with the language of religion – were also the most truthful.

DAVID: You are making an important observation here about the faithfulness of an individual story to its 'master narrative' or faith-perspective. There must be some standard by which we judge some stories as faithful to God's story and others to be wide of the mark.

GORDON: Exactly. I was thinking of our own stories that we told at the beginning of this conversation and wondering whether there was any way in which we could judge their truthfulness to the Christian story to which we both adhere.

DAVID: It seems to me that one of the ways in which we can begin to answer this question is by bringing to bear the resources of theological doctrine. Indeed, in recent years, doctrine has been likened to the 'grammar' that regulates the many stories which we tell to one another and alerts us to the complex matrix of theological beliefs against which we judge the truthfulness of what we say and do (Lindbeck 1984, pp.79–84). So, to give a very simple example, we can affirm the truthfulness of a story in which a person goes out of their way to help another on the basis of a moral framework in which the quality of self-giving love is prominent; a moral framework that is itself rooted in the gospel injunctions to love and Jesus' own parable of the Good Samaritan.

GORDON: So you could say, then, that reciting the Nicene Creed is the theological equivalent of parsing the verbs by which we learn to tell true stories.

DAVID: That is a good analogy, although we must be careful not to underestimate the complexity of the task. Take, for example, the stories of gay women and men who experience the joy of being in loving and supportive relationships. For some, these stories represent a clear violation of a Christian moral code. Clearly, however, the matter is not so easily resolved and appeal is often made to various other themes – or grammatical rules – within the 'lexical core' of the canonical scriptures. Indeed, as with our English language, the whole process is fraught with the theological equivalent of irregular verbs. So perhaps we have to accept the fact that it is not always clear what makes one story beautifully right and another dangerously wrong. That is to say, we must sometimes reserve judgement over the truthfulness of the stories that we tell.

GORDON: It is interesting, as I look back upon my own story, how little explicit reference I chose to make to the Christian tradition. And when I do refer to my Christian beliefs, it is to correct a theological or 'grammatical' error which I perceived to be present in the worshipping community of which I was a part. Their story, as I understood it, was one formulated by cultural and religious suspicion; a story which simply did not cohere with the principles of love and mutual respect.

DAVID: So what you seem to be highlighting for us is the fact that sometimes a group narrative will appear theologically incorrect. When such anomalies occur they often require only minor changes in the grammatical structure of the story. For example, in the case of the Nicene Creed, it is interesting how many churches are currently amending the line 'For us men and for our salvation' by removing the masculine noun. A simple act of grammatical editing, but one that enables a more truthful rendition of the story of good news to all people – women and men alike. At other times, however, especially when a number of anomalies are present within a single story, it becomes increasingly difficult to remain an 'inhabitant' of that particular story-world (Polanyi 1983, pp.15–16); so difficult, in fact, that the only option – as Stephen Crites (1989) once put it – is to 'break the story to tell a truer story' (p.72).

GORDON: I understand what you are saying. Indeed, this talk of a paradigmatic shift in our story-world reminds me of the work of Rosemary Radford Ruether (Ruether 1986) who breaks with the most misogynist stories of the Christian tradition to embrace those stories that more truly narrate the experience of womanhood. Of course, there are those who have argued that this kind of theological reshaping does not go far enough and remains too tied to the grammar of the Christian tradition (Schüssler Fiorenza 1983, pp.17–18). For the purposes of this discussion, however, her work appears to be a good example of the tensions that can arise when the implicit grammar of a particular story-world is called into question.

DAVID: So what we seem to be dealing with here is the thorny issue of whether the stories of our personal experience have authority to subvert and challenge the authoritative narratives of our faith tradition.

GORDON: Yes, I think you are right. I was wondering myself whether the revelation of God's story in scripture really is beyond dispute or whether these ancient texts should be approached with some degree of suspicion whereby their usefulness and vested interests are challenged?

DAVID: This is a difficult question. Nevertheless, let me make two brief responses in the hope that it that might help us to begin to discern an answer. My first response concerns what it is that makes scripture authoritative. Let me state my conviction that God's story is always more than the written texts of scripture. Thus although there will be aspects of the biblical narrative that we will want to call into question – for example, its presentation of mental illness in demonic categories – the authority of this ancient text does not lie in any inherent property it may have but in its unique ability to mediate Christ's presence to us in the here and now (Kelsey 1975, pp.39–50). I am therefore prepared to admit to the difficulties of particular narratives, but would want to argue that these stories are still worth telling for the way in which they reveal God to us and transform the way in which we see the world.

GORDON: And what is your second response?

DAVID: My second response to your question concerns the authority that we attribute to personal experience if we insist upon adopting a critical stance in respect of the stories of our tradition. Whilst the reintroduction of personal experience into theological discourse, largely due to the insistence of practical theologians that our stories of faith arise out of and relate back to the lived experience of women and men, is to be welcomed, I often wonder on what basis we judge our stories to be more truthful than the stories of the tradition? Are we not in danger of giving too much privilege to the present over against the biblical texts? (Thiselton 1992, p.557).

GORDON: But are you simply trying to justify what has happened in our own conversation?

DAVID: I am not sure I understand what you mean.

GORDON: Our aim was to explore various issues concerning the role and function of narrative in relation to the original stories that we wrote to one another. Yet I am painfully aware of how difficult it has been to live up to this aim and how easily we have tended towards the abstract. By devaluing the status of personal experience, could it be that you are simply trying to rationalize our failure to consider our own stories in greater depth?

DAVID: Your specific question will be one for others to deliberate. On a more general level, however, I guess that there is an underlying issue about the way in which narrative theologians have occasionally tended to become abstract in their discussion of stories. Like those who theorize about play, it is perhaps all too easy to become too serious about our play and too abstract about our stories. After all, is it not the case that the best way to learn about stories is to tell them?

GORDON: So surely we must return to our own stories and reflect upon the fact that all our ideas, our insights and considered knowledge, are but grammatical footnotes upon these attempts to narrate the truth of what has happened to us: nothing more, nothing less. Of course, it is hoped that by rehearsing our theological grammar in this way we will be better able to articulate and embody the stories that we tell. But conversations such as these can never be the last word.

DAVID: I cannot begin to sum up the terrain that we have covered in the course of this conversation. In response to what you have said, I am left with a strong sense of how important, and how difficult it is, to remain at the level of story. We shall, no doubt, return to this point as we turn to the role of narrative in the practice of pastoral care and counselling. Allow me at this point, however, simply to leave you with a tale that speaks of God, a theologian, and a story:

> When the great Rabbi Israel Shem Tov saw misfortune threatening the Jews, it was his custom to go into a certain part of the forest to meditate. There he would light a fire, say a special prayer, and the miracle would be accomplished and the misfortune averted. Later, when his disciple, the celebrated Magrid of Mezritch, had occasion, for the same reason, to intercede with heaven, he would go to the same forest and say: 'Master of the Universe, listen! I do not know how to light the fire, but I am still able to say the prayer,' and again the miracle would be accomplished. Still later, Rabbi Moshe-leib of Sasov, in order to save his people once more, would go into the forest and say, 'I do not know how to light the fire. I do not know the prayer, but I know the place and this must be sufficient.' It was sufficient and the miracle was accomplished. Then it fell to Rabbi Israel of Rizhyn to overcome misfortune. Sitting in his armchair, his head in his hands, he spoke to God: 'I am unable to light the fire, and I do not know the prayer, and I cannot even find the place in the forest. All that I can do is to tell the story, and this must be sufficient.' And it was sufficient. God made man because he loves stories. (Bausch 1991, pp.15–16)

Editorial Note:

1   The following extract is taken from a Contact Pastoral monograph under the same title in which the authors attempt to explore the significance of narrative for pastoral theology and practice. This particular extract is the third chapter of this monograph. In the chapters preceding it, Lynch and Willows have discussed the growth of interest in narrative in academic circles and have told stories from their own experience which they try to use as a basis for reflection in the rest of the monograph. In the second chapter of the monograph, this reflection focuses on the social, psychological and existential functions of narrative. This leaves the way open, in the following extract, for a more explicitly theological discussion of the nature and role of story in our lives.

21

The Challenge of Creativity
(1999)

David Aldridge

To make a challenge is both to claim and to accuse. It can also mean to invite or summon, to call into question, to make demands on, and is a call to engage in some sort of activity. This is what I shall be talking about in the course of this paper: how creativity challenges us to engage. I am also aware, however, that the word is related to Latin *caluminia* – the word we know as calumny, and that is to make a false claim. As soon as we talk about being creative, then, we are prey to hubris and the possibility of making claims for something that we perhaps do not possess. The modern meaning of creativity is to produce, to cause to grow, to cause to come into existence (from the Latin *creare*), and also means to be engaged in creative work. Yet, in earlier centuries, to make the claims of being creative would suffer the consequence of being branded a blasphemer. After all, there was only one Creator. It is thus perhaps as well to begin by reminding ourselves of this ancient wisdom; for 'creativity' can surely inflate the ego beyond the boundaries of what is reasonable.

Creativity, the breakthrough moment of 'Aha' or 'Eureka', is common to both the arts and the sciences and the biologist, Konrad Lorenz (Cavanaugh 1994) reminds us that all discovery has the same origin. Biologically and conceptually, the earliest phases are the same. Day by day our senses observe and our subconscious stores data and ideas that are shuffled into theories and hypotheses, ideas that eventually merge into consciousness like underground water emerges as a spring of consciousness or a fountain if it is channelled.

The process of creativity is allied to how children acquire language. While they learn to use words, the epistemological process of knowing, thinking and deciding is not word-dependent. Language comes late in the epistemological narrative. We know about the world by being in it. Experience is lived and only through living can we experience its significance. Our bodies know and therefore communicate a bodily sense of being here, but we create our knowledge as a process of being and acting in the world. How we describe that process – how that knowledge becomes expressed as words – is a part of the narrative. Eventually, when leaving those bodies, we must call upon another set of knowledge, which some of us refer to as spiritual. The soul has its own epistemology, its own way of knowing. Improvised music, then, is the consequence of this expressive stream that comes before words. I shall return to this idea later when I consider dialogue.

The challenge for counsellors and therapists is to promote the creative moment. It is more likely to occur in the prepared person than the unprepared. Or as the Sufis say: the person has to be turning in his or her sleep. It's no use if they are asleep, they are better left undisturbed and if they are already awake, then there is no need to do anything.

How we understand creativity and how we bring that into our daily lives is a challenge – a call to engagement – and as we are talking here about working in the hospice, a call to engagement in the lives of others. Modern thinking about creativity concentrates less on the created product and emphasizes more the process of creating. Rather than isolating the artist and the finished work, there is an emphasis on the artist and the spectator, or in many cases, the performer and the participator. We have then a move from an objective aesthetic, where objects are discussed, to that of a relationship. And it is here that we have the relevance for counselling and the creative arts therapies. It is this concept of relationship that offers a bridge to the consideration of intimacy.

Intimacy

When we come to consider intimacy; then we have another word that is as challenging as creativity. Intimate denotes a warm personal relationship that is deeply personal, private or secret (from the Latin *intimus* – a very close friend – innermost, deepest). Because of the intimations of secrecy and closeness, the term has, in recent years, become euphemistic for a sexual relationship. It is this connotation that brings us difficulty in using intimate in its broader sense; for we have to explain with what we are becoming intimate. In therapy, as in friendship, it is the intimacy of two souls. For the dying, the body is being left behind, and the sexual creativity of reproduction is no longer appropriate. What is necessary is that closeness of human warmth where selves experience understanding. We need to be intimate with the other to come into dialogue, in that dialogue we experience ourselves through others. Creativity is that coming into being with another, being made new, the basis of which is intimacy. Again, we see how the idea of creating something new, that idea of reproductive fruitfulness, could easily be translated into a sexual understanding. And for those of us that have had the opportunity to work creatively, then it is that same vitality and excitement that imbues creative work whether it be artistic or scientific.

This intimacy, like creativity as we read earlier, is not language dependent, it allows for the privacy and primacy of expression within relationship. It is not public like language and therefore not social in its broadest sense. Although to talk about it we have to translate that experience into language, which is dependent upon culture. The experience itself, the knowledge of the world, its epistemology, can be based upon sounds, smells, movements or images. Again, if we reflect upon the sensuality of experience, then we see how intimacy can easily be misinterpreted in terms of sexual connotation. In the intimate creative moment we can experience the consequence of being ourselves as we appear in a relationship. This enables us to express our inner potential for being, something new can emerge, and emerges in the company of another human being. I sometimes think, watching and listening to music therapy sessions, that this is maybe the first time that a person has had chance to listen to themselves, albeit through dialogue with the other. We see and hear ourselves reflected in and through the other and this is a central core of music therapy technique.

Creativity and intimacy also have a relationship to prayer. If prayer is resting intimately in God, then what emerges as an answer to prayer is also an expression of creativity – something new emerging from an intimate relationship.

Dialogue

When we engage communicatively with another then we partake in creating dialogue. A central feature of dialogue is the need to listen to the other. The 'other' is necessary because it allows a distance from narcissism and room for disclosure (Schalow 1998, p.143). The self is opened up to the potential of 'what can be', where the power to speak arises at the threshold of intelligibility. The creative arts are the domain of this threshold of intelligibility, such that what can be can be expressed is expressed but not necessarily in words.

Dialogue is the common *logos* (word) running through two persons together. We are thus endowed with a structure in which our expressions can find a mutual form. Discourse is always with others. We need the other to share the world with and thus experience the very consequences of our being. When we engage in dialogue then we are participating in a reciprocal engagement in truth. We allow something to be seen. We allow something to be heard. We avoid one-sidedness by listening for what governs the dialogue and that is the logic of the mutuality of the form. This is often expressed as harmony between people. Such harmony is not the pursuit of homogeneity but the search for tolerance where we endure the tension of self and other.

Listening is important in dialogue because it is only by entering into the depths of human suffering that we can discern the potential for change. If we allow the other to disclose itself, then we have the allowance of difference and the potential for an acceptance of the other. Unfolding ourselves in this space of reciprocity allows both distance and intimacy to emerge, whereby we can hear the distance between us. Such relationships allow for companionship, whether this is friendship or the more formal relationships of counselling and therapy. If we introduce the concept of silence into this world of relationship, then we leave behind the world and its public sphere and experience the other in privacy. Silence may be the primary realm where we experience the intimacy of conversation. From out of this silence, music and the creative arts can build bridges into a public world of language through varying media of expression.

Inspiration

The link between heart and the organs of sense is not simple mechanical sensationalism; it is aesthetic. That is, the activity of perception or sensation, in Greek is *aisthesis* which means at root 'taking in' and 'breathing in' – a gasp, that primary aesthetic response (Hilman 1981, p.31).

If we are listening, and listening at the deepest level, then we are taking in the other person, and it is this 'taking in' that is seen as being fundamentally aesthetic, which gives us a link to the arts therapies, but also provides us with a link to the concept of inspiration and creativity. Inspiration is often seen as a basis for those significant moments in our lives that we relate to being creative. The ancient Muses inspiring creativity, where transcendental knowledge was brought to human beings, achieved this by whispering, breathing and singing (Hart 1998). It is this inspiration that seems to get the process of creativity going, where an expectant sensitivity of the imminent allows something new to emerge. Again, I would return us to the importance of silence, prayer and meditation for the creative process to begin. A feature of such conditions is an openness to other realms of perception that are sometimes referred to as synaesthetic and are invariably described as being vital and direct and rarely willed.

Creativity then, which is not language dependent, takes place in an intimate relationship of mutual acceptance from out of which emerges something that is new. The possibility is of transcendence and that I shall be arguing later is the basis of hope, and hope is the spiritual force that drives our therapeutic endeavours (Aldridge 1993).

Music therapy in the hospice

Within the past decade music therapists have developed their work with people who have life-threatening illnesses and with those who are dying. Working together, in a creative way, to enhance the quality of living can help patients make sense of dying. It is important for the dying, or those with terminal illness, that approaches are used that integrate the physical, psychological, social and spiritual dimensions of their being (Aldridge 1987, 1996; Greisinger *et al* 1997; Kotarba and Hurt 1995). In addition, how we care for the sick and dying, no matter how they contracted their disease, is a matter of our own personal responsibility and a collective measure of our humanity. Hospice care has met this multifaceted challenge and creative arts therapies are being increasingly used in such situations.

One of the concepts of hospice is to maximize the available quality of life for the terminally-ill resident in the face of impending death. To achieve privacy for patients and their families, while optimizing medical capability, has been a singular aim for many hospice planners. As part of this designed environment, the quality of artworks and the aesthetics of the sound environment makes sense too, and this has led to cooperative initiatives between artists, musicians and clinical staff. Indeed, some clinicians believe that the physical environment has an impact on the treatment process and its outcome (Gross and Swartz 1992). Such considerations are not new, in the ancient Persian system traditional forms of architecture were related to rhythms in music thus defining sacred spaces within the house as within the soul (Bakhtiar 1976). Recently architects and artists have also taken up the challenge to meet the health care needs of patients (Scher 1996).

Creativity

But why be creative, what is the value of the arts in such a situation? Surely modern science has enough to offer us at this time? There lies the difficulty, for although modern medicine uses a scientific basis for much that it does, there are also other perspectives on the world that art and religion bring. Indeed, William James criticizes the scientific ways of viewing the world as colourless and lifeless and we need to develop a vivid face on the world (Capps 1996).

Enabling another to communicate is at the basis of the creative arts therapies, that this communication must not be words alone is at the heart of music therapy (Ansdell 1995; Bruscia 1991; Bunt 1994; Lee 1995). However, whether we use words, vocal sounds or noises, we have a being in the world that is essentially articulated as form, and in the performance of this form – I should say forming – we give creation to that which is within us. When we perform music together, or articulate a poem, then the difference 'me' and 'the other' falls away, and that is perhaps the key to much of what we do as artist-therapists. But forming alone, as an active element, is not enough, there has to be a stuff of which ideas are realized. Music is sensuous. Tones have timbre and can be heard. It is in the forming of the sensuous that we find the creative act, whether it be making music, painting, sculpting or dancing.

In another context I propose that our very identity is a work of art, akin to a piece of music that must be daily improvised (Aldridge 1996; Aldridge in Olesen 1997). Part of our work in life is to clarify that identity we have of ourselves, and to do that we need others. This principle is a basis of therapy, whereby one person helps the other to clarify their true self. That is why we also fall in love, so that our true self is realized by another. One knows oneself by being known by another. Finding out who we are is not simply asking ourselves the question 'Who am I?' but discerning our potential self in another. Thus, falling in love, or the creative intimacy of the therapeutic relationship, are chances we take with another to discover who we are. It is a basic act of recognition. Recognition in the creative act of coming into being and is fundamental to the mutual recognition of mother and infant (Capps 1996). That is why creative intimacy is important for the therapeutic relationship but demands an awareness such that professional boundaries are not transgressed.

A basic tenet of psychotherapy has been that therapists need supervision to manage such dilemmas of distance and is vital for the protection of both therapist and patient. Norman Fischer (1997) writes:

Aesthetically the work of art creates a world with its own logic, one that is simply not dictated by the facts. The two ideas, a work of art with its own logic and of ethical principles that in reflecting on the world present reasons that are not in the world, are united through the common denominator of distance. (p.377)

This tension of intimacy and distance reflects the inner tensions of arts that are also therapies. There is an internal aesthetic that must comply to an external pragmatic; individual creativity conforming to a public expectancy within a helping relationship. This is the challenge of creativity in the arts therapies.

My friend George

Each individual composes the music of his own life. If he injures another he breaks the harmony, and there is discord in the melody of life (Khan 1979).

I would like to conclude with an example of how music, at the initiative of a friend who was dying, promoted various creative responses from family and friends. My friend George was diagnosed as having a chronic form of leukaemia. We were both at that time in our mid-thirties. We both had families, each having children of the same school ages, and we both were moderately successful in our careers in health-care practice. All seemed rosy in the garden. We both liked to run. George, however, decided that he needed a challenge in his life and running a marathon would be just what he needed. So, to satisfy the race rules, he went for a medical check-up. Until then he felt well enough to run. Check-ups are dangerous. Something was very wrong with his blood, he discovered. Within days he was in hospital awaiting a bone-marrow transplant. Road runner to invalid in one fell swoop.

In the hospital he couldn't sleep and asked me to help him with relaxation techniques and hypnosis that he was already acquainted with through his reading, not practice. These simple techniques worked, and when he was first released from hospital we talked about what other techniques could be used to combat what was to be a long and tiring series of treatments. I use the word combat here as that was exactly as George saw the task before him, an uphill struggle against an unseen enemy. That was his metaphor, a battle, and from that he gained strength.

Through the following months we used guided imagery to bring about a progressive relaxation and to help him through the anxiety of the consultations and to motivate him through treatment. I worked closely with his haematologist and oncologist who too was interested in how we could address the many problems facing George as it became clear that the techniques to heal his bone marrow were without success. Each treatment would bring expectations and each set of tests would end in despair. George was a believer in technology and his beloved technology was letting him down. We also went to the same church and I guess his beloved God was letting him down too.

At that time the local church was engaged in a healing ministry. Friends and family would work with the parish priest to visit the sick, to administer the sacrament of healing and to celebrate the Eucharist in the patients home. This was an ecumenical initiative that brought many people together within a small community. Some medical practitioners were actively supported as the parish served a local general hospital, others were sceptical but saw little threat from a well-meaning laity. A contact with the local hospice was also encouraged as the healing ministry of the church offered a long-term contact before the acute stages of dying. George and his wife were pleased to have other congregation members into their home. While the future looked bleak, there was temporary relief and always the opportunity for him to talk about what was important at the time with his friends. This could be planning the future schooling of the children, the best possible diet for promoting energy, the meaning of the sacrament of the blood of Christ (to someone with leukaemia this has an urgent meaning), or what relaxation technique to use next.

One day we knew that the bone marrow changes would not work. George was dying. His oncologist didn't know what to do and I didn't know what to do. So standing awkward and helpless in George's living room one day, I had to admit to him that I was running out of ideas. Now, how do you say that as a practitioner of any persuasion? But it was true, and George was my friend, and that made it even more tragic. 'Why don't you sing for me', he said. At that time I had not heard of music therapy. I couldn't chicken out and ask for a music therapist. So, I sang. We sang. We were both fans of the English folk-song revival and had similar record collections. From our common geographical backgrounds we enjoyed the robustness of the 'Watersons'. We could also belt out a convincing repertoire of Church hymns even though the words may not have been entirely correct and true to the original. In that moment, music brought us to another level of intimacy within a friendship that was important. If the reader has an image of boys in a choir then he or she will not be far wrong.

We had of course prayed and meditated. I was teaching meditation techniques to other groups at that time. But music was something that we could do together, the mutuality of listening and singing had an extra dimension. And it was in the use of songs that we could explore those feelings about our lives that we would not have addressed in conversation. As Englishmen, there were some things that we didn't talk about openly, like tenderness and vulnerability. Indeed, we had been actively encouraged not to talk about such things, particularly at school, as people would think we were sissy. Yet, such expressions were going to be vital because George had a family that needed his tenderness and he needed theirs in return. Expressing his vulnerability, previously disguised as irritation, would be an important milestone along his own personal way towards death. In a world where emotions are expressed publicly, it can all too often seem that only the loudest, coarsest expressions are appreciated. Yet many of us know that what contributes to our value is those feelings that are private and subtle. Music therapy, with its potential for the quiet and the delicate, as well as the loud and the coarse, lends itself to the exposition of that which we may call sublime.

The church group coming to visit him also sang for him too. From these songs, George could plan his funeral and it was through these songs that we had our deepest personal memories of him. It was in song too that I could express to George what friendship meant to me and what happens when friends don't see each other any more.

In song, we had both the possibilities for creating personal intimacy, of saying what lay upon our hearts. But there was also a social function of shared music. Family and friends could gather together and sing with him, there were the possibilities of expression already present in well-known songs that could be activated for those who were singing.

Songs took George into the future of his funeral where he would be remembered, but we could also remember him too. Undoubtedly this helped us in our grieving. But there is another important factor in that when I hear those songs today I remember our friendship, George and his family, in all its depth and closeness. This reminiscence is also important for those who grieve and remain.

22

Passion and Pain

Conceiving Theology out of Infertility (1999)

Heather Walton

Moving in the shadows; joined into a circle; beaten like a drum. Women in a hospital for wombs.

I have come to this place. I came after a long journey but I am still not sure I should be here. I feel it may be a mistake but that cannot be seen yet. I am the last to arrive. It is past the time printed on my official 'invitation' card. The other women have made camp already. There is one who smiles and introduces herself. 'I am a minister's wife.' She has already submitted and removed her clothes. She sits neatly in her petalled night-dress and matching dressing gown which buttons to the floor. Already there are flowers on her bedside cabinet. Lemon carnations, gypsophelia and fern.

The woman who wears her husband's big shirt as hospital costume over her gently swelling stomach has no flowers, no sponge bag, towel or new soap. There is no travelling bag beside her bed or books or magazines. All she has is the shirt she took off her man's back and she was lucky he was with her when she went for her normal outpatients appointment at the antenatal clinic. They admitted her straight away, two storeys up from the place of pregnancy, and this is all she could think of to wear.

Her baby is dead. The baby has been dead for a while but she still looks rosy and fruitful. Her pregnancy makes her appear childlike and tender. We all wish to nurture and protect her. No one can really believe that the baby is dead. She felt fine this morning, feels fine now. Her husband will come back in the evening with her suitcase and the flowers. Maybe we will all believe it then. I do not think we can grasp that the doctors are allowing a dead child to spread its arms around a living body like this. It has been left for a night to celebrate a warm, blood and salt wake with her. If the baby were really dead surely they would have moved heaven and earth; altered all the schedules and taken it away. Pumped out all the traces.

We are three children but there is another person in this place. We have to comfort a beautiful, wise, fat old mother. She gathers us together and she is going to protect us all, the minister's wife, the woman with her lost baby and even me. We sit upon her bed and begin to chatter like girls just home from school telling the day. Soon we are laughing. 'Well,' says our mother, 'we might as well enjoy ourselves tonight because we won't be doing any dancing in the morning.'

If we are not chattering tomorrow hers will be the deepest silence. She will not be dancing for many days because they are going to cut her womb right away. For several years they have been demanding to do this but always before she said no. She does not know why she said yes now except that it came to her to do so while she was on holiday in Spain. And she recently moved away from Birmingham which was a city she never liked.

So there are four of us together on this little side ward but really it is only an alcove; part of a much longer ward. When evening visiting is over we venture out to meet the other women from the shadows. Of all the women I am the only one still wearing her own clothes, her own shoes and scent. Everyone else is wearing a long gown to celebrate her part in our collective rite. Despite this I am welcomed into the flickering intimacy of the TV room – we are all welcome here.

One woman begins to tell her story. 'Before I had my baby I had already lost one fallopian tube. Then after I'd had her I went for family planning and they asked me what I'd like and I said I don't know. The easiest.'

This woman is eating chocolate. She is twenty-five years old and she is very thin. The story goes on,

'Well they gave me an injection it was depot provera. After that it was awful. I had pain and bleeding. Now they tell me my other tube might need to be removed. I don't think what they did was right. They never asked me my medical history or anything. Just stuck the needle in and that was that.'

I can't get over the fact that this woman, who is young and middle class, who is married to a dentist for goodness sake, would go around allowing people to stick needles into her like that. Where has she been for all her life not to have known about the dangers of such treatment? But I do not say anything to criticize. I do not open my mouth and voice my feelings. Not tonight in this place. We are telling tales of fate not judgement.

I know this to be the case when my turn comes; when the lot falls to me. A woman turns to me and asks 'You haven't any little ones yourself?'

Tears come to the back of my eyes and flow out with the answer. They have been waiting there for months. This is so. I have no children. The minister's wife and myself have only a partial claim to our place amongst the women. We wish to, but we do not conceive.

I have no children and in the outside world I have denied that I desire them. I do not admit this limitation of my powers. I am a strong person. I have not taken off my clothes like these others. I don't wear slippers to walk along silently by their side.

But here I can be pitied. See how much I need this pity. I need it even more than the minister's wife because in her community such a loss is public knowledge. There is always someone considered wise at the end of a telephone line and her elderly parents support her with encouragement prayer. The younger women always come and tell her first about their pregnancies and she can prepare herself with dignity. She does not have to hear of other women's 'visitations' on crowded social occasions. She does not have to clap and kiss and laugh – and pray the tears will not break through.

The woman who rocks her dead baby inside her rocks me in her arms. There are tears running along her cheeks as she holds me fiercely and those tears are flowing for me. 'At least I've got three lying safe in bed at home.' I have never in my life seen anything so powerfully sad as a woman in the fullness of pregnancy whose baby lies dead in the safe bed inside her. She holds me pressed against it; against her. She knows I have inside me countless dead babies who have not even the grave mound of her own. She recognizes them. She sees them although outside this place they are never seen. I do not cry loudly. We drink tea in the television room and most of the women smoke.

Lying in the bed I cannot decide whether to listen to the radio or to try to sleep. My cubicle is next to the window. We are on the third floor and overlook the living city. My home is not far away. My partner and my friends are sleeping. Two floors up women are giving birth but their cries cannot reach me here.

My operation is not scheduled till 11am but still they wake me at 6.30am and say I must shower. The minister's wife says, and our mother agrees, that you absolutely must not use soap when you wash before an operation. They say this is definitely true and it is for medical reasons although they don't know what they are. 'But,' I say, 'nobody has told us not to use soap.' It is difficult to think well because we are not allowed tea or even water to rinse our mouths. We are in danger of quarrelling over this soap issue so I withdraw. I sit on my bed and think what reason might there be not to use soap. I cannot think of any. I will act like a grown woman and use the nice soap I bought. On an empty stomach its scent is very strong. I feel a bit sick.

What you must wear is a cotton robe that has a slit down the back. It is supposed to tie with strings but it is very old and there are none. I fasten mine with a safety pin from my purse. If I did not have this I would have needed to lie on my back for all the hours before they come to me. But I am up and I am walking.

I go to visit the woman who was given depot provera. She has already had a pre-med and looks relaxed and content. She must be lucid though because she is doing a crossword. I try to tell her what I have been thinking. Other women need to be protected against what has happened to her. She must write it all down. There is an organization that is campaigning. They will not betray any confidences. I know someone she can contact who is very nice. I have her address here, write it on the corner of her magazine.

But she is at peace and smiling. I feel like someone trying to turn a bride against marriage. She is set on her own course now and all she can offer me is kindness. I shiver because her calm acceptance has turned me into a bitter barren woman. I just return to my bed and lie back passive like the others. Back on my side ward the minister's wife has drawn her curtains and I assume that she is praying. The other two are drowsy and silent. I take the pre-med tablets for something to do and let the voices from the radio speak to each other over my headphones as the slow minutes pass.

The minister's wife has already been taken but it is only ten o'clock and I am not ready when the cheerful porter comes for me. I tell him that I'm not scheduled till eleven but he doesn't listen. They may give me the wrong operation and I will wake up without a womb at all. Sit up as the porter wheels me through the corridors on a trolley. This doesn't feel too safe around the corners. I would have walked but even with the safety pin this gown offers little cover.

I am frightened. Not because I think I might not wake up but in case I am awake all the time. When I say this they laugh. The anaesthetist says not to worry. This injection is not like the one you have at the dentists. There will be just a little scratch and then nothing at all.

When I become conscious again the brilliant thoughts that have been tumbling through my brain move beyond my reach. I know that they were there but now I cannot grasp them. This is a grief feeling, and a feeling of loss, and then there is pain. They have blown up my stomach with CO_2 and inserted a camera through a small cut into my belly. They are attempting to see my infertility. What they have done in my vagina, to the cervix, the neck of the womb, I do not know. I just know there is pain there too. The worst feelings come from the air that is still in my stomach and is gripping me with cramps. I lie still and hope it will all pass and that I might sleep again soon.

And then, at the second surfacing, thoughts are clearer and the pain is worse. It is lunch time in the recovery room and there are no porters to take us back to the ward. Two nurses are talking softly and a woman is being sick. I have said twice that I am awake but nobody answers. The canvas sheet beneath me (this is used to tip you from stretcher to bed) is soaked through. I don't know whether it is blood or urine. I manage to sit up. That brings a nurse to me. 'Don't try to move.' I tell her I am wet and in pain and want some water. She brings a lint square lined with plastic and places it under me. The comfort is immediate. She replaces the wet towel beneath my legs with a dry one. She wets my lips with water and I am comforted. Lying back on the stretcher I try to enter their conversation. I think I am intelligent and funny. They take no notice of me at all.

When the porter comes I make a great show of being alert. He says, 'It's the heavy drinkers always come round first.' Because I am so well recovered, he asks me if I want to edge myself from the stretcher to the bed. Because of my pride, I say yes but it is almost more than I can manage.

I only wish to sleep and when my partner comes in the afternoon I look how I did not imagine I would look. I am like the rest: a patient in a hospital bed. My hands are limp and my face is pale. I am still wearing the white gown. I am unresponsive and have no resistance left but he has brought me a gift. It is exactly the right gift. Tall, full, wide goblet tulips. Scarlet with black at the centre. Velvet petals from scarlet to black. Flowers of passion and pain opening wider and wider in the warmth of the hospital ward.

It is only much later when I begin to think about those around me. The minister's wife is clutching a cardboard dish into which she tries to vomit, but nothing comes up with her retching. The green curtains are tightly drawn around the bed of our mother. I am surprised to see that the pregnant woman is sat in her chair reading a magazine. She is eating biscuits. It is not a quick recovery. She has not been to theatre. No anaesthetist was available for her! Why not, for her alone? She was the one most in need of all. I feel ashamed but she seems glad that someone has regained sense enough to talk to her. She helps me take off the white gown and slips the new night-dress I bought for this wedding over my head.

In the morning, I am well enough to eat breakfast and to look strong and capable for the doctors when they come on their visit. Again the minister's wife is called for first and, although they draw the curtains around her bed, I can hear every word. They say one tube is atrophied and useless the other tube is also damaged and she has scars that have come from menses which bleed wrongly on the inside of her body.

'The cure we use for this condition is the contraceptive pill but of course you want to conceive. And you are not getting any younger. If you take the pill your insides will heal and there will be a better environment to conceive. But if you stop taking the pill there is no guarantee that the bleeding will not start again. This will bring you back to the start of the cycle.'

They should not give this woman such cruel riddles.

They say to her that *in vitro fertilization* must be her best option but I already know that this woman would accept any miracle, any intervention by the hand of God; but not this one. Not from human hands. There could be no worse news. Briskly, they draw the curtains open and reveal her sitting upright and shocked. They come to enclose me in a green cave.

I am fortunate because I have no scars inside and no bleeding. My tubes are delicate and supple. They move gently to deliver the egg each month to exactly the right place. They have observed all these things and they tell me they are beautiful.

But I too am left with a riddle. 'You can of course conceive, but you do not in fact conceive.' Perhaps I am possessed. They say, 'to you too we can offer the exorcism of IVF. We have no weaker medicine today.' I detain them with questions which they cannot answer and they are impatient to move on. The walls of the cave are drawn back again. I go to embrace the minister's wife. She has no problems about weeping in the arms of a feminist. We are all together here.

At coffee time the two of us are pale but dressed and wearing shoes. We sit with our drinks in the day room waiting to be collected. The pregnant woman is with us and she still has not heard when her operation will be. Also with us, in the day room, is a young woman who has just arrived. She wears metal-rimmed glasses and has a cardboard suitcase with a metal handle. She shrinks away from us. She creates a screen with a novel and French cigarettes. She has a great horror of us but I am rude enough to break in.

'It's for a termination. An abortion. I'm really sorry. I know it must seem awful to you. Obscene. God they shouldn't put women desperate to get rid and women miscarrying everything together. They shouldn't mix us together like this. I'm sorry.'

I try to remember how I once felt about this issue. In the abstract it seemed awful putting women needing abortions with women losing babies, unable to conceive. In reality it feels there can't be another way. We are together in this place and that doesn't seem like an awful thing, not to any of us, even the minister's wife. We are only sorry that she feels so alone, so strained.

I reach for her hand. Dear little sister, when we are here we tell tales of fate and judgement. Even if you clutch your suitcase, your novel and your cigarettes, you won't be excluded. I will leave you my flowers. They are special. They are not anaemic carnations or embryo roses. They are tall goblet tulips brimming with passion and pain. You will like them. I came here in secret too and I am leaving unbowed as you will.

Moving in the shadows; joined into a circle; beaten like a drum. Women in a hospital for wombs.

This hospital is the same place exactly as the whole universe. I have brought you to a place in which you may recognize God and know yourself. When you understand this you can smile at the small stories of human freedom and divine judgement which are told for children. They are charms recited to protect against the passion and the pain. There are darker, deeper tales to tell.

You begin to understand when you hold your sister to you. Her baby is dead inside her. Or perhaps she is preparing to end a life that was ill conceived. Maybe, just perhaps, in the future the almost impossible birth might take place in one of us. But not yet. All of your life you have been told only to look towards the light. Now you may begin to see beyond the little lights and into the greater darkness.

Here is your faith
God is God
Of the Living and the Dead.
This is how theology is done.

References

Aldridge, D. (1987) 'Families, cancer and dying.' *Family Practice 4*, 212–218.

Aldridge, D. (1993) 'Hope, meaning and the creative art therapies in the treatment of AIDS.' *The Arts in Psychotherapy 20*, 285–297.

Aldridge, D. (1996) *Music Therapy Research and Practice in Medicine: From Out of the Silence.* London: Jessica Kingsley Publishers.

Aldridge, D. (1997) 'Lifestyle, charismatic ideology and a praxis aesthetic.' In S. Olesen *et al.* (eds) *Studies in Alternative Therapy 4: Lifestyle and Medical Paradigms.* Odense: Odense University Press.

Aldridge, D. (1999) 'The challenge of creativity.' *Contact: The Interdisciplinary Journal of Pastoral Studies 129*, 3–11.

Alexander, M. (ed) (1966) *The Earliest English Poems.* Harmondsworth: Penguin Books.

Alves, R. (1984) *What is Religion?* Mary Knoll, NY: Orbis Books.

Ansdell, G. (1995) *Music for Life: Aspects of Creative Music Therapy with Adult Clients.* London: Jessica Kingsley Publishers.

Arbuckle, D. (ed) (1967) *Counselling and Psychotherapy.* New York: McGraw.

Association for Pastoral Care and Counselling (1974) *Constitutional Papers.* London: APCC.

Auerbach, E. (1953) *Mimesis: The Representation of Reality in Western Literature.* Princeton, NJ: Princeton University Press.

Bakhtiar, L. (1976) *Sufi: Expressions of the Mystic Quest.* London: Thames & Hudson.

Ballard, P.H. (ed) (1986) *The Foundations of Pastoral Studies and Practical Theology.* Cardiff: Faculty of Theology, University College, Cardiff.

Ballard, P.H. (1992) 'Can theology be practical?' *Contact: The Interdisciplinary Journal of Pastoral Studies 109*, 3–11.

Barnhouse, R.T. (1979) 'Spiritual direction and psychotherapy.' *Journal of Pastoral Care 33*, 149–163.

Barr, J. (1973) *The Bible in the Modern World.* London: SCM Press.

Bausch, W. (1991) *Storytelling: Imagination and Faith.* Mystic, CT: Twenty-Third Publications.

Bennett, A. (1998) *The Complete Talking Heads.* London: BBC Worldwide.

Berger, P. (1980) *The Heretical Imperative: Contemporary Possibilities of Religious Affirmation.* London: Collins.

Berhorst, C. (1974) 'The Chimaltenango project – Guatemala.' *Contact: Christian Medical Commission of the WCC, 19.*

Billings, A. (1992) 'Pastors or counsellors?' *Contact: The Interdisciplinary Journal of Pastoral Studies 108*, 3–9.

Bion, W.R. (1961) *Experiences in Groups: And Other Papers.* London: Tavistock Publications.

Birchenall, P. and Birchenall, M. (1986) 'Caring for mentally handicapped people: the community and the church.' *The Professional Nurse 1, 6*, 150ff.

Black, D. (1991) *A Place for Exploration: The Story of the Westminster Pastoral Foundation 1969–1990*. London: Westminster Pastoral Foundation.

Blake, W. (1961) *Poetry and Prose of William Blake*. London: Nonesuch Press.

Bloomfield, I. (1978) 'Religion and psychotherapy: friends or foes?' *Contact: The Interdisciplinary Journal of Pastoral Studies 61*, 3–12.

Bondi, R.C. (1983) 'Apophatic theology.' In J. Bowden and A. Richardson (eds) *A New Dictionary of Christian Theology*. London: SCM Press.

Bowden, J. (1988) *Jesus, The Unanswered Questions*. London: SCM Press.

Boyd, K. (1980) 'Pain, sickness and suffering.' *Contact: The Interdisciplinary Journal of Pastoral Studies 69*, 23–31.

Browning, D. (1977) 'Pastoral care and models of training in counselling.' *Contact: The Interdisciplinary Journal of Pastoral Studies 57*, 12–19.

Browning, D. (ed) (1983a) *Practical Theology: The Emerging Field in Theology, Church and World*. San Francisco: Harper & Row.

Browning, D. (1983b) *Religious Ethics and Pastoral Care*. Philadelphia: Fortress Press.

Browning, D. (1991) *A Fundamental Practical Theology: Descriptive and Strategic Proposals*. Minneapolis, MN: Fortress Press.

Bruscia, K. (1991) *Case Studies in Music Therapy*. Phoenixville, PA: Barcelona Publishers.

Buber, M. (1963) *Werke* (vol. III). München: Kösel-Verlag.

Bunt, L. (1994) *Music Therapy: An Art Beyond Words*. London: Routledge.

Burkhart, J. (1983) 'Schleiermacher's vision for theology.' In D. Browning (ed) *Practical Theology: The Emerging Field in Theology, Church and World*. San Francisco: Harper & Row.

Byrne, L. and Jenkins, D. (1994) 'Catholicism in the future: a dialogue.' In J. John (ed) *Living the Mystery: Affirming Catholicism and The Future of Anglicanism*. London: Darton, Longman & Todd.

Campbell, A.V. (1979) 'The politics of pastoral care.' *Contact: The Interdisciplinary Journal of Pastoral Studies 62*, 2–15.

Campbell, A.V. (1986) *Rediscovering Pastoral Care* (second edn). London: Darton, Longman & Todd.

Campbell, A.V. (ed) (1987) *A Dictionary of Pastoral Care*. London: SPCK.

Campbell, J. (1976) *The Masks of God: Creative Mythology*. Harmondsworth: Penguin Books.

Capps, D. (1996) 'Erikson's "inner space": where art and religion converge.' *Journal of Religion and Health 35*, 93–115.

Capra, F. (1982) *The Turning Point: Science, Society and the Rising Culture*. London: Fontana.

Caussade, J-P. de (1959) *Self Abandonment to Divine Providence*. London: Burns & Oates.

Cavanaugh, M. (1994) 'The precursors of the Eureka moment as a common ground between science and theology.' *Zygon 29*, 191–203.

Chesterton, G.K. (1961) *Orthodoxy*. London: Fontana

Church of England. Commission on Urban Priority Areas (1985) *Faith in the City: A Call for Action by Church and Nation*. London: Church House Publishing.

Church of England. House of Bishops (1991) *Issues in Human Sexuality*. London: Church House Publishing.

Clebsch, W.A. and Jaekle, C.R. (1964) *Pastoral Care in Historical Perspective.* New Jersey: Prentice-Hall.

Clinebell, H.J. (1965) *Mental Health Through Christian Community: The Local Church's Ministry of Growth and Healing.* Nashville, TN: Abingdon Press.

Clinebell, H.J. (1966) *Basic Types of Pastoral Counselling: Resources for the Ministry of Healing and Growth.* Nashville, TN: Abingdon Press.

Clinebell, H.J. and Seifort, H. (1969) *Personal Growth and Social Change: A Guide for Ministers and Laymen as Change Agents.* Philadelphia, PA: Westminster Press.

Collins, G. (1980) *Christian Counselling.* Berkhamsted: Word Books.

Connolly, J. (ed) (1978) *Therapy Options in Psychiatry.* Tunbridge Wells: Pitman Medical.

Coulson, J. (1970) *Newman and the Common Tradition: A Study in the Language of Church and Society.* Oxford: Clarendon Press.

Crabb, L. (1985) *Effective Biblical Counselling.* London: Marshall-Pickering.

Crites, S. (1989) 'The narrative quality of experience.' In S. Hauerwas and L. Gregory Jones (eds) *Why Narrative? Readings in Narrative Theology.* Grand Rapids, MI: Eerdmans.

Cupitt, D. (1991) *What is a Story?* London: SCM Press.

Daly, M. (1979) *Gyn/Ecology: The Metaethics of Radical Counselling.* London: The Women's Press.

Daly, M. (1984) *Pure Lust.* London: The Women's Press.

De Gruchy, J. (1986) *Theology and Ministry in Context and Crisis: A South African Perspective.* London: Collins.

Dodson Gray, E. (ed) (1988) *Sacred Dimensions of Women's Experience.* Wellesley, MA: Roundtable Press.

Dostoyevsky, F. (1958) *The Brothers Karamazov.* Harmondsworth: Penguin Books.

Duke, J.O. and Stone, H. (1988) *Christian Caring: Selections from Practical Theology.* Philadelphia, PA: Fortress Press.

Dyson, A.O. (1982) 'Theology and the educational principles in ministerial training.' *Kairos 6,* 4–15.

Dyson, A.O. (1983) 'Pastoral theology: towards a new discipline.' *Contact: The Interdisciplinary Journal of Pastoral Studies 78,* 2–8.

Eckhart, M. (1980) *Breakthrough: Meister Eckhart's Creation Spirituality in New Translation.* New York: Doubleday.

Epston, D. and White, M. (1990) *Narrative Means to Therapeutic Ends.* London: Norton.

Erikson, E.H. (1968) *Identity, Youth and Crisis.* London: Faber.

Evans, R.A. and Parker, T.D. (eds) (1976) *Christian Theology: A Case Method Approach.* New York: Harper & Row.

Eysenck, H.J. and Eysenck, M.W. (1985) *Personality and Individual Differences: A Natural Science Approach.* New York: Plenum Press.

Eysenck, S.B.G., Eysenck, H.J. and Barrett, P. (1985) 'A revised version of the psychoticism scale.' *Personality and Individual Differences 6,* 21–29.

Farley, E. (1983) *Theologia: The Fragmentation and Unity of Theological Education.* Philadelphia, PA: Fortress Press.

Farley, E. (1987) 'Interpreting situations: an inquiry into the nature of practical theology.' In L.S. Mudge and J.N. Poling (eds) *Formation and Reflection: The Promise of Practical Theology.* Philadelphia, PA: Fortress Press.

Fierro, A. (1977) *The Militant Gospel: An Analysis of Contemporary Political Theologies.* London: SCM Press.

Fischer, N. (1997) 'Frankfurt school of Marxism and the ethical meaning of art: Herbert Marcuse's "The Aesthetic Dimension".' *Communication Theory 7,* 362–381.

Foskett, J. (1985) 'Pastoral counselling.' *British Journal of Guidance and Counselling 13,* 1, 98–111.

Foskett, J. (1994) 'Seeing is believing.' *Journal of Pastoral Care 48,* 363–369.

Foskett, J. and Lyall, D. (1988) *Helping the Helpers: Supervision and Pastoral Care.* London: SPCK.

Foucault, M. (1977) *Discipline and Punish: The Birth of Prison.* London: Allen Lane.

Foucault, M. (1978) *The History of Sexuality.* London: Allen Lane.

Francis, L.J. (1991) 'The personality characteristics of Anglican ordinands: feminine men and masculine women?' *Personality and Individual Differences 12,* 1133–1140.

Francis, L.J. (1992) 'Male and female clergy in England: their personality differences, gender reversal?' *Journal of Empirical Theology 5,* 2, 31–38.

Francis, L.J., Fulljames, P. and Kay, W.K. (1992) 'The functioning of the EPQ lie scale among religious subjects in England.' *Journal of Psychology and Christianity 11,* 255–261.

Francis, L.J. and Pearson, P.R. (1991) 'Personality characteristics of mid-career Anglican clergy.' *Social Behaviour and Personality 19,* 81–84.

Francis, L.J. and Rodger, R. (1994) 'The personality profile of Anglican clergymen.' *Contact: The Interdisciplinary Journal of Pastoral Studies 113,* 27–32.

Francis L.J. and Thomas, T.H. (1992) 'Personality profile of conference-going clergy in England.' *Psychological Reports 70,* 682.

Frankl, V. (1964) *Man's Search For Meaning.* Harmondsworth: Penguin Books.

Frankl, V. (1973) *The Doctor and the Soul: From Psychotherapy to Logotherapy.* Harmondsworth: Penguin Books.

Furnham, A. (1992) *Personality at Work: The Role of Individual Differences in the Workplace.* London: Routledge.

Gennep, A. van (1960) *The Rites of Passage.* London: Routledge & Kegan Paul.

Geertz, C. (1991) *The Interpretation of Cultures: Selected Essays.* London: Fontana.

Gibran, K. (1976) *The Prophet.* London: Heinemann.

Glasse, J.D. (1972) *Putting it Together in the Parish.* Nashville, TN: Abingdon Press.

Glaz, M. and Moessner, J. (1991) *Women in Travail and Transition: A New Pastoral Care.* Minneapolis, MN: Fortress Press.

Goodacre, D. (1980) 'Politics and perennial tragedy.' *Careme,* August, 32.

Graham, E. (1994) 'Truth or dare? Sexuality, liturgy and pastoral theology.' *Contact: The Interdisciplinary Journal of Pastoral Studies 115,* 3–9.

Graham, E. and Halsey M. (eds) (1993) *Lifecycles: Women and Pastoral Care.* London: SPCK.

Graham, G. (1990) *The Idea of Christian Charity: A Critique of Some Contemporary Conceptions.* London: Collins.

Grainger, R. (1988) *The Message of the Rite: The Significance of Christian Rites of Passage.* Cambridge, MA: Lutterworth.

Green, L. (1987) *Power to the Powerless: Theology Brought to Life.* Basingstoke: Marshall, Morgan & Scott.

Green, L. (1990) *Let's Do Theology: A Pastoral Cycle Resource Book.* London: Mowbray.

Greisinger, A. *et al* (1997) 'Terminally ill cancer patients: their most important concerns.' *Cancer Practice 5,* 147–154.

Gerkin, C. (1984) *The Living Human Document: Re-visioning Pastoral Counselling in a Hermeneutical Mode.* Nashville, TN: Abingdon Press.

Groome, T. (1987) 'Theology on our feet: a revisionist pedagogy for healing the gap between Academia and Ecclesia.' In L.S. Mudge and J.N. Poling (eds) *Formation and Reflection: The Promise of Practical Theology.* Philadelphia, PA: Fortress Press.

Gross, J.L. and Swartz, R. (1992) 'The effects of music therapy on anxiety in chronically ill patients.' *Music Therapy 2,* 43–52.

Gutierrez, G. (1974) *A Theology of Liberation: History, Politics and Salvation.* London: SCM Press.

Halmos, P. (1965) *The Faith of the Counsellors.* London: Constable.

Halmos, P. (1978) *The Personal and the Political: Social Work and Political Action.* London: Hutchison.

Hamilton, W. (1993) *A Quest for the Post Historical Jesus.* London: SCM Press.

Hampshire, S. (ed) (1978) *Public and Private Morality.* Cambridge: Cambridge University Press.

Hampshire, S. (1978) 'Public and private morality.' In S. Hampshire (ed) *Public and Private Morality.* Cambridge: Cambridge University Press.

Hart, T. (1998) 'Inspiration: exploring the experience and its meaning.' *Journal of Humanistic Psychology 38,* 7–35.

Hauerwas, S. (1981) *A Community of Character: Toward a Constructive Christian Social Ethic.* Indiana, IN: University of Notre Dame.

Hauerwas, S. and Gregory Jones, L. (eds) (1989) *Why Narrative? Readings in Narrative Theology.* Grand Rapids, MI: Eerdmans.

Hesse, H. (1978) *Siddhartha.* London: Picador.

Higher Education Policy Group (1974) *Some Policy Issues in Higher Education: A Group Report.* London: The Group.

Hilman, J. (1981) *The Thought of the Heart.* Dallas, TX: Spring.

Hiltner, S. (1958) *Preface to Pastoral Theology.* Nashville, TN: Abingdon Press.

Holeton, D. (1990) 'Liturgical research and pastoral liturgy.' *Anglican Theological Review 72,* 3, 313–323.

Hopewell, J.F. (1989) *Congregation: Stories and Structures.* Philadelphia, PA: Fortress Press.

Houston, D. (1978) 'Affirmation and sacrifice in everyday life and in social work.' In N. Timms and D. Watson (eds) *Philosophy of Social Work.* London: Routledge & Kegan Paul.

Hurding, R. (1985) *Roots and Shoots: A Guide to Counselling and Psychotherapy.* London: Hodder & Stoughton.

Jacobs, M. (1982) *Still Small Voice: A Practical Introduction to Counselling for Pastors and Other Helpers.* London: SPCK.

Jacobs, M. (1985a) *The Presenting Past: An Introduction to Practical Psychodynamic Counselling*. London: Harper & Row.

Jacobs, M. (1985b) 'Pastoral counselling and psychotherapy.' *Contact: The Interdisciplinary Journal of Pastoral Studies 86*, 2–8.

Jacobs, M. (1987) 'Counselling.' In A.V. Campbell (ed) *A Dictionary of Pastoral Care*. London: SPCK.

Jacobs, M. (1988) 'The use of story in pastoral care.' *Contact: The Interdisciplinary Journal of Pastoral Studies 95*, 14–21 and *96*, 12–17.

James, W. (1956) *The Will to Believe*. London: Constable.

Jones, D. and Francis, L.J. (1992) 'Personality profile of Methodist ministers in England.' *Psychological Reports 70*, 538.

Jung, C.J. (1973) *Memories, Dreams, Reflections*. London: Fontana.

Kelsey, D.H. (1975) *The Uses of Scripture in Recent Theology*. London: SCM Press.

Khan, S.I. (1979) *The Bowl of Saki*. London: Sufi Publishing Company Ltd.

Kierkegaard, S. (1941) *Training in Christianity*. Oxford: Oxford University Press.

Kirk, K. (1939) *The Study of Theology*. London: Hodder & Stoughton.

Kitwood, T. (1990) *Concern for Others: A New Psychology of Conscience and Morality*. London: Routledge.

Klinkenbeard, H. (1984) 'Mental handicap chaplaincy.' (unpublished paper delivered to conference on Mental Handicap at Woodlands Hospital in Aberdeen).

Knox, J. (1994) *John Knox: On Rebellion*. Cambridge: Cambridge University Press.

Kotarba, J.A. and Hurt, D. (1995) 'An ethnography of an AIDS hospice: towards a theory of organizational pastiche.' *Symbolic Interaction 18*, 413–438.

Lake, F. (1966) *Clinical Theology: A Theological and Psychiatric Basis to Clinical Pastoral Care*. London: Darton, Longman & Todd.

Lake, F. (1980) 'The theology of pastoral counselling.' *Contact: The Interdisciplinary Journal of Pastoral Studies 68*, 1–48.

Lamb, M. (1976) 'The theory-praxis relationship in contemporary Christian theologies.' *Proceedings of the Catholic Theological Society of America*. (conference paper).

Lambourne, R.A. (1971) 'Objections to a national pastoral organization.' *Contact: The Interdisciplinary Journal of Pastoral Studies 35*, 24–31.

Lambourne, R.A. (1974) 'Personal reformation and political formation in pastoral care.' *Contact: The Interdisciplinary Journal of Pastoral Studies 44*, 30–40.

Lambourne, R.A. (1983) 'Personal reformation and political formation.' In M. Wilson (ed) *Explorations in Health and Salvation: A Selection of Papers*. Birmingham: University of Birmingham. Institute for the Study of Worship and Religious Architecture.

Lartey, E.Y. (1987) *Pastoral Counselling in Inter-Cultural Perspective: A Study of Some African (Ghanian) and Anglo-American Views on Human Existence*. Berne: Peter Lang Press.

Lartey, E.Y. (1996) 'Practical theology as a theological form.' *Contact: The Interdisciplinary Journal of Pastoral Studies 119*, 21–25.

Lash, N. (1981) *A Matter of Hope: A Theologian's Reflections on the Thought of Karl Marx*. London: Darton, Longman & Todd.

Lee, C. (1995) *Lonely Waters*. Oxford: Sobell House.

Lee, R.S. (1968) *Principles of Pastoral Counselling*. London: SPCK.

Leech, K. (ed) (undated) *Contemplation and Resistance.* London: Church Literature Association.

Liddell, P. (1983) *A Handbook of Pastoral Counselling.* London: Mowbray.

Lindbeck, G. (1984) *The Nature of Doctrine: Religion and Theology in a Postliberal Age.* London: SPCK.

Loughlin, L. (1996) *Telling God's Story: Bible, Church and Narrative Theology.* Cambridge: Cambridge University Press.

Lyall, D. (1989) 'Pastoral action and theological reflection.' *Contact: The Interdisciplinary Journal of Pastoral Studies 100,* 3–7.

Lyall, D. (1995) *Counselling in the Pastoral and Spiritual Context.* Buckingham: Open University Press.

Lynch, G. (1996) 'Where is the theology of British pastoral counselling.' *Contact: The Interdisciplinary Journal of Pastoral Studies 121,* 22–28.

Lynch, G. and Willows, D. (1998) *Telling Tales: The Narrative Dimension of Pastoral Care and Counselling.* Edinburgh: Contact Pastoral.

Malan, D.H. (1976a) *The Frontier of Brief Psychotherapy: An Example of the Convergence of Research and Clinical Practice.* New York: Plenum Medical Books.

Malan, D.H. (1976b) *Toward the Validation of Dynamic Psychotherapy: A Replication.* New York: Plenum Medical Books.

Mance, J. (undated) *A Comparison between Counselling and Psychoanalysis.* London: Guild of Pastoral Psychology.

Marinker, M. (1975) 'Why make people patients?' *Journal of Medical Ethics 1,* 2, 81–84.

Masson, J. (ed) (1990) *Against Therapy.* London: Fontana/Collins.

Mathers, J. (1976) 'A healthy society?' *Contact: The Interdisciplinary Journal of Pastoral Studies 55,* 14–20.

Maurice, F.D. (1837) *The Kingdom of Christ* (two volumes). London: James Clarke.

May, R. (1991) *The Cry for Myth.* New York: Norton.

McFague, S. (1987) *Models of God.* London: SCM Press.

McFague, S. (1993) *The Body of God.* London: SCM Press.

McKeown, T. (1976) *The Role of Medicine: Dream, Mirage or Nemesis?* London: Nuffield Provincial Hospitals Trust.

Melinsky, M.A.H. (1970) *Religion and Medicine* (vol. one). London: SCM Press.

Midgley, M. (1992) *Science as Salvation: A Modern Myth and Its Meaning.* London: Routledge.

Moltmann, J. (1974) *The Crucified God.* London: SCM Press.

Moltmann, J. (1978) *The Church in the Power of the Spirit.* London: SCM Press.

Monteith, W.G. (1987) *Disability: Faith and Acceptance.* Edinburgh: St Andrew's Press.

Moore, S. (1977) *The Crucified is no Stranger.* London: Darton, Longman & Todd.

Morris, J. (ed) (1992) 'Personal and political: a feminist perspective on researching physical disability.' *Disability, Handicap and Society 7,* 2, 157–166.

Mowrer, O.H. (1961) *The Crisis in Psychiatry and Religion.* Princeton, NJ: Van Norstrand.

Mowrer, O.H. (1964) *The New Group Therapy.* Princeton, NJ: Van Norstrand.

Mudge, L.S. and Poling, J.N. (eds) (1987) *Formation and Reflection: The Promise of Practical Theology.* Philadelphia, PA: Fortress Press.

Murdoch, I. (1970) *The Sovereignty of Good*. London: Routledge & Kegan Paul.

Nauss, A.H. (1973) 'The ministerial personality: myth or reality?' *Journal of Religion and Health 12*, 77–96.

Neibuhr, R. (1963) *Moral Man and Immoral Society: A Study in Ethics and Politics*. London: SCM Press.

Nelson, J. (1992) *Intimate Connection: Male Sexuality, Masculine Spirituality*. London: SPCK.

Northcott, M. (1990) 'The case study method in theological education.' *Contact: The Interdisciplinary Journal of Pastoral Studies 103*, 26–32.

Nouwen, H. (1972) 'Education to the ministry.' *Theological Education 9*, 48–57.

Nouwen, H. (1994) *The Wounded Healer*. London: Darton, Longman and Todd.

Nouwen, H. (1986) *The Road to Day Break*. New York: Cross Roads.

Oakley, J. (1992) *Morality and the Emotions*. London: Routledge.

Oden, T. (1967) *Contemporary Theology and Psychotherapy*. Philadelphia, PA: Westminster Press.

Oden, T. (1979) *Agenda for Theology*. San Francisco: Harper & Row.

Olesen, S. *et al* (eds) (1997) *Studies in Alternative Therapy 4: Lifestyle and Medical Paradigms*. Odense: Odense University Press.

Parish, A. (ed) (1987) *Mental Handicap*. Basingstoke: Macmillan.

Pattison, S. (1980) 'Images of inadequacy: some theoretical models of hospital chaplaincy.' *Contact: The Interdisciplinary Journal of Pastoral Studies 69*, 6–15.

Pattison, S. (1982) 'Pastoral care in psychiatric hospitals: an approach based on some insights and the methods of liberation theology.' (Unpublished PhD dissertation.)

Pattison, S. (1986) 'The use of behavioural sciences in pastoral studies.' In P.H. Ballard (ed) *The Foundations of Pastoral Studies and Practical Theology*. Cardiff: Faculty of Theology, University College, Cardiff.

Pattison, S. (1988) *A Critique of Pastoral Care*. London: SCM Press.

Pattison, S. (1989) 'Some straw for the bricks: a basic introduction to theological reflection.' *Contact: The Interdisciplinary Journal of Pastoral Studies 99*, 2–9.

Pattison, S. (1994) *Pastoral Care and Liberation Theology*. Cambridge: Cambridge University Press.

Pattison, S., Bellamy, P. and Easter, B. (1989) 'Evaluating pastoral studies placements.' *Contact: The Interdisciplinary Journal of Pastoral Studies 99*, 9–14.

Pattison, S. with Woodward, J. (1994) *A Vision of Pastoral Theology: In Search of Words that Resurrect the Dead*. Edinburgh: Contact Pastoral.

Patton, J. (ed) (1990) *From Ministry to Theology*. Nashville, TN: Abingdon Press.

Pervin, L.A. (ed) (1990) *Handbook of Personality: Theory and Research*. New York: Guildford Press.

Phillips, A. (ed) (1993) *On Kissing, Tickling and Being Bored: Psychoanalytic Essays on the Unexamined Life*. London: Faber.

Polanyi, M. (1958) *Personal Knowledge*. Chicago: University of Chicago Press.

Polanyi, M. (1983) *The Tacit Dimension*. London: Peter Smith.

Preston, R.H. (1991) *Religion and the Ambiguities of Capitalism*. London: SCM Press.

Pruyser, P.W. (1987) *Changing Views of the Human Condition*. Macon: Mercer University Press.

Ramshaw, E. (1987) *Ritual and Pastoral Care*. Philadelphia, PA: Fortress Press.

Richardson, A. (1969) *Dictionary of Christian Theology*. London: SCM Press.

Rorty, R. (1989) *Contingency, Irony and Solidarity*. Cambridge: Cambridge University Press.

Ruether, R. (ed) (1985) *Women-Church: Theology and Practice of Feminist Liturgical Communities*. San Francisco: Harper & Row.

Ruether, R. (1986) 'Feminism and religious faith: renewal or creation?' *Religion and Intellectual Life 3*, Winter.

Sayers, D. (1941) *The Mind of the Maker*. London: Methuen.

Schalow, F. (1998) 'Language and the roots of conscience: Heidegger's less travelled path.' *Human Studies 21*, 141–156.

Scher, P. (1996) *Patient-focused Architecture for Health Care: A Study for Arts for Health*. Manchester: Faculty of Art and Design, Manchester Metropolitan University.

Schön, D. (1991) *The Reflective Practitioner: How Professionals Think in Action*. Aldershot: Avebury.

Schreiter, R.J. (1985) *Constructing Local Theologies*. London: SCM Press.

Schumacher, E.F. (1973) *Small is Beautiful: A Study of Economics as if People Mattered*. London: Blond & Briggs.

Schüssler Fiorenza, E. (1983) *In Memory of Her: A Feminist Theological Reconstruction of Christian Origins*. London: SCM Press.

Segundo, J. (1976) *The Liberation of Theology*. Maryknoll, NY: Orbis Books.

Sergeant, J. and Sergeant H. (eds) (1968) *Poems from Hospital*. London: Allen & Unwin.

Shannon, R. (1975) *The Peacock and the Phoenix: Poems, 1963–1971: Designs and Texts, 1970-1975*. Millbrae, CA: Celestial Arts.

Smith, S. (1962) *Selected Poems*. London: Longmans.

Sölle, D. (1981) *Choosing Life*. London: SCM Press.

Sölle, D. (1993) *On Earth as in Heaven*. Louisville, KY: Westminster/John Knox Press.

Sontag, S. (1979) *Illness as Metaphor*. London: Allen Lane.

Soskice, J. (1985) *Metaphor and Religious Language*. Oxford: Clarendon Press.

St. Hilda Community (1991) *Women Included: A Book of Services and Prayers*. London: SPCK.

Stout, J. (1988) *Ethics After Babel: The Languages of Morals and Their Discontents*. Cambridge: James Clarke.

Stuart, E. (ed) (1992) *Daring to Speak Love's Name: A Gay and Lesbian Prayer Book*. London: Hamish Hamilton.

Swinton, J. (1997) 'Friendship in community: creating a space for love.' *Contact: The Interdisciplinary Journal of Pastoral Studies 122*, 17–22.

Swinton, J. (2000) *From Bedlam to Shalom: Towards a Practical Theology of Human Nature, Interpersonal Relationships and Mental Health Care*. New York: Peter Lang Press.

Tagore, R. (1974) *Gitanjali*. London: Macmillan.

Thiselton, A. (1992) *New Horizons in Hermeneutics*. London: HarperCollins.

Thomas, R.S. (1992) *Mass for Hard Times*. Newcastle upon Tyne: Bloodaxe Books.

Thurneysen, E. (1962) *A Theology of Pastoral Care*. Louisville, KY: John Knox Press.

Tinsley, E.J. (1983) 'Via negativa.' In J. Bowden and A. Richardson (eds) *A New Dictionary of Christian Theology*. London: SCM Press.

Towler, R. and Coxon, A.P.M. (1979) *The Fate of the Anglican Clergy: A Sociological Study*. London: Macmillan.

Tracy, D. (1975) *Blessed Rage for Order: The New Pluralism in Theology*. New York: Seabury Press.

Vanier, J. (ed) (1982) *Community and Growth*. London: Darton, Longman & Todd.

Vanstone, W.H. (1977) *Love's Endeavour, Love's Expense: The Response of Being to the Love of God*. London: Darton, Longman and Todd.

Walton, H. (1999) 'Passion and pain: conceiving theology out of infertility.' *Contact: The Interdisciplinary Journal of Pastoral Studies 130*, 3–9.

Ward, K. (1976) *The Divine Image: The Foundations of Christian Morality*. London: SPCK.

Watts, A. (1976) *The Wisdom of Insecurity*. London: Rider & Co.

Weil, S. (1951) *Waiting on God*. London: Routledge & Kegan Paul.

Wesson, J. (1986) 'How Cinderella must get to the ball: Pastoral studies and its relation to theology.' In P.H. Ballard (ed) *The Foundations of Pastoral Studies and Practical Theology*. Cardiff: Faculty of Theology, University College, Cardiff.

Williams, H.A. (1976) *Tensions: Necessary Conflicts in Life and Love*. London: Mitchell Beazley.

Williams, R. (1979) *The Wound of Knowledge*. London: Darton, Longman & Todd.

Willimon, W. (1979) *Worship as Pastoral Care*. Nashville, TN: Abingdon Press

Willows, D. (1999) 'By faith transformed: education and therapy.' *Journal of Health Care Chaplaincy 2*, 14, 60–66.

Wilson, M. (ed) (1983) *Explorations in Health and Salvation: A Selection of Papers*. Birmingham: University of Birmingham Institute for the Study of Worship and Religious Architecture.

Wilson, M. (1985) 'Personal care and political action.' *Contact: The Interdisciplinary Journal of Pastoral Studies 87*, 12–22.

Woodward J. (ed) (1990) *Embracing the Chaos*. London: SPCK.

Contributors

Professor David Aldridge is Professor for Qualitative Research in Medicine at the University of Witten Herdecke, Germany.

The Revd Professor Paul Ballard is Professor of Religious and Theological Studies at Cardiff University and President of the British and Irish Association of Practical Theology.

The Revd Dr Alan Billings was previously Principal of the West Midlands Ministerial Training Course at Queens College, Birmingham. He is currently a Parish Priest and Director of the Centre for Practical Christianity, Kendal.

Irene Bloomfield was co-founder of the Association of Pastoral Care and Counselling. She has been actively involved in national and international activities in pastoral care and counselling and was President of APCC from 1995–1998.

The Revd Dr Kenneth Boyd was Editor of *Contact* from 1974–1984. He is currently a Senior Lecturer in Medical Ethics at the University of Edinburgh and Research Director of the Institute of Medical Ethics. He is a minister in the Church of Scotland.

Professor Alastair Campbell was Editor of *Contact* from 1970–1974. He is currently the inaugural Professor of Ethics in Medicine in the School of Medicine at the University of Bristol and Director of the Centre for Ethics in Medicine.

The Revd Professor Anthony Dyson (1936–1998) was Professor of Social and Pastoral Theology at the University of Manchester between 1980 and 1998.

The Revd Professor Leslie Francis is Director of the Welsh National Centre for Religious Education and Professor of Practical Theology at the University of Wales, Bangor.

Professor Elaine Graham is Samuel Ferguson Professor of Social and Pastoral Theology at the University of Manchester. She was a founder member and former Chairperson of the British and Irish Association of Practical Theology.

Michael Jacobs worked at the University of Leicester until 1999. During part of that time he was also Director of Pastoral Care and Counselling in three dioceses. He is now an independent consultant, trainer and supervisor.

Dr Frank Lake (1914–1982) was formerly a medical missionary and Fellow of the Royal College of Psychiatrists. He was also founder of the Clinical Theology Association.

Dr Robert Lambourne (1917–1972) was formerly a general medical practitioner and Fellow of the Royal College of Psychiatrists. He was also a Lecturer in Pastoral Studies at the University of Birmingham.

The Revd Dr Emmanuel Lartey is a Senior Lecturer in Pastoral Studies at the University of Birmingham. He is also currently Chairperson of the British and Irish Association of Practical Theology.

The Revd Dr David Lyall was Editor of *Contact* from 1984–1992. Formerly a parish minister and hospital chaplain, he is now a Senior Lecturer in Christian Ethics and Practical Theology at the University of Edinburgh and Principal of New College.

Dr Gordon Lynch is a Lecturer in Social and Pastoral Theology at the University of Birmingham and a trained counsellor.

Dr James Mathers (1916–1986) was formerly a Fellow of the Royal College of Psychiatrists and Honorary Lecturer in Pastoral Studies at the University of Birmingham.

The Revd Dr Michael Northcott is a Senior Lecturer in Christian Ethics and Practical Theology at the University of Edinburgh.

Stephen Pattison was Editor of *Contact* from 1992–1997. Formerly a Lecturer in Pastoral Studies at the University of Birmingham, he is now a Senior Lecturer in Practical Theology at Cardiff University.

The Revd Canon Raymond Rodger has served as a Parish Priest in the Church of England for twenty-nine years. Since 1992 he has been Personal Assistant to the Bishop of Lincoln.

The Revd Dr John Swinton is the present Editor of *Contact*. With a background in psychiatric nursing and hospital chaplaincy, he is currently also a Lecturer in Practical Theology at the University of Aberdeen and a minister in the Church of Scotland.

Dr Heather Walton is a Lecturer in Practical Theology at the University of Glasgow. Previously she worked in ministerial training in Manchester and Oxford.

The Revd Dr David Willows was Editor of *Contact* from 1997– 2000. A former mental health chaplain, he is currently Director of Research and Development at the Paternoster Centre and Examining Chaplain for Educational Studies to the Bishop of London.

The Revd Dr Michael Wilson (1916–1999) was formerly a Senior Lecturer in Pastoral Studies at the University of Birmingham and Member of the Royal College of Physicians.

The Revd Dr James Woodward is Master of the Foundation of Lady Katherine Leveson. He is also Bishop's Advisor on health and social care.in the diocese of Birmingham and Honorary Research Fellow at Cardiff University.

Subject Index

Author Index